See the Wider picture

The curious Cube Houses, Rotterdam, the Netherlands

These strange houses were designed in the 1970s. They are made in cube shapes turned on their points. This gives space for people to walk underneath. From a distance they look like a forest and the people who live in them feel like they are living in a tree village.

Would you like to live in a house like this?

CONTENTS

STARTER UNIT My world	0.1 I'M ... *to be*; subject pronouns; possessive adjectives; the alphabet; spelling pp. 4–5		0.2 MY THINGS Possessions; plural nouns; demonstrative pronouns; colours p. 6
	VOCABULARY	GRAMMAR	READING and VOCABULARY	GRAMMAR

	VOCABULARY	GRAMMAR	READING and VOCABULARY	GRAMMAR
UNIT 1 People are people	Talk about family and nationalities pp. 10–11	Use *can* to talk about abilities p. 12 VOX POPS	Find specific detail in an article and talk about general appearance and personality p. 13 VOX POPS	Use *have got* to talk about possession VIDEO *To the Max* p. 14
UNIT 2 It's delicious!	Talk about food and drink pp. 22–23	Use *there is/there are* to talk about places to eat in town p. 24	Find specific detail in a blog entry and talk about preparing food p. 25 VOX POPS	Use countable and uncountable nouns and talk about quantities of food • Quantifiers VIDEO *To the Max* p. 26 VOX POPS
UNIT 3 Every day	Talk about daily routines pp. 34–35	Use the Present Simple to talk about pets and their habits • Present Simple (affirmative and negative) p. 36 VOX POPS	Find specific detail in an article and talk about free time activities p. 37 VOX POPS	Use the Present Simple to ask about routines • Present Simple (questions and short answers) VIDEO *To the Max* p. 38
UNIT 4 Love to learn	Talk about classroom objects and school subjects pp. 46–47	Use the Present Continuous to talk about things happening now p. 48	Find specific detail in a short story and talk about making friends p. 49 VOX POPS	Talk about what usually happens and what is happening now • Present Simple and Present Continuous VIDEO *To the Max* p. 50
UNIT 5 The music of life	Talk about types of music and musical instruments VOX POPS pp. 58–59	Make comparisons • Comparative adjectives p. 60	Find specific detail in reviews and give opinions about musicals p. 61	Use superlatives to compare more than two people or things VIDEO *To the Max* p. 62
UNIT 6 A question of sport	Talk about sports and sportspeople VOX POPS pp. 70–71	Use *was/were* to talk about events in the past p. 72	Find specific detail in a text and talk about places to play sport p. 73	Use the Past Simple to talk about events in the past • Past Simple affirmative (regular and irregular verbs) VIDEO *To the Max* p. 74
UNIT 7 The time machine	Talk about technology and important moments in the past VOX POPS pp. 82–83	Use the Past Simple negative to talk about events in the past p. 84	Find specific detail in an article and talk about everyday technology p. 85	Use the Past Simple to ask and answer questions about the past • Past Simple (questions and short answers) VIDEO *To the Max* p. 86
UNIT 8 Talking to the world	Talk about different countries VOX POPS pp. 94–95	Use *have to/don't have to* and *mustn't* to talk about cultural rules • Modal verbs: *have to/don't have to, mustn't* p. 96	Find specific detail in an article and talk about learning languages p. 97 VOX POPS	Use *a/an* and *the* to talk about places in town • Articles: first and second mention VIDEO *To the Max* p. 98
UNIT 9 Getting around	Talk about means of transport and travel VOX POPS pp. 106–107	Use the Present Continuous to talk about future arrangements p. 108	Find specific detail in a text and talk about holidays p. 109	Use *going to* to talk about future plans VIDEO *To the Max* p. 110

IRREGULAR VERBS LIST p. 127   STUDENT ACTIVITIES pp. 128–129   CLIL ART: Still life p. 136   LITERATURE: Poetry p. 137

2 Contents

0.3 IN MY CLASS Imperatives; classroom language; object pronouns p. 7	0.4 MY BIRTHDAY IS ... Days of the week; months; seasons; cardinal and ordinal numbers; dates p. 8	0.5 WHAT'S YOUR ... ? Telling the time; saying phone numbers; wh- questions p. 9		
LISTENING and VOCABULARY	SPEAKING	WRITING / ENGLISH IN USE		BBC CULTURE
Identify specific detail in a conversation and talk about clothes p. 15	Greet and introduce people AUDIO *To the Max* p. 16	Write a short description of a person p. 17	WORDLIST p. 18 REVISION p. 19 GRAMMAR TIME 1 p. 118	Can you remember thirty numbers? VIDEO *Child prodigies* pp. 20–21
Identify specific detail in a conversation and talk about shopping for food p. 27	Order food and drink AUDIO *To the Max* p. 28	Use *too much/ too many* and *not enough* to talk about quantities p. 29	WORDLIST p. 30 REVISION p. 31 GRAMMAR TIME 2 p. 119	Can a robot cook? VIDEO *Tomorrow's food* pp. 32–33
Identify specific detail in a radio programme and talk about feelings p. 39	Talk about likes and dislikes AUDIO *To the Max* p. 40	Write about a daily routine p. 41	WORDLIST p. 42 REVISION p. 43 GRAMMAR TIME 3 p. 120 EXAM TIME 1 pp. 130–131	Do child actors go to school every day? VIDEO *A typical day?* pp. 44–45
Identify specific detail in a radio programme and talk about boarding schools p. 51	Make and respond to polite requests AUDIO *To the Max* p. 52	Use prepositions of place to describe position p. 53 VOX POPS	WORDLIST p. 54 REVISION p. 55 GRAMMAR TIME 4 p. 121	Can students learn without a timetable or classrooms? VIDEO *Byron Court School* pp. 56–57
Identify specific detail in a radio programme and talk about live music p. 63 VOX POPS	Make and respond to suggestions AUDIO *To the Max* p. 64	Write short messages (texts and tweets) p. 65	WORDLIST p. 66 REVISION p. 67 GRAMMAR TIME 5 p. 122	Why do we play musical instruments? VIDEO *National Youth Orchestra of Iraq* pp. 68–69
Identify specific detail in a radio sports programme and talk about a sports match p. 75 VOX POPS	Talk about hobbies and interests AUDIO *To the Max* p. 76	Use *ago* to talk about events in the past p. 77	WORDLIST p. 78 REVISION p. 79 GRAMMAR TIME 6 p. 123 EXAM TIME 2 pp. 132–133	When did football begin? VIDEO *Rugbynet* pp. 80–81
Identify specific detail in a radio interview and talk about my childhood p. 87 VOX POPS	Agree and disagree with statements AUDIO *To the Max* p. 88	Write a personal email with news p. 89	WORDLIST p. 90 REVISION p. 91 GRAMMAR TIME 7 p. 124	Are museums boring? VIDEO *The Black Museum* pp. 92–93
Identify specific detail in a conversation and talk about communication p. 99	Check if people understand me and say if I understand AUDIO *To the Max* p. 100	Use verb + preposition collocations to talk about successful vlogging p. 101	WORDLIST p. 102 REVISION p. 103 GRAMMAR TIME 8 p. 125	Can you send postcards from Antarctica? VIDEO *The Penguin Post Office* pp. 104–105
Identify specific detail in conversations and talk about the weather p. 111 VOX POPS	Ask for and give directions AUDIO *To the Max* p. 112	Write an invitation email p. 113	WORDLIST p. 114 REVISION p. 115 GRAMMAR TIME 9 p. 126 EXAM TIME 3 pp. 134–135	Are there ghosts in the Underground? VIDEO *Travelling on the Tube* pp. 116–117

BIOLOGY: Exercise p. 138   HISTORY: Mummies p. 139   SCIENCE: Hot-air balloons p. 140
CULTURE 1: Explore the English-speaking world p. 141   2: Explore the UK p. 142

0

 **0.1 I'M ...**

to be; subject pronouns; possessive adjectives; the alphabet; spelling

My world

VOCABULARY
Alphabet | Possessions | Colours | Classroom language | Cardinal and ordinal numbers | Days of the week | Months | Seasons | Dates | Telling the time

GRAMMAR
to be | Subject pronouns | Possessive adjectives | Demonstrative pronouns | Plural nouns | Imperatives | Object pronouns | *wh-* questions

A    B    C    D    E

1 Study the Grammar A box. In pairs, match sentences 1–5 with photos A–E. How do you say the underlined words in your language?

Grammar A	Subject pronouns
I you he she it we they	

1 Karolina and Kasia are friends. <u>They</u>'re thirteen and they're from Krakow.
2 Here's Marie and George. <u>She</u>'s a doctor and <u>he</u>'s a teacher. They aren't at work today.
3 This is a photo of me and my friend Fraser. <u>We</u>'re from Edinburgh.
4 I'm Katie Skinner. <u>I</u>'m not from London. I'm here on holiday! <u>It</u>'s a great city.
5 A: Excuse me, are <u>you</u> really the Queen?
   B: No, I'm not. I'm Mary Reynolds. I'm an actor!

2 Study the Grammar B box. Find examples of *to be* in the sentences in Exercise 1.

Grammar B	to be
+	**−**
I'm (am) Julie. You/We/They're (are) friends. He/She's (is) a teenager.	I'm not (am not) an actor. You/We/They aren't (are not) students. He/She isn't (is not) from London.
?	**Short answers**
Are you a student? Is she a teacher? Are they from Paris?	Yes, I am./No, I'm not. Yes, she is./No, she isn't. Yes, they are./No, they aren't.

3 Complete the sentences about the people in Exercise 1 with *is/isn't* or *are/aren't*.
1 Karolina and Kasia *aren't* from Edinburgh.
2 George _____ a doctor.
3 Marie _____ teacher.
4 Fraser and I _____ teenagers.
5 Katie _____ from London.
6 Mary _____ an actor.

4 Replace the words in bold in Exercise 3 with subject pronouns.
1 They are from Edinburgh.

5 Make questions with *to be*. In pairs, ask and answer the questions.
1 Karolina / thirteen / ?
 A: Is Karolina thirteen?
 B: Yes, she is.
2 Kasia / fifteen / ?
3 Marie and George / students / ?
4 Katie / in Paris / ?
5 Mary / at work now / ?

6 Study the Grammar C box. Choose the correct option.

Grammar C		Possessive adjectives				
I	you	he	she	it	we	they
my	your	his	her	its	our	their

1 My sister is ten. *His / Her* name is Kirsty.
2 We're at Greenwood School. *Your / Our* English teacher is Mrs. Smith.
3 A: Hi! What are *your / our* names?
 B: I'm Todd and he's Dan.
4 Our two cats are great. *Our / Their* names are Fiona and Minka.
5 This is my friend from America. *His / Her* name is Tom.
6 Here's a photo of my dog. *Its / Their* name is Rocky.
7 Hi! *My / Our* name's Pierre Dubois and I'm from France.
8 This is Anna, my friend. And that's *his / her* brother, Louis.

7 🔊 **1.02** Listen to the alphabet and repeat. Say the alphabet round the class from *A* to *Z*. Then from *Z* to *A*!

8 🔊 **1.03** Study the Watch out! box. Listen and write down the names. Then spell your first name and your surname.

Spelling	
Geeta = G-double E-T-A Harry = H-A-double R-Y	**Watch OUT!**

1 _____   4 _____
2 _____   5 _____
3 _____   6 _____
I'm _____.

9 Complete the sentences to make them true for you. Use the correct form of *to be*.
1 I _____ sixteen years old.
2 My best friend _____ fifteen.
3 My English teacher _____ from London.
4 Our school _____ great.
5 My parents _____ teachers.
6 My mobile phone _____ new.

10 Turn the sentences in Exercise 9 into questions. In pairs, ask and answer the questions.
 A: Are you sixteen years old?
 B: No, I'm not.

0.2 MY THINGS

Possessions; plural nouns; demonstrative pronouns; colours

1. ____ is my bike!
2. ____ are my watches!
3. ____ are my bags!
4. ____ is my laptop!

This is my mobile phone! These are my books!

GARAGE SALE. Help dogs. Buy Our Things!

Hey, that's my skateboard! Those are my guitars!

1 In pairs, look at the picture of a garage sale. What is the money for?

2 Study the Vocabulary box. Check that you understand the words. Which things can you see in the picture?

Vocabulary	Possessions
bag bike book computer guitar key laptop mobile phone skateboard teddy TV wallet watch	

3 Study the Grammar A box. Write the plural form of the words in the Vocabulary box.

bag – bags

Grammar A	Plural nouns
Regular	
cat → cats apple → apples class → classes	
match → matches baby → babies monkey → monkeys	
Irregular	
man → men woman → women child → children	

4 Study the Grammar B box. Complete the speech bubbles in the picture with words from the box.

Grammar B	Demonstrative pronouns
Singular	**Plural**
↓ this → that	↓ these → those

5 Choose the correct option.
1 *This /* (*These*) films are very interesting.
2 *That / Those* book is great!
3 *This / These* men are our friends!
4 *That / Those* watches are old.
5 *That / Those* phone is new.
6 *That / Those* women are teachers.
7 *This / These* apples are good!

6 In pairs, look at the picture in Exercise 1 and find something:

1 **red**
2 **yellow**
3 **blue**
4 **green**
5 **brown**
6 **black**
7 **orange**

This T-shirt is blue. This …

7 Work in pairs. What are your favourite colours?

My favourite colours are …

Starter unit

0.3 IN MY CLASS

Imperatives; classroom language; object pronouns

1 Complete the classroom rules for an English class with the verbs below.

talk   watch   write

Our rules
- ¹_____ in English – don't talk in your language!
- ²_____ in your exercise book. Don't write in your coursebook!
- Learn English at home too. Read websites in English. ³_____ YouTube videos in English.

3 🔊 1.04 Match verbs 1–6 with pictures A–F. Listen and follow the instructions.
1 ☐ ask/answer   4 ☐ repeat
2 ☐ stand (up)   5 ☐ sit (down)
3 ☐ open/close your book   6 ☐ turn to page 93

A Thirty / Thirty   B (arrow up, person standing)   C 93
D (arrow down, person sitting)   E Are you from London? Yes, I am.   F WIDER WORLD

4 🔊 1.05 Match questions 1–4 with answers a–d. Listen and check.
1 What's the English word for 'katastrofa'?
2 Excuse me, which page are we on?
3 What's the spelling of *exercise*?
4 What's the homework?

a Exercise 5 on page 4.
b Catastrophe.
c E-X-E-R-C-I-S-E.
d Page 9.

5 Study the Grammar B box. Complete the sentences with object pronouns.

Grammar B	Object pronouns					
I	you	he	she	it	we	they
me	your	him	her	it	us	them

1 Magda's a nice girl. Talk to *her*.
2 Excuse _____, is this your pen?
3 Mum and I are here now. Please phone _____.
4 Wow! Listen to _____! He's fantastic!
5 Don't look at your phone! Put _____ in your bag.
6 Thanks for your help. This present is for _____.
7 Look at _____ – they're great!

2 Study the Grammar A box. In pairs, find examples of imperatives in Exercise 1.

Grammar A	Imperatives
+	
Watch this film!	
Write the words in your books.	
–	
Don't eat in class!	
Don't talk!	

6 Ask your teacher two questions from Exercise 4.

What is the English word for 'chico'?

And YOU

Starter unit 7

0.4 MY BIRTHDAY IS …

Days of the week; months, seasons; cardinal and ordinal numbers; dates

1 🔊 **1.06** Write the missing days of the week. Listen and check your spelling.

1 Monday
2 _____
3 _____
4 _____
5 Friday
6 _____
7 Sunday

2 🔊 **1.07** Complete the calendar with the months below. Listen and check.

August   February   May   November

January

March

April

June

July

September

October

December

3 In pairs, write the months for each season. Use the pictures in Exercise 2 to help you.

Summer: June, _____, _____
Autumn: _____, _____, _____
Winter: _____, _____, _____
Spring: _____, _____, _____

4 Count around the class.

1 Count backwards from 30 to 0: *30, 29, …*
2 Count to 30 in twos: *2, 4, 6, …*
3 Count to 36 in threes: *3, 6, …*
4 Count to 50 in fives: *5, 10, …*

5 🔊 **1.08** Study the Watch out! box. Listen and write the numbers you hear.

> **Watch OUT!**
> **Saying numbers**
> 300 = three hundred (**not** three hundreds)
> 511 = five hundred and eleven
> 4,000 = four thousand (**not** four thousands)
> 8,921 = eight thousand nine hundred and twenty-one

a *thirteen*   e _____
b _____   f _____
c _____   g _____
d _____   h _____

6 Write the ordinal numbers in words.

1st	*first*	15th	
2nd	second	20th	twentieth
3rd		21st	twenty-first
8th		26th	
10th	tenth	30th	thirtieth

7 🔊 **1.09** Study the Watch out! box. Listen and choose the date you hear.

> **Watch OUT!**
> **Saying dates**
> In British English, we write *1st November*. We say 'November the first' or 'the first of November'.

1 a 1st January   b 11th January
2 a 13th March   b 30th March
3 a 29th July   b 20th July
4 a 13th October   b 30th October
5 a 21st December   b 23rd December

8 In pairs, ask and answer the questions.

1 What day is it today?
2 What day is it tomorrow?
3 What's your favourite day of the week?
4 What's your favourite month and season?
5 When's your birthday?

Starter unit

0.5 WHAT'S YOUR ... ?

Telling the time; saying phone numbers; wh- questions

Excuse me, what's the time?

It's ten past four.

1 🔊 **1.10** In pairs, complete the times for the clocks in the picture. Listen and check.

1 It's *eight* o'clock.
2 It's half past _____ ./It's seven thirty p.m.
3 It's a quarter to _____ ./It's _____ forty-five a.m.
4 It's ten _____ four.
5 It's _____ to _____ .
6 It's twenty-five _____ _____ ./It's one _____ _____ .

2 🔊 **1.11** Listen to six short dialogues and write the times.

1 *3.00 p.m.*   4 _____
2 _____   5 _____
3 _____   6 _____

3 Make questions.

1 your / what / name / is / ?
   What is your name?
2 where / you / from / are / ?
   _____
3 is / when / birthday / your / ?
   _____
4 who / best friend / your / is / ?
   _____
5 are / how old / you / ?
   _____
6 your / what / favourite thing / is / ?
   _____
7 phone number / is / what / your / ?
   _____

4 🔊 **1.12** Complete the interview with the questions in Exercise 3. Listen and check.

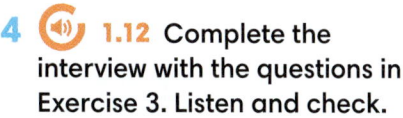

A: ᵃ*1*
B: I'm Jake.
A: ᵇ_____
B: Fifteen.
A: ᶜ_____
B: Bolton, a big town near Manchester.
A: ᵈ_____
B: 6th November. I'm a Scorpio!
A: ᵉ_____
B: 038744 3219.
A: ᶠ_____
B: My mum, probably!
A: ᵍ_____
B: Probably my new skateboard.

5 Study the Watch out! box. In pairs, take it in turns to say the phone numbers.

> **Saying phone numbers**
> We write *038744 3219*.
> We say 'oh three eight seven double four, three two one nine'.
>
> **Watch OUT!**

1 69330 554   3 10 982 633
2 774 649 085   4 416 887 602

6 In pairs, ask and answer the questions in Exercise 3. Tell the class three interesting things about your partner.

Starter unit

1

1.1 VOCABULARY
Nationalities, family, adjectives to describe people

I can talk about family and nationalities.

People are people

VOCABULARY
Nationalities | Family | Adjectives to describe people | Verbs | Personality adjectives | Clothes and footwear

GRAMMAR
can for ability | have got

Grammar: Welcome to my life!

Speaking: She's famous

BBC Culture: Child prodigies

Workbook p. 17

BBC VOX POPS ▶
CLIL 1 > p. 136

My multinational family

My name's Asha. I'm a teenager – I'm thirteen years old. I'm English and French, but my family is multinational.

My mum's name is Sonia. She's English. My dad's name is Henri. He's French. My granny Cara (my mum's mother) is Irish and my grandpa Abe is from the USA. My other grandfather, Gus (my dad's father), is Argentinian and my grandma Miyo is from Japan.

My auntie Rita (my mum's sister) is married. Her husband's name is Alex. He's Scottish. Their son's name is Tommy. He's my baby cousin – only nine months old. My uncle Antoine (my dad's brother) is married too. His wife's name is Ola. She's from Poland. Their daughter (my cousin Ana) is thirteen years old too. We're good friends.

1 🔊 **1.13** Look at the photos. How many people are there in the family? Read the text and write the names of the people.

2 🔊 **1.14** Complete the Vocabulary A box with countries and nationalities from the text. Listen and check. What nationality is Asha? Can you add more countries and nationalities to the list?

Vocabulary A	Countries and nationalities	
England – ¹*English*	Argentina – ⁵____	Germany – German
France – ²____	⁶____ – Japanese	Italy – Italian
Ireland – ³____	Scotland – ⁷____	Holland – Dutch
⁴____ – American	⁸____ – Polish	

3 🔊 **1.15** Study the Vocabulary B box. Write the words in the correct group. One word can go in both groups. Listen and check.

Vocabulary B	Family
aunt brother cousin daughter father grandfather grandmother husband mother sister son uncle wife	

♀ *aunt*, ____, ____, ____, ____, ____

♂ *brother*, ____, ____, ____, ____, ____

4 Find other words in the text on page 10 for these words. In pairs, use words from Exercises 2–4 to ask and answer questions about Asha and her family.

1 aunt — *auntie*   4 grandfather ____
2 mother ____   5 grandmother ____
3 father ____

A: *Is Asha's mum French?*
B: *No, she isn't.*

5 Study the Watch out! box. Read the text on page 10 again and rewrite the sentences using 's. Who says these sentences?

> **Watch OUT!**
> **Possessive 's**
> We use 's to talk about our family members, names, appearance and possessions.
> *Asha's mother is English.*
> *My uncle's car is electric.*
> *Gus's hair is grey.*
> *My grandparents' home is in L.A.*

1 The name of my mum is Sonia.
  My mum's name is Sonia. (Asha)
2 The name of my brother is Antoine.
3 The name of my husband is Gus.
4 The son of my sister is a baby.
5 The mother of my husband is Japanese.
6 The names of my cousins are Asha and Tommy.
7 The sister of my wife is married to Henri.
8 The wife of my uncle is Polish.

6 🔊 **1.16** **WORD FRIENDS** In pairs, check you understand the words below. Then write them in the correct column. Some words can go in more than one column. Listen and check.

~~big~~   ~~blonde~~   blue   brown   dark
green   grey   long   old   red
short   slim   small   tall   young

Eyes	Hair	General appearance
big	*blonde*	*big*

7 Look at the photos on page 10 and correct the sentences.

1 Asha's hair is blonde.
  Asha's hair isn't blonde. It's dark.
2 Asha's eyes are blue.
3 Ana is old.
4 Henri's hair is long.
5 Tommy is big.
6 Gus is young.

8 In pairs, ask and answer questions about the people in the photos on page 10. Use words from Exercise 6.

A: *Is Cara's hair long?*
B: *No, it isn't. It's short. Is Rita old?*

9  In pairs, take it in turns to say sentences about people in your family. Your partner guesses if your sentences are true or false.

A: *My aunt Justine, my mum's sister, is from Montreal. She's Canadian.*
B: *False.*
A: *No, it's true.*

Unit 1   11

1.2 GRAMMAR *can*

I can use *can* to talk about abilities.

1 In pairs, match one of the words/phrases below with each photo (A–D). Read and check.

| dance   fly   jump   run   stay under water
| sing   speak a foreign language   swim

Aida's blog
Fantastic people

A

Tara Davis is a sixteen-year-old Californian athlete. She can't fly, but she can jump 6.41 metres!

Tom Sietas is from Germany. He can stay under water for twenty-two minutes and twenty-two seconds.

B

C

Chen Liting and her friends are from Beijing. They can't walk, but they can dance in their wheelchairs.

Marlon Couto Ribeiro is a young man from Brazil. He can speak eleven languages, e.g. Spanish, Japanese and French.

D

Comments

Marilo, 19.17: Hi, Aida. Can you dance?
Aida, 19.20: No, I can't. ☹
Jma, 19.39: Can Marlon Couto Ribeiro speak Spanish?
Aida, 19.50: Yes, he can.
Jma, 19.54: How many languages can you speak, Aida?
Aida, 19.58: I can speak two languages – English and Arabic.

2 Study the Grammar box. Read the text again and complete the sentences with *can* or *can't*.
1 Marlon *can* speak Japanese.
2 Tom _____ stay under water for a long time.
3 Chen Liting and her friends _____ dance, but they _____ walk.
4 Tara _____ fly, but she _____ jump.

Grammar	*can*

We use *can* and *can't* to talk about abilities.

+	–
They can dance.	She can't fly.
?	

Can he speak English? Yes, he can. / No, he can't.
How many languages can you speak?

GRAMMAR TIME ▶ PAGE 118

3 🔊 **1.17** Can you guess what famous people can or can't do? In pairs, make sentences with *can* or *can't*. Listen and check.
1 Katy Perry / sing / dance in a wheelchair
   Katy Perry can sing but she can't dance in a wheelchair.
2 Beyoncé / speak Japanese / dance
3 Stephen Hawking / talk using a computer / walk
4 Ronaldo and Neymar / play football / jump six metres
5 Shakira / speak Italian / speak German

4 Write six questions with *can* and the words/phrases in A and B below.

| **A**   you   your brother/sister   your friend   your parents

| **B**   dance   jump three metres   sing   speak English   speak three languages   stay under water for one minute   swim one kilometre

Can you dance?
Can your parents speak English?

5 [VOX POPS ▶ 1.1] In pairs, ask and answer the questions in Exercise 4.

A: *Can you dance?*
B: *No, I can't but I can sing.*

Unit 1

1.3 READING and VOCABULARY — The different faces of Jennifer Lawrence

I can find specific detail in an article and talk about general appearance and personality.

1 [CLASS VOTE] Who is your favourite actor?

2 🔊 1.18 Match photos A–D below with the sentences 1–4. Read the text and check.
1. ☐ Her make-up is perfect.
2. ☐ She's poor.
3. ☐ She's a mutant.
4. ☐ She can shoot arrows.

3 Read the text again. Mark the sentences ✓ (right), ✗ (wrong) or ? (doesn't say).
1. ☐ Jennifer is American.
2. ☐ Ree is a teenager.
3. ☐ Rosalyn can't shoot arrows.
4. ☐ Katniss' hair is short.
5. ☐ Raven is a young woman.
6. ☐ Raven and Jennifer are 100 percent different.

4 Study the Vocabulary box. Find the words in the text. How do you say the words in your language?

Vocabulary	Personality adjectives
brave clever friendly funny nervous nice quiet	

5 In pairs, write sentences about the people below. Use adjectives from the Vocabulary box.

Bart Simpson   Lisa Simpson   Mr Bean
Batman   my mum/dad   my best friend

Bart Simpson is funny. He isn't quiet.

6 [VOX POPS ▶ 1.2] Choose the correct options to make the sentences true for you. You can choose more than one option. In groups, compare your answers.
- My eyes are *blue / brown / green / other* (____).
- My hair is *long / short / not long or short*.
- My hair is *black / blonde / brown / other* (____).
- I'm *short / tall*.
- I'm *brave / clever / nice / quiet / nervous / friendly / funny*.

A: *My eyes are green. My hair is long and brown. I'm friendly and happy.*
B: *My eyes are green too, but my hair is short and black. I'm quiet and …*

The different faces of Jennifer Lawrence

Jennifer Lawrence is twenty-six. She's from Kentucky, USA. She's friendly and funny. She's slim, tall (1.75 m) and pretty. Her eyes are blue and her hair is blonde. But Jennifer is an actor and actors can change their appearance.

In *Winter's Bone* Jennifer is Ree, a quiet seventeen-year-old girl from a poor family. She's unhappy. Her hair is long and dirty.

In *American Hustle* she's Rosalyn, a nervous woman with beautiful blonde hair and perfect make-up.

In *The Hunger Games* Jennifer is Katniss, a teenage girl with long dark hair and grey eyes. She's brave and strong and she can shoot arrows.

In *X-Men* Jennifer is the mutant Raven. Raven's clever, she can speak fourteen languages, but she isn't very nice. She's very different from Jennifer. She's over 100 years old. Her hair is red, her eyes are yellow and her skin is blue! But Raven and Jennifer are not completely different: Raven can change her appearance too.

Unit 1   13

1.4 GRAMMAR *have got*

I can use *have got* to talk about possession.

VIDEO   WELCOME TO MY LIFE!

Max: Hi and welcome to *To The Max*. I'm Max Gregg and I'm thirteen. My family and I are from Boston in the United States, but at the moment our hometown is Rye in England.

I'm a dance fanatic. I've got my own dance studio in our garage at home. I've also got a video blog about dance. It's got some great tips about how to do different kinds of modern dance. My video blog hasn't got any fans at the moment. It's a shame!

I've got a big sister, Lily. She's nineteen and she's at university. Has she got any hobbies? Well, her hobby is learning languages. She can speak four languages: English, German, Polish and Russian. She's really smart!

Rye has got a castle and lots of old houses, but it hasn't got much for teenagers. Our house is twenty minutes from the sea, but I can't swim!

I haven't got a big family. Just me, Lily and Dad. We haven't got any pets. Dad's got a job at a university near here. He's OK, but he's got a really uncool car and he can't drive very well, especially in London. Oh, and he can't cook.

| Hi there!   It's a shame. | **OUT of class** |

1 Look at the photo. What can Max do?

2  1.3 1.19 Watch or listen and answer the questions.
1 What is Max's surname?
2 How old is Max?
3 Where does he come from?

3 Study the Grammar box. Find examples of *have got* in the text.

Grammar	*have got*
+	−
I've got (have got) a sister.	He haven't got (have not got) a big family.
?	
Have they got a pet? Yes, they have./No, they haven't. What have you got?	

GRAMMAR TIME > PAGE 118

4 1.20 Complete the text about Max's best friend with the correct form of *have got*. Listen and check.

Sol Gardner is English and he's my best friend. The Gardners ¹_____ a big flat in my street. Mr Gardner is an actor and his wife is a singer. Sol ²_____ short hair and brown eyes. He ³_____ two sisters, Carla and Nikki. They ⁴_____ a Labrador, Charlie. The Gardners ⁵_____ a car, but Mr Gardner has got a motorbike. Sol is an uncle now – his sister Carla is married and they ⁶_____ a daughter, Ida.

5 Make questions with *have got*. In pairs, ask and answer the questions.
1 Max / a sister / ?
  Has Max got a sister?
2 Max / a blog / ?
  _____
3 Max's dad / a job / ?
  _____
4 the Greggs / a garage / ?
  _____
5 Sol / any brothers / ?
  _____

A: *Has Max got a sister?*   B: *Yes, he has.*

6 In pairs, ask and answer the questions. Tell the class about your partner.
- Have you got any brothers or sisters/ a blog/friends in another country?
- Have you and your family got a house or a flat/a car?
- Has your best friend got a big family/a pet?

A: *Have you got any brothers or sisters?*
B: *Yes, I have. I've got two brothers. Have you …*

14 Unit 1

1.5 LISTENING and VOCABULARY Fashion

I can identify specific detail in a conversation and talk about clothes.

The Newport Look

3 May

NO RAIN TODAY. MAYBE SUMMER IS HERE! ☺

And here are some of the fantastic summer styles on the streets of Newport this morning. It's not true that Newport isn't a fashionable city! ;-)

1 Look at the pictures and read the blog. In your opinion, which person (A–D) has got great style?

2 🔊 **1.21** Listen and match the names with pictures A–D.
1 ☐ Duncan   3 ☐ Sam
2 ☐ Marc   4 ☐ Donna

3 🔊 **1.21** Listen again. Mark the sentences T (true) or F (false).
1 ☐ Chrissy is a fan of Donna's hair.
2 ☐ Donna's sunglasses are from a supermarket.
3 ☐ Sam is fifteen years old.
4 ☐ Sam's boots are Spanish.
5 ☐ Duncan is a student.
6 ☐ Marc's bike is from France.

4 Study the Vocabulary box. Complete the sentences about the people in the photos.

Vocabulary	Clothes and footwear

Clothes: dress hat jacket jeans shirt shorts skirt sweater sweatshirt T-shirt tracksuit trousers
Footwear: boots shoes trainers
Other: hat (sun)glasses

1 Duncan has got a pink *jacket*, a blue _____ and white _____.
2 Donna has got a pink _____, a short _____ and green _____.
3 Sam has got a brown _____, blue _____ and brown _____.
4 Marc has got blue _____ and a blue _____.

5 🔊 **1.22** **DICTATION** Listen to a recording about Chrissy. Listen again and write down what you hear. Then make similar sentences about yourself.

6 🔊 **1.23** Order the words to make compliments. Listen and check.

1 trainers / your / are / really cool / !

2 style / you / great / 've got / !

3 fantastic / your shirt / is / ! / colour / really nice / it's a / !

7 In pairs, make compliments about your partner's clothes. Use Exercise 6 to help you. Be nice!

A: Your sunglasses are great!
B: Thanks! Your sweater is really nice!

1.6 SPEAKING — Greeting people

I can greet and introduce people.

AUDIO — SHE'S FAMOUS

Max: Hey, Sol. That girl in the red T-shirt!
Sol: What about her?
Max: That's Clare Philips. She's famous. She's a TV presenter. Come on! … Excuse me! Hi!
Girl: Hello.
Max: How are you?
Girl: I'm fine, thanks. How are you?
Max: I'm good. I'm Max.
Girl: Pleased to meet you. I'm …
Max: This is my friend, Sol.
Sol: Hi. How's it going?
Girl: Fine, thanks, but …
Sol: Nice to meet you.
Girl: Yeah, nice to meet you too.
Max: Oh, this is really cool.
Girl: What is?
Max: The famous Clare Philips in the park in my town! I think you're wonderful.
Girl: Thanks, but I'm not Clare Philips. My name's Jenny Dobbs. I'm not famous.
Max: Oh. I'm sorry. I …
Girl: No worries! See you.
Max: Bye … Sorry!
Sol: Oh, Clare! You're wonderful!

OUT of class
What about her?   Come on!
Excuse me!   Really cool!
I'm sorry!   No worries!

1 CLASS VOTE Write a list of six famous people. Compare with your classmates. Who is popular in the class?

2 🔊 1.24 Look at the photo and choose the correct option. Read or listen and check.
1 Max and Sol are *in the park* / *at school*.
2 The girl *is* / *isn't* Max's sister.
3 She *is* / *isn't* famous.

3 Study the Speaking box. Find the phrases in the dialogue.

> **Speaking — Greeting people**
>
> Hello!/Hi!
> How are you?/How's it going?
> I'm fine/good, thanks.
> My name's …/I'm …
> Pleased/Nice to meet you.
> This is my friend, Sol.
> Bye./Goodbye./See you (later).

4 Complete the sentences with the words below.

bye   fine   hi   how   I'm   it   meet   ~~this~~

a *This* is my friend, Ian.
b Hi, Al. _____ Jo.
c I'm good. _____ are you?
d Nice to _____ you, too.
e I'm _____, thanks. My name's Al.
f _____, Ian. Nice to meet you.
g Oh! Look at the time! _____!
h Hi, how's _____ going?

5 🔊 1.25 Complete the dialogue with sentences from Exercise 4. Listen and check.

Jo: Hello!
Al: ¹ *h*
Jo: ²____
Al: ³____
Jo: ⁴____
Al: This is my friend, Ian.
Jo: ⁵____
Ian: ⁶____
Jo: ⁷____
Al: Goodbye!
Ian: See you!

6 In groups of three, practise the dialogue in Exercise 5.

7 In groups of three, have a conversation. Follow these steps. Then swap roles.
• You meet in a café.
• Student A, greet Student B.
• Student B, introduce Student C to Student A.
• Say goodbye.

1.7 WRITING A description

I can write a short description of a person.

1 CLASS VOTE Read the texts quickly. In your opinion, are Jade and Lionel heroes?

A

My hero
by Karin

My hero is my friend Jade Pryce. She's thirteen years old and she's a student at my school. She's English but her mother is from Spain. Jade is short and she's got dark hair.

Life is very difficult for Jade. She's a good student but she's got big problems with her health and she's often not at school. But Jade is very brave and she's always very happy, friendly and funny. That's why she's my hero.

B

My hero
by Paulo

My hero is the sportsman Lionel 'Leo' Messi. He's about thirty and he's a footballer. Messi is from Argentina and he can speak Spanish and English. He's married and he's got two children. He's got dark hair and he isn't very tall.

Leo Messi is one of the world's top football players and he's got a lot of money. He's very rich but he's a very nice person. He's got a charity for children with problems. He's my favourite football player and my hero.

2 In pairs, read the texts again. Mark the sentences T (true) or F (false).
1 ☐ Jade hasn't got an easy life.
2 ☐ Jade isn't clever.
3 ☐ Leo Messi is Spanish.
4 ☐ He's got a wife and children.

3 Underline the examples of *can* and *have got* in the texts in Exercise 1.

4 In pairs, tick the things Karin and Paulo mention in their descriptions in Exercise 1.
1 ☐ personality
2 ☐ nationality/languages
3 ☐ hobbies
4 ☐ appearance
5 ☐ age/job

5 Study the Writing box and check your answers in Exercise 4.

Writing | **A description of a person**

Introduce the person
My hero is my friend …/ the singer …
My favourite sports star/ actor is …

Age/Occupation
She's thirteen and she's a student.
He's about thirty and he's a footballer.

Nationality/Languages/ Family
He's from Argentina.
She can speak three languages.
He's married and he's got two children.

Appearance
She's tall and slim.
She's got glasses.
He's got black hair and brown eyes.

Personality/Positive things about the person
She's got a difficult life but …
He's got a lot of money but …
She's brave/clever/friendly.
He's a great person.

and, but
She can dance. She can sing too. → She can dance **and** she can sing.
He can dance. He can't sing. → He can dance **but** he can't sing.

---

6 Look at the examples in the Writing box. Join the sentences with *and* or *but*.
1 She can run. She can't swim.
   She can run but she can't swim.
2 He's got dark hair. He's got brown eyes.
3 She's quiet. She's very funny.
4 He's Italian. He can't speak Italian.

Writing Time

7 Write a description of your hero. Use the texts in Exercise 1 and the Writing box to help you. Write about:
• his/her age, job, nationality and appearance.
• his/her personality.

TIP
Connect your ideas with *and* or *but*.

WORDLIST
Nationalities | Family | Appearance adjectives | Personality adjectives | Clothes and footwear

American /əˈmerɪkən/ adj
appearance /əˈpɪərəns/ n
Argentina /ˌɑːdʒənˈtiːnə/ n
Argentinian /ˌɑːdʒənˈtɪniən/ adj
aunt /ɑːnt/ n
auntie /ˈɑːnti/ n
big /bɪɡ/ adj
boots /buːts/ n
brave /breɪv/ adj
brother /ˈbrʌðə/ n
children /ˈtʃɪldrən/ n
clever /ˈklevə/ adj
clothes /kləʊðz/ n
cool /kuːl/ adj
country /ˈkʌntri/ n
cousin /ˈkʌzən/ n
dad /dæd/ n
dance /dɑːns/ n
daughter /ˈdɔːtə/ n
different /ˈdɪfərənt/ adj
dirty /ˈdɜːti/ adj
dress /dres/ n
easy /ˈiːzi/ adj
England /ˈɪŋɡlənd/ n
English /ˈɪŋɡlɪʃ/ adj
face /feɪs/ n
family /ˈfæməli/ n
famous /ˈfeɪməs/ adj
fashionable /ˈfæʃənəbəl/ adj
father /ˈfɑːðə/ n
footwear /ˈfʊtweə/ n
France /frɑːns/ n
French /frentʃ/ adj
friendly /ˈfrendli/ adj
funny /ˈfʌni/ adj
German /ˈdʒɜːmən/ adj

Germany /ˈdʒɜːməni/ n
(sun)glasses /ˈsʌnˌɡlɑːsɪz/ n
grandfather /ˈɡrændˌfɑːðə/ n
grandma /ˈɡrænmɑː/ n
grandmother /ˈɡrænˌmʌðə/ n
grandpa /ˈɡrænpɑː/ n
granny /ˈɡræni/ n
happy /ˈhæpi/ adj
hat /hæt/ n
hobby /ˈhɒbi/ n
husband /ˈhʌzbənd/ n
Ireland /ˈaɪələnd/ n
Irish /ˈaɪərɪʃ/ adj
Italian /ɪˈtæliən/ adj
Italy /ˈɪtəli/ n
jacket /ˈdʒækət, ˈdʒækɪt/ n
Japan /dʒəˈpæn/ n
Japanese /ˌdʒæpəˈniːz/ adj
jeans /dʒiːnz/ n
make-up /ˈmeɪkʌp/ n
married /ˈmærɪd/ adj
mother /ˈmʌðə/ n
mum /mʌm/ n
nationality /ˌnæʃəˈnæləti, ˌnæʃəˈnælɪti/ n
nervous /ˈnɜːvəs/ adj
nice /naɪs/ adj
old /əʊld/ adj
personality /ˌpɜːsəˈnæləti, ˌpɜːsəˈnælɪti/ n
Poland /ˈpəʊlənd/ n
Polish /ˈpəʊlɪʃ/ adj
poor /pɔː/ adj
pretty /ˈprɪti/ adv
quiet /ˈkwaɪət/ adj
Scotland /ˈskɒtlənd/ n
Scottish /ˈskɒtɪʃ/ adj
shirt /ʃɜːt/ n

shoes /ʃuːz/ n
short /ʃɔːt/ adj
shorts /ʃɔːts/ n
sister /ˈsɪstə/ n
skirt /skɜːt/ n
slim /slɪm/ adj
small /smɔːl/ adj
smart /smɑːt/ adj
son /sʌn/ n
strong /strɒŋ/ adj
style /staɪl/ n
sweater /ˈswetə/ n
sweatshirt /ˈswetʃɜːt/ n
tall /tɔːl/ adj
teenager /ˈtiːneɪdʒə/ n
the USA /ðə ˌjuː es ˈeɪ/ n
tracksuit /ˈtræksuːt, -sjuːt/ n
trainers /ˈtreɪnəz/ n
trousers /ˈtraʊzəz/ n
T-shirt /ˈtiː ʃɜːt/ n
uncle /ˈʌŋkəl/ n
unhappy /ʌnˈhæpi/ adj
wife /waɪf/ n
young /jʌŋ/ adj

WORD FRIENDS

best friend
big/blue/brown/dark/green/small eyes
blonde/brown/dark/grey/long/red/short hair
dance fanatic
drive well
learn a language
play football
speak a foreign language

VOCABULARY IN ACTION

1 Use the wordlist to find:
1 ten nationalities *English, …*
2 seven personality adjectives
3 seven appearance adjectives

2 Complete the pairs with words from the wordlist.
1 father and *mother*
2 mum and _____
3 sister and _____
4 son and _____
5 husband and _____
6 grandma and _____
7 uncle and _____

3 Complete the table with clothes and footwear from the wordlist.

❄	☀
b o o t s	d _ e _ s
j _ _ k _ _ _	h _ _
j _ _ n s	s _ o _ t _
s _ e _ _ e _	sk _ _ t
s _ e _ t h _ r _	s _ _ _ l _ s _ s
tr _ c _ _ u _ _	T- _ _ _ r

4 🔊 **1.26** PRONUNCIATION Listen to how we pronounce the /ɪ/ sound. Listen again and repeat.

b<u>i</u>g <u>E</u>nglish ch<u>i</u>ldren

5 🔊 **1.27** PRONUNCIATION In pairs, say the sentences. Listen, check and repeat.
1 My s<u>i</u>ster <u>i</u>s pr<u>e</u>tty and sl<u>i</u>m.
2 <u>I</u>t's d<u>i</u>fferent <u>i</u>n <u>I</u>taly.

Revision

VOCABULARY

1 Complete the text with the words below.

> ~~American~~ brother children cousins daughter
> English famous France quiet wife

My uncle Mike is ¹*American* – he's from Oregon in the USA. He's my mother's ² _____ . He's a very ³ _____ person but I like him a lot. He's married. His ⁴ _____ 's name is Diane. She's an ⁵ _____ woman from London. She's an actor but she isn't very ⁶ _____ . Mike and Diane's home is in Paris, in ⁷ _____ . They have got three ⁸ _____ – two sons and one ⁹ _____ . They are my favourite ¹⁰ _____ .

2 Look at the picture. Complete the words in the description of Emily.

Emily is a very ¹*friendly* person. She's fourteen years ²o_____ . She's short and ³s_____ . She's got a ⁴p_____ face and long, brown ⁵h_____ . Today she's got a white ⁶s_____ , a blue ⁷T-_____ , black ⁸s_____ and pink ⁹s_____ .

3 Look at the picture in Exercise 2 and write a description of Richie. Write about his clothes, appearance and personality.

Richie is fifteen years old. He's …

4 Complete the questions with words from the Word Friends list. In pairs, ask and answer the questions.

1 Are you a _____ fanatic?
2 Can your grandmother _____ football?
3 Can your dad drive _____ ? What about your mum?
4 How many foreign _____ can you speak?
5 Is it possible to _____ a language in a day?

GRAMMAR

5 Order the words to make sentences. Use *be* and the possessive *'s*.

1 grandma / grey / hair / my
  My grandma's hair is grey.
2 blue / English teacher / eyes / our
3 best friend / my / name / Paul
4 car / dad / my / very old
5 clothes / cool / my / sister

6 Make sentences about Janey. Use *can/can't*.

1 dance well (✓)   drive a car (✗)
  Janey can dance well but she can't drive a car.
2 speak Spanish (✓)   speak Polish (✗)
3 swim (✓)   fly (✗)
4 cook (✓)   jump six metres (✗)

7 Make sentences about Janey. Use *has got/ hasn't got*.

1 two grannies (✓)   a big family (✗)
  Janey has got two grannies but she hasn't got a big family.
2 blonde hair (✓)   blue eyes (✗)
3 a cool T-shirt (✓) a football shirt (✗)
4 an interesting hobby (✓) a pet (✗)

8 In pairs, ask and answer questions about your best friend. Use *can*, *have got* and phrases from Exercises 6 and 7.

A: *Can your friend cook?*   B: *Yes, he can.*
A: *Has he got a pet?*   B: *No, he hasn't.*

SPEAKING

9 Work in pairs. You meet at a new school. Student A, follow the instructions below. Student B, go to page 128.

Student A, have a conversation with Student B, using these phrases in the correct order. You start.

- My name's …
- Hello!
- Oh! Look at the time! Bye!
- This is my friend, Jim.
- I'm good. How are you?

DICTATION

10 🔊 1.28 Listen. Then listen again and write down what you hear.

Can you remember thirty numbers?

The UK National Junior Memory Championship

Some people are very clever and have got wonderful memories. But can you learn to be a memory champion?

In the UK there's a memory competition for children. It's the National Junior Memory Championship. The children's schools are a bit different. They have reading lessons and writing lessons, but there are also memory lessons!

This year the competition is at London Zoo. The children have different tests. They've got a list of numbers. They've got a list of words. They've got a list of names and they've got information about London Zoo. And they've only got five minutes.

Joachim can remember forty-seven words – that's fantastic! Iris can remember forty names – that's fantastic too. But the winner is Lily-Rose. She can remember thirty numbers, thirty-five names and ninety percent of the information. Wow!

Look at the numbers above for 30 seconds. Then close the book and write down as many as you can.

GLOSSARY
champion (n) a person who is the best at a sport, game, etc.
competition (n) a game or test that people try to win
information (n) facts or details about something
memory (n) the ability to remember things
winner (n) a person that wins a game, competition, etc.

EXPLORE

1 In pairs, ask and answer the questions.
  1. Have you got a good memory?
  2. How many numbers can you remember in a list?
  3. What things can you remember? What things can you not remember?
  4. Have you got a very clever friend? What can he or she do?

2 Read the article. Mark the sentences T (true) or F (false). Correct the false sentences.
  1. ☐ The competition is in the USA.
  2. ☐ The children can do memory lessons at school.
  3. ☐ The competition is at a school.
  4. ☐ There are two tests in the competition.
  5. ☐ Joachim is the winner.

3 Work in pairs. Write a list of fifteen English words and give it to your partner. Study each other's lists for three minutes. How many words can you remember?

4 Is it a good idea to have memory lessons at school? Why? / Why not?

EXPLORE MORE

5 You are going to watch part of a BBC programme about clever children. Read an advert for the programme. Can you remember any famous clever children from the past?

Child prodigies

There are many famous child prodigies: Mozart (Music), Pascale (Maths), Picasso (Art), etc. In this series, we can learn about some child prodigies of today.

6 ▶ 1.4 Watch Part 1 of the video. What is it about?
  a ☐ a famous place in London
  b ☐ a famous violinist called Yehudi Menuhin
  c ☐ a competition for young violin players

7 ▶ 1.4 Watch again. Tick the countries you hear about in the video.
  ☐ England ☐ France ☐ Germany
  ☐ Japan   ☐ Poland ☐ Singapore
  ☐ the USA

8 Complete the sentences with one or two words in each gap.
  1. Samuel Tan is _____ years old.
  2. For Juliet, playing the violin is _____.
  3. This year is Yehudi Menuhin's _____ birthday.

9 ▶ 1.5 Watch Part 2 of the video. Complete the fact file about the girl.

  NAME: _____
  AGE: _____
  NAME OF CLUB: _____
  HOBBIES: _____
  DREAM JOB: _____

10 In pairs, ask and answer the questions.
  1. Is there a boy or girl like Anushka in your family?
  2. What's your dream job?

YOU EXPLORE

11 **CULTURE PROJECT** In groups, write a fact file about a child prodigy in your country.
  1. Use the internet to research famous young children.
  2. Find some pictures or videos.
  3. Write your fact file.
  4. Share it with the class.

2 It's delicious!

2.1 VOCABULARY   Food and drink, meals

I can talk about food and drink.

VOCABULARY
Food and drink | Meals
Places to eat | Cooking
Popular supermarket foods

GRAMMAR
there is/there are + some/any
Countable and uncountable nouns
Quantifiers | too much/too many, not enough

Grammar: I'm starving!

Speaking: Anything else?

BBC Culture:
Tomorrow's food

Workbook p. 29

BBC VOX POPS ▶

What is 200 calories?

Fruit is good for us. 200 calories is 385 grams of apples or 444 millilitres of orange juice. But other things aren't good for us. 200 calories is one small packet of crisps (37 grams) or only 34 grams of bacon.

What about the other things in the pictures?
How many grams or millilitres is 200 calories?

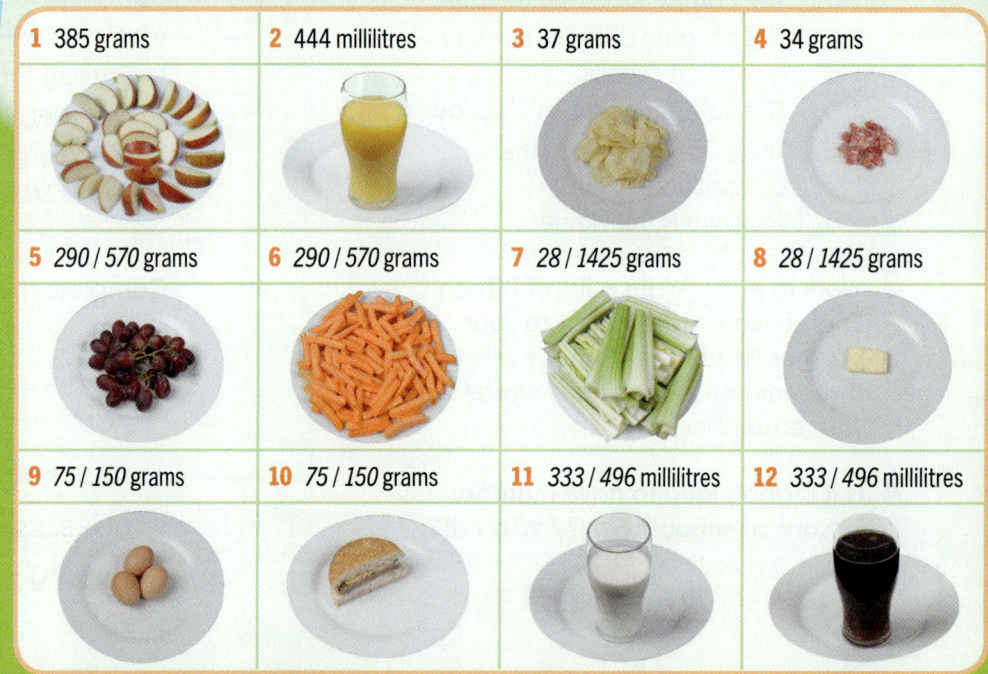

1 385 grams
2 444 millilitres
3 37 grams
4 34 grams
5 290 / 570 grams
6 290 / 570 grams
7 28 / 1425 grams
8 28 / 1425 grams
9 75 / 150 grams
10 75 / 150 grams
11 333 / 496 millilitres
12 333 / 496 millilitres

1 Look at the photos. Which things can you name?

2 🔊 1.29 Study the Vocabulary A box. Match photos 1–12 with the words. Listen and check.

Vocabulary A	Food and drink		
Fruit:	☐ apples	☐ grapes	
Vegetables:	☐ carrots	☐ celery	
Meat:	☐ bacon	☐ cheeseburger	
Drinks:	☐ cola	☐ orange juice	☐ milk
Other:	☐ butter	☐ crisps	☐ eggs

3 🔊 1.30 Add the words below to the correct group in the Vocabulary A box. Listen and check. Can you think of any more types of food and drink?

bananas   biscuits   breakfast cereal   chicken   milkshake
muffins   potatoes   yoghurt

4 CLASS VOTE What are your favourite types of food and drinks? Are they good or bad for you?

I like crisps but they're not very good for you. My favourite drink is milk. It's good for you too.

5 🔊 1.31 Read the text on page 22 and look at the photos. Guess the correct option for photos 5–12. Listen and check.

6 Study the Vocabulary B box. How do you say the words in your language?

Vocabulary B	Meals
breakfast lunch dinner	

7 🔊 1.32 Listen to two friends talking and complete the times in the table.

	Breakfast	Lunch	Dinner
Ian	1 7.30 a.m.	3 _____	4 _____
Lee	2 _____	5 _____	6 _____

8 In pairs, ask and answer the questions.
1. What time is breakfast/lunch/dinner in your house?
2. What is a typical breakfast/lunch/dinner for you?

Breakfast in my house is at seven o'clock. A typical breakfast for me is milk, breakfast cereal and …

9 🔊 1.33 Look at the menu. Then listen and complete Ian's notes below. How many calories are in his menu for a day? Is that good or bad?

Your menu for a day – choose from these options

0 calories	water
50 calories	an apple; two small carrots; some grapes
100 calories	toast and butter; a small glass of cola or orange juice; a large banana; one fruit yoghurt
200 calories	a large glass of milk; a small packet of crisps; a celery, apple and yoghurt salad; bacon and eggs; a small cheese sandwich; breakfast cereal with milk; three biscuits
400 calories	a muffin, a cheeseburger; a bacon sandwich; chicken with potatoes

Breakfast: orange juice; ¹_____; ²_____; muffin
Lunch: ³_____; celery, apple and yoghurt salad; ⁴_____; cola
Dinner: bacon sandwich; ⁵_____; ⁶_____; water

10 In pairs, use these prompts to choose food and drink from the menu in Exercise 9. Work out how many calories are in your menu. Go to page 128 and check.
- For breakfast …
- That's … calories for breakfast.
- What about lunch?
- Your menu for the day has … calories.

2.2 GRAMMAR *there is/there are*

I can use *there is/there are* to talk about places to eat in town.

1 **CLASS VOTE** Study the Vocabulary box. Have you got these places in your country? Vote for your favourite place to eat.

Vocabulary	Places to eat

burger bar   café   fast food restaurant
pizzeria   restaurant   sandwich bar
vegetarian café

My favourite place to eat is a …

2 Read the blog post. Which places from the Vocabulary box are in Brixton Village Market?

Bibi's Brixton Eating out

London is an expensive city but in Brixton Village Market there are some cheap restaurants. There are two fantastic pizzerias. My favourite is Franco Manca££ – the pizzas are fantastic. There's a good burger bar, Honest Burgers££ – the cheeseburgers are great. And there's a cool café called Rosie's£. The cakes are delicious, there's free wi-fi and Rosie is really friendly.

FAQs

Q: Is there a McDonald's in Brixton Village Market?
A: No, there isn't, but there are some good fast food restaurants.

Q: Are there any vegetarian cafés in Brixton?
A: Yes, there are. There aren't any vegetarian cafés in the market but there's a place called The Veg Bar ££ about 1 km away.

cheap: £££££   expensive: £££££

3 Study the Grammar box. Find examples of *there is/there are* in the blog post.

Grammar	*there is/there are*	
	Singular	Plural
+	There's a sandwich bar.	There are some burger bars.
–	There isn't a vegetarian café.	There aren't any pizzerias.
?	Is there an Italian restaurant? Yes, there is./No, there isn't.	Are there any cafés? Yes, there are./No, there aren't.

GRAMMAR TIME > PAGE 119

4 Complete the sentences about restaurants in Brixton with the correct form of *there is/there are*.

1 <u>There's</u> a café called Black and White. ✓
2 _____ some excellent burger bars. ✓
3 _____ a cheap vegetarian café. ✗
4 _____ an African restaurant. ✓
5 _____ any Polish restaurants. ✗
6 _____ a German sandwich bar? ?

5 🔊 1.34 Read the description of the market and choose the correct option. Listen and check.

In the market in my town there are ¹(some)/ *any* great restaurants. ²*There / There's* a café with delicious cakes. It's called The Savoy. There's ³*a / an* Indian restaurant, Delhi Deli. It's very good. There ⁴*aren't / isn't* a Japanese restaurant but ⁵*it's / there's* a Chinese place called the Red Dragon. There ⁶*are / is* two pizzerias, Mario's and Pomodoro. Mario's pizzas are brilliant. There's ⁷*a / some* vegetarian café, Vegatastic. There aren't ⁸*any / some* burger bars but there ⁹*are / 's* a sandwich bar – Slices. It's cheap and the sandwiches are good.

6 Cover the text in Exercise 5. In pairs, take it in turns to ask and answer questions from the prompts. Look at the text and check.

1 an Indian restaurant?
2 a Japanese restaurant?
3 a Chinese restaurant?
4 any pizzerias?
5 any burger bars?
6 any sandwich bars?

7 In pairs, take it in turns to play the role of a tourist in your town. Ask about places to eat. Your partner answers your questions.

Unit 2

2.3 READING and VOCABULARY — What can you do with an egg?

I can find specific detail in a blog entry and talk about preparing food.

OLLIE
the teenage chef

What can you do with an EGG?

There are lots of great recipes with eggs. You can beat them with salt and pepper and make scrambled eggs. You can fry them in oil and have them for breakfast with bacon – it's not good for you, but it's delicious! You can boil an egg in water and eat it with toast. It's great and a boiled egg only has seventy-two calories! There's a fantastic Italian pasta meal with eggs: spaghetti carbonara. It's 'delizioso'! There are delicious egg desserts too: you can bake a cake or make a chocolate mousse.

I'm from London but my favourite egg recipe isn't English; it's Spanish omelette. It's very easy. The ingredients are potatoes (500 grams), one large onion, six eggs, oil, salt and pepper. Cut up the potatoes and onion and fry them in oil. Then beat the eggs in a bowl with a fork. Add the potatoes, onion, salt and pepper. Cook it in a frying pan with some oil. Then use a plate to turn the omelette over and cook the other side. Olé!

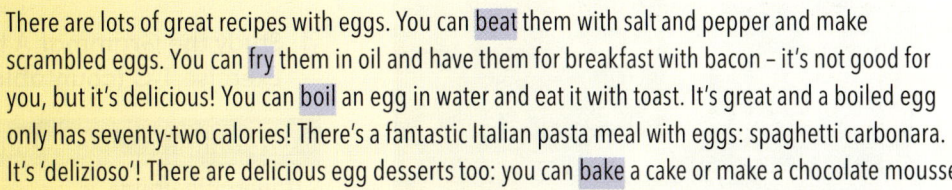

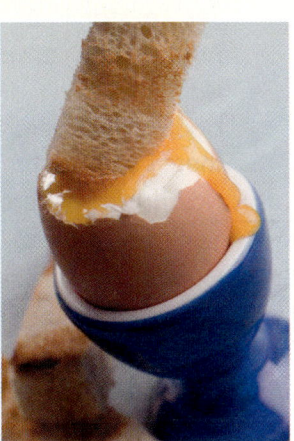

1 CLASS VOTE Can you cook?

| ☺ I'm an expert chef! | 😐 I can cook a little. | ☹ I can't make toast! |

2 Study the Vocabulary box. Match the words with A–F in the photos. Can you add more words to the box?

Vocabulary	Cooking		
A bowl	frying pan	plate	
fork	pepper	salt	

3 🔊 1.35 Read the text and answer the questions.
1. Which egg recipe is not very good for you?
2. What has seventy-two calories?
3. What nationality is Ollie?
4. How many eggs are there in the recipe for Spanish omelette?
5. How many ideas for cooking eggs are there in the text?

4 🔊 1.36 WORD FRIENDS Complete the phrases with the highlighted verbs in the text. Listen and check.

¹ *boil* water
² *bake* a cake
³ _____ an onion
⁴ _____ an egg
⁵ _____ salt
⁶ _____ potatoes

5 🔊 1.37 Complete the recipe with words from Exercises 2 and 4. Listen and check.

Egg-mayo sandwich

Boil two eggs. Take off the shells and put the eggs in a ¹b_____. ²C_____ up a small onion. Use a ³f_____ to mix the onion with the eggs. ⁴A_____ salt and mayonnaise. Put two slices of bread on a ⁵p_____ and add the egg-mayo mixture. Enjoy!

6 [VOX POPS ▶ 2.1] In pairs, talk about your favourite recipes with eggs.

My favourite recipe is banana bread. The ingredients are bananas, eggs, sugar …

Unit 2

2.4 GRAMMAR Quantifiers

I can use countable and uncountable nouns and talk about quantities of food.

VIDEO   I'M STARVING!

Sol: Are you hungry?
Max: Yes, I'm starving!
Sol: Are there any crisps?
Max: No, there aren't, and there aren't any biscuits. But there's a lot of celery and there's some ketchup.
Sol: No, thanks! Is there any cheese?
Max: Yes, there is.
Sol: How much cheese is there?
Max: Eh … Oh! There isn't much cheese. But there are some eggs. And there are a lot of potatoes.
Sol: How many eggs are there?
Max: Seven. Catch! Oops! Six!
Sol: OK, let's make a Spanish omelette!
Max: Can you do that?
Sol: Of course I can.
Max: There aren't many onions. Just two small ones.
Sol: That's fine.
Max: Oh no! There isn't any oil! Here it is.
Sol: OK, I've got the potatoes. Can you do the onions?
Max: Yeah.

Later:

Sol: Max, keep an eye on it! I've got a phone call.
Dad: Max! Where are you? Can you give me a hand?

> I'm starving!   Let's make … !
> Of course.   Keep an eye on it.
> Can you give me a hand?   **OUT of class**

1 In pairs, look at the photo. Which of the ingredients below can you see?

> biscuits   celery   cheese   crisps   eggs
> ketchup   oil   onions   potatoes

2 ▶ 2.2 🔊 1.38 Watch or listen. What's Sol's idea for a meal? Do they make it?

3 Study the Grammar A box. Mark the words in Exercise 1 C (countable) or U (uncountable).

Grammar A   Countable and uncountable nouns

Countable nouns
Singular: a banana, an apple   Plural: bananas, apples

Uncountable nouns
bread, milk

I've got three apples.   ~~I've got three milks.~~

GRAMMAR TIME > PAGE 119

4 Study the Grammar B box. Find examples of quantifiers in the dialogue.

Grammar B   Quantifiers

	Countable nouns	Uncountable nouns
?	How many apples are there? Are there any bananas?	How much milk is there? Is there any milk?
+	There's an apple (a banana). There are some apples. There are a lot/lots of apples.	There's some milk. There's a lot/lots of milk.
–	There aren't any biscuits. There aren't many bananas.	There isn't any cola. There isn't much water.

GRAMMAR TIME > PAGE 119

5 🔊 1.39 Choose the correct option. Listen and check.

Sol: OK, banana bread … Is there ¹*a /* (any) butter?
Max: Yes, there ²*is / are*.
Sol: How ³*any / much* butter is there?
Max: There's ⁴*a lot of / many* butter – half a kilo. It's very hard.
Sol: ⁵*Are / Is* there any bananas?
Max: Yes, ⁶*are / there are*.
Sol: ⁷*Are / How* many bananas are there?
Max: There aren't ⁸*many / much* bananas – just three.

6 [VOX POPS ▶ 2.3] Write about the food and drink in your kitchen. Then, in pairs, ask and answer to find out what's in your partner's kitchen.

*In my kitchen, there's some milk but there isn't …
Is there any … in your fridge?
How much … is there?*

2.5 LISTENING and VOCABULARY   Shopping for food

I can identify specific detail in a conversation and talk about shopping for food.

A 26p   B   C   D   E

1 Look at photos A–E. Which things can you name?

2 Match photos A–E with the words in the Vocabulary box. Then answer the questions below.

Vocabulary	Popular supermarket foods
☐ beans	A cheese and onion crisps
☐ brownies	☐ chocolate chip cookies
☐ fish fingers	

1 Which of the foods in the photos come in packets? Which come in tins?
2 Can you buy these things in your country?

3 1.40 Listen to Greg and his parents. Complete the shopping list with words from the Vocabulary box.

tea	apples	1 _____
bread	ice cream	2 _____
milk	yoghurt	3 _____

4 1.41 Study the Watch out! box. Listen to how we say prices. Then write the prices below in words.

Watch OUT!

How to say prices:
35p = thirty five p/pence
£1.56 = one pound fifty-six (pence)
£2.70 = two pounds seventy (pence)

1 26p   *twenty-six pence*
2 70p   _____
3 £2.10 _____
4 £2.28 _____
5 £4.15 _____

5 1.42 Greg and his parents are at a supermarket. Listen and match the prices in Exercise 4 with photos A–E above.

6 1.43 Greg and his friend Lucy are at the supermarket. Complete their conversation with the words below. Listen and check.

about ~~buy~~ cheap expensive get
good much

Greg: Let's ¹ *buy* some fruit.
Lucy: Yes, ² _____ idea. I like bananas. How ³ _____ are they?
Greg: They're ⁴ _____. A kilo of bananas is only 64p!
Lucy: OK, let's ⁵ _____ some bananas.
Greg: What ⁶ _____ chocolate biscuits?
Lucy: No, they're ⁷ _____.

7 1.44 Listen to the whole conversation and complete the supermarket leaflet. Which things do Greg and Lucy buy?

Fantastic prices!
- 1 kg of bananas: ¹_____p
- chocolate biscuits: ²£_____
- ³_____ : £1.95
- muffins: ⁴£_____
- 250 ml of ⁵_____ : £1.25
- 1 litre of cola: ⁶_____p

8 **And YOU** In groups, look at the prices in photos A–E and in the leaflet in Exercise 7. You have ten pounds. Use these phrases to make a shopping list for a party. Then compare your list with another group.

- Let's buy/get …
- What about…?
- How much is it/are they?
- Yes, good idea./No, it's/they're expensive.
- It's/They're cheap.
- They're only one pound twenty.

Unit 2 27

2.6 SPEAKING Ordering food

I can order food and drink.

AUDIO — ANYTHING ELSE?

Max:	Is it vegetarian here?
Lily:	It's vegan. No meat, eggs or cheese. Just fruit and vegetables and …
Ginny:	Hi. What would you like?
Lily:	<u>Thai noodles for me, please.</u>
Max:	A soya burger with chips, please. Can I have some ketchup with that?
Ginny:	Of course.
Dad:	Can I have a hamburger?
Lily:	Dad! They haven't got any meat here!
Dad:	Oh sorry! An omelette then.
Ginny:	This is a vegan café, sir. There isn't any meat or eggs or …
Dad:	A cheese sandwich?
Ginny:	Or cheese!
Dad:	Salad Surprise.
Ginny:	OK. Anything else?
Lily:	No, thanks.
Ginny:	<u>Can I get you some drinks?</u>
Dad:	Yes, please. A big glass of milk! Just joking!

At the table:

Ginny:	Is everything OK?
Lily:	It's delicious!
Dad:	<u>Excuse me</u>, have you got any salt and pepper?
Ginny:	Sure. Here you are.

Later:

Ginny:	Any desserts?
Dad:	I'd like some ice cream. Never mind!

Time to pay:

Dad:	How much is that?
Ginny:	That's £24.80, please.
Dad:	<u>Here you are.</u>
Ginny:	Everything OK?
Dad:	Oh yes! Delicious!

> Just joking!   Sure.   Never mind!

OUT of class

1 CLASS VOTE Look at the snacks below. What are the three favourite snacks in your class?

> burger   chips   hot dog   kebab   noodles
> pizza   sandwich

2 🔊 1.45 Look at the photo. Listen and answer the questions.
1 Max, Lily and Dad are in a café. What kind of café is it? What things are on the menu?
2 Is Max happy with his meal? Lily? Dad?

3 Study the Speaking box. Complete the gaps with the underlined phrases in the dialogue.

Speaking — Ordering in a café

Waiter	Customer
What would you like?	¹_____/A burger, please./
Of course.	Can I have a burger?/I'd like some
Anything else?	ice cream.
Is that all?	Can I have some ketchup with that?
² _____	No, thanks./Yes, please./Yes, thanks.
Here you are.	³ _____, have you got any salt?
(Is) everything OK?	It's delicious.
Any desserts?	How much is that?
That's £24.80, please.	⁴ _____

4 🔊 1.46 Complete the dialogue with words from the Speaking box. Listen and check. In pairs, practise reading the dialogue.

Kezia:	Hi! What ¹_____ you like?
Dad:	A hot dog, ²_____.
Kezia:	³_____ else?
Dad:	Yes, can I ⁴_____ some chips?
Kezia:	OK, a hot dog with chips. ⁵_____ you are.
Dad:	Thanks. Oh, ⁶_____ I have some ketchup with that?
Kezia:	Sure. Can I ⁷_____ you a drink?
Dad:	No, ⁸_____. How ⁹_____ is that?
Kezia:	¹⁰_____ £2.95.
Dad:	Here you ¹¹_____. Thanks.

5 In pairs, take it in turns to order food from Exercise 1. Use the dialogue in Exercise 4 to help you.

28 Unit 2

2.7 ENGLISH IN USE *too much/too many, not enough*

I can use *too much/too many* and *not enough* to talk about quantities.

Too many cooks spoil the broth

There's too much meat on that plate.

There aren't enough chips on that plate.

There isn't enough salt in that sauce.

There's too much salt!
There isn't enough meat!
There are too many chips!

1 Read the cartoon and answer the questions.
1. How much meat is there on the woman's plate – a lot or not much?
2. How many chips are there – a lot or not many?
3. How much salt is there in the sauce – a lot or not much?
4. Is the woman happy with her meal?

Language	*too much/too many, not enough*

When we aren't happy because there is a lot of something, we use *too much*/*too many*.
There's *too much salt* in this sauce.
There are *too many chips* on my plate.

When we aren't happy because there isn't much of something, we use *not enough*.
There is*n't enough meat* on my plate.
There are*n't enough chips* on that plate.

3 🔊 **1.47** Look at the list for a picnic for twelve people. Write sentences with *too much/too many* and *not enough*. Listen and check.

There's too much celery.

> <u>Food and drink for the picnic</u>
> - 12 kilos of celery
> - 10 grams of chocolate
> - 18 melons
> - 2 packets of crisps
> - 3 sandwiches
> - 72 boiled eggs
> - 50 litres of cola
> - 1 bottle of water

2 Study the Language box and look at the pictures. Complete the sentences with the correct form of *be* and *too much/too many* or *not enough*.

1 There *isn't enough* milk in my glass!

2 There _____ milk in my glass!

3 There _____ grapes on my plate!

4 There _____ grapes on my plate!

4 In pairs, write a list of eight types of food and drink for a picnic for your class. Say the quantity, e.g. *three bananas*. Then compare your lists with another pair. Use *not enough* and *too much/many* to comment on your classmates' lists.

A: There isn't enough fruit in your list.
B: Yes? Well, there's too much cheese in your list.
C: And there are too many biscuits. They're not good for you.
D: There aren't enough crisps and …

Unit 2

WORDLIST   Food and drink | Snacks | Cooking | Places to eat | Meals

apple /ˈæpəl/ n
bacon /ˈbeɪkən/ n
banana /bəˈnɑːnə/ n
beans /biːnz/ n
biscuit /ˈbɪskət, ˈbɪskɪt/ n
bowl /bəʊl/ n
bread /bred/ n
breakfast /ˈbrekfəst/ n
breakfast cereal /ˈbrekfəst ˌsɪəriəl/ n
brownie /ˈbraʊni/ n
burger/hamburger /ˈbɜːɡə/ ˈhæmbɜːɡə/ n
burger bar /ˈbɜːɡə bɑː/ n
butter /ˈbʌtə/ n
café /ˈkæfeɪ/ n
cake /keɪk/ n
carrot /ˈkærət/ n
celery /ˈseləri/ n
cheap /tʃiːp/ adj
cheese /tʃiːz/ n
cheeseburger /ˈtʃiːzbɜːɡə/ n
chicken /ˈtʃɪkən, ˈtʃɪkɪn/ n
chips /tʃɪps/ n
chocolate /ˈtʃɒklət, ˈtʃɒklɪt/ n
chocolate chip cookie /ˈtʃɒklət tʃɪp ˈkʊki/ n
chocolate mousse /ˈtʃɒklət muːs/ n
cola /ˈkəʊlə/ n
cook /kʊk/ v
crisps /krɪsps/ n
delicious /dɪˈlɪʃəs/ adj
dessert /dɪˈzɜːt/ n
dinner /ˈdɪnə/ n
drink /drɪŋk/ v
egg /eɡ/ n

expensive /ɪkˈspensɪv/ adj
fast food restaurant /fɑːst fuːd ˈrestərɒnt/ n
fish fingers /fɪʃ ˈfɪŋ ɡəz/ n
food /fuːd/ n
fork /fɔːk/ n
fruit /fruːt/ n
frying pan /ˈfraɪɪŋ pæn/ n
grape /ɡreɪp/ n
hot dog /hɒt dɒɡ/ n
hungry /ˈhʌŋɡri/ adj
ice cream /aɪs kriːm/ n
kebab /kəˈbæb, kɪˈbæb/ n
ketchup /ˈketʃəp/ n
kitchen /ˈkɪtʃən, ˈkɪtʃɪn/ n
lunch /lʌntʃ/ n
mayonnaise /ˌmeɪəˈneɪz/ n
meal /miːl/ n
meat /miːt/ n
menu /ˈmenjuː/ n
milk /mɪlk/ n
milkshake /ˈmɪlkˌʃeɪk/ n
muffin /ˈmʌfən, ˈmʌfɪn/ n
noodles /ˈnuːdəlz/ n
oil /ɔɪl/ n
omelette /ˈɒmlət, ˈɒmlɪt/ n
orange juice /ˈɒrəndʒ dʒuːs/ n
pasta /ˈpæstə/ n
pepper /ˈpepə/ n
pizza /ˈpiːtsə/ n
pizzeria /ˌpiːtsəˈriːə/ n
plate /pleɪt/ n
potato /pəˈteɪtəʊ/ n
price /praɪs/ n
recipe /ˈresəpi, ˈresɪpi/ n

restaurant /ˈrestərɒnt/ n
salad /ˈsæləd/ n
salt /sɔːlt/ n
sandwich /ˈsænwɪdʒ/ n
sandwich bar /ˈsænwɪdʒ bɑː/ n
snack /snæk/ n
soup /suːp/ n
spaghetti /spəˈɡeti/ n
sugar /ˈʃʊɡə/ n
supermarket /ˈsuːpəˌmɑːkət, ˈsuːpəˌmɑːkɪt/ n
tea /tiː/ n
toast /təʊst/ n
tomato /təˈmɑːtəʊ/ n
vegetable /ˈvedʒtəbəl/ n
vegetarian café /ˌvedʒəˈteəriən ˈkæfeɪ/ n
water /ˈwɔːtə/ n
yoghurt /ˈjɒɡət/ n

WORD FRIENDS

add salt
bake a cake
beat an egg
boil water
boiled eggs
cut up (an onion, a potato)
fried eggs
fry potatoes
(a) glass of milk
(a) packet of crisps
scrambled eggs
(a) tin of beans

VOCABULARY IN ACTION

1 Use the wordlist to find:
1. seven types of fruit and vegetable *apple, …*
2. seven places to eat
3. six drinks

2 Complete the names of meals a–c. Then complete gaps 1–8 with the food words below.

brownie ~~cereal~~ chips dessert milk
salad sandwich tomato

My favourite meals	
ᵃ **B r e a k f a s t**	fruit and ¹cereal, a glass of ² _____
ᵇ **L _ _ c _**	³ _____ soup and a bacon ⁴ _____
ᶜ **D _ _ _ _ r**	chicken and ⁵ _____, a vegetable ⁶ _____ and cola; a ⁷ _____ with ice cream for ⁸ _____

3 Complete the sentences with words from the Word Friends list.

1. Can you give me a **g**_____ of milk?
2. Oh no! For lunch we've got two **p**_____ of crisps and a **t**_____ of beans.
3. You can have boiled eggs, fried eggs or **s**_____ eggs.
4. To make chips, **c**_____ up some potatoes, then **f**_____ them in a frying pan. **A**_____ salt and pepper. Enjoy!

4 🔊 1.48 **PRONUNCIATION** Listen to how we pronounce the /ɪ/ and /iː/ sounds. Listen again and repeat.

/ɪ/: ch**i**cken cr**i**sps   /iː/: thr**ee** m**ea**ls

5 🔊 1.49 **PRONUNCIATION** In pairs, say the phrases. Listen, check and repeat.

1. m**i**lk **i**n the k**i**tchen
2. **ea**t m**ea**t
3. ch**ea**p ch**i**ps
4. f**i**sh for t**ea**
5. a t**i**n of b**ea**ns
6. ch**ee**se and b**i**scu**i**ts

Revision

VOCABULARY

1 Choose the odd word out. Say why.

1 apple	banana	grape	(yoghurt)
2 bread	carrot	celery	potato
3 bacon	burger	cheese	chicken
4 cola	egg	juice	milk
5 brownie	cake	ice cream	ketchup
6 bowl	fork	pepper	plate
7 hot dog	kebab	fish fingers	pizza
8 burger bar	café	lunch	restaurant

1 Yoghurt is different. It's not a fruit.

2 Write the correct word for each definition.
1. In this place you can eat vegetables but you can't eat meat. v_____ r_____
2. A big shop with lots of different food. s_____
3. A restaurant with a typical Italian meal. p_____
4. A room where you can cook. k_____
5. Fried potatoes in a packet. c_____
6. Hot fried potatoes on a plate. c_____
7. A type of chocolate cake. b_____
8. Hot bread for breakfast. t_____
9. You can read it in a restaurant. m_____

3 Look at the picture. Name the ten things on the table. Use the wordlist to help you. Don't write the words down.

4 Look at the picture in Exercise 3 for one minute and then close your books. In pairs, write down the ten things on the table. Can you remember them all?

three bananas, …

GRAMMAR

5 Write sentences about the picture in Exercise 3. Use *there is/there are*.

There are three bananas. There's …

6 Complete the dialogue with one word in each gap.

A: Are there ¹*any* fish fingers in the fridge?
B: No, ²_____ aren't.
A: Is there ³_____ ice cream?
B: Yes, there's ⁴_____ chocolate ice cream.
A: How ⁵_____ ice cream is there?
B: There's a ⁶_____ of ice cream – two litres!
A: How ⁷_____ apples are there?
B: There ⁸_____ many apples – only two.

7 Work in pairs. Write a list of six things in your fridge. Don't show the list to your partner. Ask questions to find out what is in your partner's fridge.

Are there any fish fingers in your fridge?
How many …?

8 Look at the pictures and complete the sentences. Use *not enough* and *too much/too many*.

1 There _____ chips on my plate.
2 There _____ cola in the bottle.

3 There _____ apples in the bowl.
4 There _____ cheese in the sandwich.

SPEAKING

9 Work in pairs. Student A, follow the instructions below. Student B, go to page 128. Student B starts. Then change roles and have the conversation again.

Student A, you are in your favourite restaurant. Student B is your waiter.
- Order a big meal with drinks and a dessert.
- Ask for extras (e.g. ketchup or salt).
- Ask how much it is.

DICTATION

10 🔊 1.50 Listen. Then listen again and write down what you hear.

CULTURE

Can a robot cook?

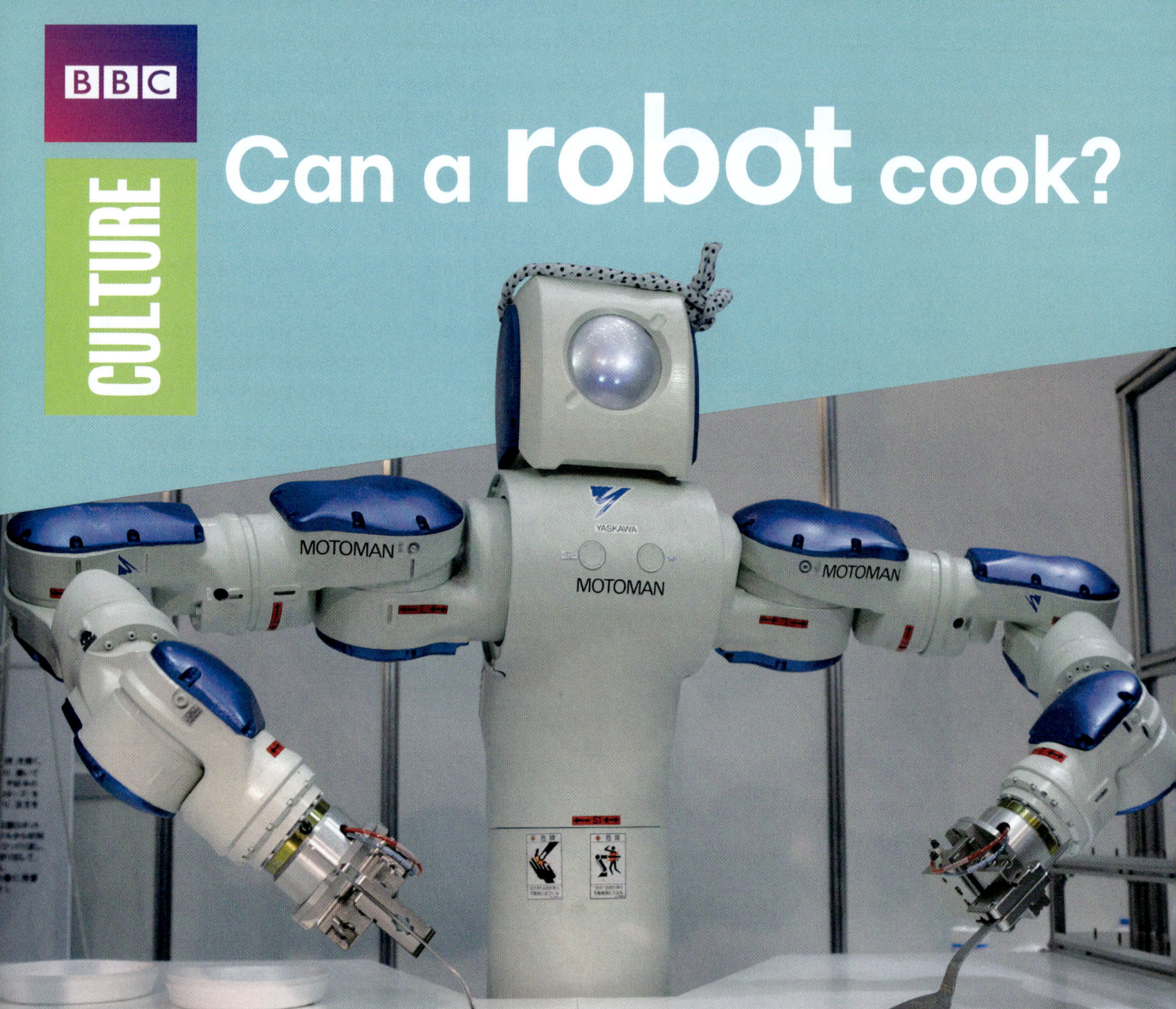

Unusual restaurants in the UK

There are lots of cafés and fast food restaurants in the UK. We can eat cheap food there. But sometimes it's fun to eat in unusual places. Here are some very unusual restaurants in the UK.

1 The Bel Canto
Do you like music with your meal? Then the Bel Canto in London is the restaurant for you. The name is Italian, but the food here is French. What makes the Bel Canto special? Its food and its opera-singing waiters! At the Bel Canto, you can enjoy a delicious French meal while your waiter is singing opera for you.

2 The Tea Cosy
In Brighton there's a very special restaurant. It's called the Tea Cosy and it's a Tea Room. You can have a traditional English afternoon tea here with tea, some cakes and small sandwiches. It's an amazing place. There are a lot of pictures and memorabilia of the English Royal Family here.

3 Dans Le Noir ?
The name of this unusual London restaurant is French for 'In the Dark ?'. Here you can't see any food on the table – there aren't any lights! There aren't any menus to read and all the waiters are blind. Choose from fish, meat or vegetarian and your dinner is a surprise! You can't see your meal but you can smell and taste it, and guess the ingredients! It's delicious.

GLOSSARY
blind (adj) a person who is blind can't see
dark (n) without light
memorabilia (n) things you keep because they belonged to a famous person
royal (adj) belonging to the king or queen of a country
tea cosy (n) a cover that you put over a teapot to keep the tea hot
taste (v) have a particular flavour

EXPLORE

1 In pairs, ask and answer the questions.
   1 What's your favourite place to eat?
   2 Are there any unusual restaurants in your town?

2 Read the article. Match photos A–C with restaurants 1–3 from the article.

3 Read the text again and answer the questions.
   1 What country is the food at the Bel Canto from?
   2 What do the waiters at the Bel Canto sing?
   3 What's a traditional afternoon tea?
   4 Why is the restaurant called 'In the Dark ?'?
   5 What can you choose for a meal here?
   6 Why are the waiters unusual?

4 Would you like to go to these restaurants? Why? / Why not?

EXPLORE MORE

5 You are going to watch part of a BBC programme called *Tomorrow's Food*. Read an advert for the programme. Have you got a favourite TV programme about food?

Tomorrow's food: Episode 1

Can robots cook and serve food in restaurants? Watch tonight's programme from the series.

6 ▶ 2.4 Watch the video and answer the question in the advert in Exercise 5.

7 ▶ 2.4 Watch again and answer the questions.
   1 What's on the floor in the restaurant?
   2 Have the robots got clothes?
   3 What can the robots say?
   4 What can the robot chef do?
   5 What can the robots *not* do?

8 Would you like to have a robot waiter in a restaurant? Why? / Why not?

9 Look at the photos of two robot chefs. You can buy them for your kitchen. Which one would you like to have? Why? Discuss in pairs.

This robot chef can cook pancakes.

And this robot chef can cook anything, but you need to buy a digital recipe from an online shop.

10 Imagine another robot chef. What can it do? Tell the class.

YOU EXPLORE

11 **CULTURE PROJECT** In groups, write a presentation about an unusual restaurant in your country.
   1 Use the internet to research an unusual restaurant.
   2 Find some pictures or videos.
   3 Write your presentation.
   4 Share it with the class.

3

Every day

VOCABULARY
Verbs to describe routines | Verb collocations | Pets | Free time activities | Adjectives to describe feelings

GRAMMAR
Present Simple (affirmative and negative) | Present Simple (questions and answers)

Grammar: Max's press conference

Speaking: Sol, meet Eva!

BBC Culture: A typical day?

Workbook p. 41

BBC VOX POPS
EXAM TIME 1 > p. 130
CLIL 2 > p. 137

Yourphotos — search — Get the app — Login

My day
posted on 2 March

63 posts **90** followers **159** following

A — Oh no, it's 11.30!

B — 45 minutes later …

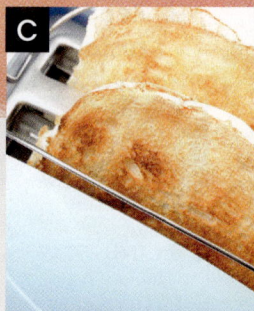
C — 12.30 p.m.

D — 1 p.m.

E — 1.30 p.m. Ooh, that's better!

F — Many things to learn! Not much time!

G — 7 p.m. A nice time with friends 😊

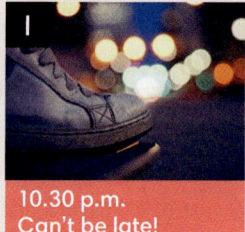
H — 10.00 p.m. Tonight's dinner

I — 10.30 p.m. Can't be late!

J — 11 p.m–3 a.m. Busy at work!

MaryB: A typical busy Friday!   **Michael:** Great photos, Mary!

3.1 VOCABULARY Verbs to describe routines

I can talk about daily routines.

1 In pairs, match the times below with the time of day.

~~1 p.m.~~   8 a.m.   8 p.m   12 a.m. (midnight)

1 in the morning _____
2 in the afternoon *1 p.m.*
3 in the evening _____
4 at night _____

34

2 CLASS VOTE What's your favourite time of day?

Morning is my favourite time of day.

3 In pairs, look at the photos of Mary's typical day on page 34. What do you think her job is? Choose from the ideas below.

actress   DJ   doctor   teacher

4 🔊 1.51 Listen and read. Check your answer to Exercise 3. How do you say the underlined words in your language?

■■■■■ often
■■■■■ sometimes
■■■■■ never

Watch OUT!

A day in the life of ...
Mary Bailey (19)

I wake up at half past ten (I <u>never</u> wake up without an alarm!) I plan my day in bed. Then I get up and I do yoga for twenty minutes. After that I have a shower and have breakfast. Then I <u>often</u> check emails and Facebook or text friends. In the afternoon I study – I want to study Medicine at college. I have lunch at three o'clock and do a little housework. In the evening I relax. I <u>sometimes</u> meet friends or we go to the cinema. I have dinner late (half past ten) and then go to work on my skateboard! I'm a DJ at the Alcatraz club in Hoxton. See you there!

5 Study the Vocabulary box. Match the verbs with photos A–J on page 34.

Vocabulary	Verbs to describe routines
exercise	have lunch/dinner
get up	have a shower
go home	relax
go to bed	study
go to work/school	wake up
have breakfast	work

6 🔊 1.52 WORD FRIENDS Complete the phrases with the verbs below. Use the text in Exercise 4 to help you. Listen and check.

check   do (x2)   ~~go~~   meet   text

<u>go</u> to the cinema/shopping
_____ / _____ friends
_____ emails/Facebook
_____ yoga/karate/taekwondo
_____ homework/housework

7 Make true sentences about you. Say which things from Exercise 6 you often/sometimes/never do. In pairs, compare your sentences. Are any things the same? Tell the class.

I often do homework.
I never go to the cinema.
We often do homework.
We never go to the cinema.

8 Make sentences about your typical day. Use the verbs/phrases in the Vocabulary box and in Exercise 6. In pairs, compare your sentences.
- In the morning I ... , ... and ...
- In the afternoon I ... , ... and ...
- In the evening I ... , ... and ...

9 In pairs, complete the sentences in the quiz with one word in each gap.

ARE YOU AN early bird or night owl?

1. ☐ I often wake a_____ before 9 a.m. on Saturday morning.
2. ☐ I love breakfast!
3. ☐ I can wake up for school without an b_____.
4. ☐ I often exercise c_____ the morning.
5. ☐ I'm never in bed before midnight.
6. ☐ Don't speak to me at breakfast!
7. ☐ I often text friends late in the evening.
8. ☐ In my opinion, the best time to d_____ homework is late at night.

10 Do the quiz in Exercise 9. Tick the sentences that are true for you. In pairs, compare your answers. Go to page 128 and check.

Unit 3

3.2 GRAMMAR Present Simple (affirmative and negative)

I can use the Present Simple to talk about pets and their habits.

1 **I KNOW!** In groups, study the Vocabulary box. How many more pets can you think of in two minutes? Have you got a family pet?

Vocabulary	Pets
budgie hamster guinea pig pony tortoise	

2 Read Lowri's post. Who is perfect in her family?

A house, not a hotel!   by Lowri, 14

'You don't help at home!' 'You spend all your time with your friends – we never see you!' 'This is a house, not a hotel!' My parents often say these things to my sister Cara and me.

But they don't say anything about George's bad habits! George sleeps all day – he doesn't do anything! When my parents come home in the evening, George wakes up, washes and gets something to eat. After that he goes out and doesn't come back all night!

In the morning when I leave for school, George walks back into the house and falls asleep. But my parents never say to George, 'This is a house, not a hotel!' In fact, Mum says he's the perfect cat!

3 Study the Grammar box. Find more examples of the Present Simple in the text in Exercise 2.

Grammar	Present Simple (affirmative and negative)
+	**–**
I eat a lot. He goes to bed late. I never exercise.	We don't listen. She doesn't help us. I don't never exercise.

GRAMMAR TIME > PAGE 120

4 🔊 1.53 Study the Watch out! box. Listen and repeat.

play → plays wash → washes	**Watch**
cry → cries	**OUT!**

5 🔊 1.54 Write the third person form of the verbs below in the correct category. Listen, check and repeat.

> finish go help kiss make miss
> stay study tidy worry

/s/ eats, _____, _____

/z/ plays, _____, _____, _____, _____, _____

/ɪz/ washes, _____, _____, _____

6 Choose the correct option.
1. I really (love)/ loves my family but I don't like / likes their bad habits!
2. In the evening Dad falls / fall asleep in his chair. He never go / goes to bed. We shouts / shout at him but it doesn't / don't help.
3. My baby brother cry / cries at night. Sometimes we doesn't / don't sleep at all!
4. Our grandparents often phone / phones us when there's something good on TV!
5. My big sister often take / takes my laptop and doesn't give / gives it back.

7 Complete the texts with the Present Simple form of the verbs in brackets.

Sadie
My dog Petra sometimes ¹*tries* (try) to sleep on me and I ² _____ (wake up). And after that I ³ _____ (not sleep) all night. She ⁴ _____ (not want) to sleep on my bed at weekends. She only ⁵ _____ (do) it on the night before an exam! 😞

Tom
We ⁶ _____ (have) a problem with our hamsters, Ben and Gerry. During the day, they're quiet and they ⁷ _____ (not come) out. But at night they ⁸ _____ (have) a big party! 😊

8 [VOX POPS ▶ 3.1] In pairs, take it in turns to tell your partner about any bad habits your pets/people in your family have. Use Exercises 6 and 7 to help you.

A: *Our dog eats my mum's shoes!*
B: *My cat sleeps on my laptop when I'm busy. In the morning my dad never stops talking!*

3.3 READING and VOCABULARY Life on the International Space Station

I can find specific detail in an article and talk about free time activities.

1 **CLASS VOTE** Which of the space adventure films below is popular in the class?

> Apollo 13   Gravity   Star Wars   Avatar   The Martian

2 Check you understand the underlined words. What do you know about the International Space Station? In pairs, tick the sentences you think are true.

1. ☐ The <u>International</u> Space Station <u>orbits</u> the Earth once every six months.
2. ☐ Astronauts are on the station for half a year.
3. ☐ Astronauts sleep in <u>sleeping bags</u>.
4. ☐ Life on the station is quiet.
5. ☐ Astronauts from different countries work on the station but never <u>at the same time</u>.

3 🔊 1.55 Read the article and check your answers to Exercise 2.

4 Match headings A–D with paragraphs 1–3 in the text. There is one extra heading.

A Free time
B History of the station
C Not an easy life
D A busy routine

5 Work in pairs. Which facts about life on the International Space Station are surprising to you?

6 **WORD FRIENDS** Check you understand the underlined phrases in the text. Then choose the correct answers.

1. In the evenings I listen ___ music.
   a at   b the   **c to**
2. When we have a long break at school, my friends and I often ___ cards.
   a write   b play   c do
3. How often do you ___ TV or films on DVD?
   a look   b see   c watch
4. I usually browse ___ for half an hour before breakfast.
   a the internet
   b TV
   c the radio
5. My friends live far from me but I often ___ with them online.
   a phone
   b contact
   c chat

Life on the International SPACE STATION

The International Space Station orbits the Earth every ninety minutes. There are normally three to ten astronauts on the station and they work there for six months.

1 _____
Astronauts have very small cabins and they sleep in sleeping bags. Many astronauts have problems sleeping. It's noisy and it's hard to stop moving. Washing is also difficult – you can't take a shower. Astronauts eat three times a day. There isn't much fresh food and a lot of the food is instant – you just add hot water.

2 _____
Astronauts work about eleven hours a day. They do experiments, write reports and talk to scientists on Earth. Sometimes they do spacewalks to check the space station. They also exercise about two hours a day. At weekends astronauts clean the station.

3 _____
There is also time to relax. There are often astronauts from different countries on the station and the atmosphere is great. Astronauts <u>watch films</u>, read, <u>listen to music</u>, <u>browse the internet</u>, <u>chat with friends online</u> or <u>play cards</u>. But their favourite activity is watching our beautiful Earth. It's never boring!

7 [VOX POPS ▶ 3.2] **And YOU**
In pairs, say what you often/sometimes/never do. Tell the class about your partner. Use the Word Friends in Exercise 6 or your own ideas.

I often watch TV in the evenings.
I sometimes play cards with my sister.
I never browse the internet in the mornings.

Dan often browses the internet. He sometimes reads but he never plays cards.

Unit 3

3.4 GRAMMAR Present Simple (questions and short answers)

I can use the Present Simple to ask about routines.

VIDEO MAX'S PRESS CONFERENCE (Part 2)

Max imagines his life as a famous dancer.

Reporter: Where do you come from?
Max: I come from Boston, Massachusetts, but I live in England.
Reporter: You live in England! Do you know the Queen?
Max: No, I don't.
Reporter: Your show *Max on Ice* is awesome! How many hours do you practise?
Max: I practise three hours in the morning and …
Reporter: Do English people really drink tea at five o'clock?
Max: Well, I don't but …
Reporter: How do you exercise?
Max: Well, I do taekwondo and …
Reporter: Do other people in your family dance?
Max: No, they don't.
Reporter: Does your father come to your shows?
Max: No, he doesn't. He's in England.
Reporter: How do you relax?
Max: Um, I listen to music.
Reporter: Do you like New York?
Max: Yes, I do. It's great to be here.
Sol: Max … Max … Hey, mate, there's a question for you on your blog.
Max: What does it say?
Sol: 'Work from home for 500 dollars a day. Check our website for more information. Click on the link.'

OUT of class
awesome   Hey, mate!

1 ▶ 3.3 🔊 1.56 Watch or listen to Part 1. Why is Max unhappy?

2 ▶ 3.4 🔊 1.57 Watch or listen to Part 2. In which city is Max in his daydream?

3 Study the Grammar box. Find examples of questions and short answers in the dialogue.

Grammar	Present Simple (questions and short answers)
Questions	**Short answers**
Do you **like** hip-hop?	Yes, I **do**./No, I **don't**.
Does he **help** you?	Yes, he **does**./No, he **doesn't**.
Wh- questions	**Answers**
Where **do** they **live**?	They **live** in Paris.
How **does** she **relax**?	She **reads**.

GRAMMAR TIME > PAGE 120

4 Complete the questions with *do* or *does*. Match the questions (1–6) with the short answers (a–f).
1 c When *do* you watch TV?
2 ☐ Where _____ your best friend come from?
3 ☐ _____ you listen to the radio?
4 ☐ What time _____ you get up?
5 ☐ _____ your mum and dad play cards?
6 ☐ _____ your best friend have a pet?

a Yes, they do.   d No, he doesn't.
b At 7.30 a.m.   e No, I don't.
c In the evening.   f Poland.

5 In pairs, ask and answer the questions in Exercise 4. Tell the class about your partner.

6 Order the words to make questions.
1 relax / do / how / you / ?
   How do you relax?
2 classmates / watch / your / TV / do / ?
   _____
3 any pets / have / your grandma / does / ?
   _____
4 do / do / when / your homework / you / ?
   _____
5 go / you / what time / do / to bed / ?
   _____
6 you / often go / to the cinema / do / ?
   _____

7 In pairs, take it in turns to ask and answer the questions in Exercise 6.

And YOU

3.5 LISTENING and VOCABULARY Feelings

I can identify specific detail in a radio programme and talk about feelings.

1 What can you see in photos A and B? In pairs, match the photos with comments 1–4.

1. ☐ I'm not a fan of winter. I feel tired and sad and I'm often ill.
2. ☐ Winter's great – I feel happy when I see the first snow of the year.
3. ☐ Winters here are cold, dark and grey. I often don't go out all day.
4. ☐ Winter is my favourite season – I love Christmas and I'm a big fan of winter sports!

2 🔊 1.58 Listen and choose the correct answers.

1. *Over to You* is
   a. a video blog on the internet.
   b. a radio programme.
   c. a TV programme.
2. 'To get the blues' means to feel
   a. cold and tired.
   b. sad and ill.
   c. tired and sad.
3. The topic today is about
   a. how to feel good about life.
   b. the weather.
   c. energy.

3 🔊 1.59 Listen to Part 2 of the radio programme. Match the speakers (1–4) with the things they do to feel happy (a–f). There are two extra ideas.

1. ☐ Mark
2. ☐ Tim
3. ☐ Lisa
4. ☐ Karen

a. eat something delicious
b. do something nice for another person
c. have a shower
d. drink hot chocolate
e. read a book
f. watch a sad film

4 Study the Vocabulary box. How do you say the words in your language? Underline the words with a positive meaning.

Vocabulary	Feelings
bored excited happy relaxed sad tired unhappy worried	

5 Complete the sentences with words from the Vocabulary box. Sometimes more than one answer is possible.

1. Sam is *worried*. He's got a lot of problems.
2. I'm so _____! I've got tickets to see my favourite band.
3. Tom feels _____. He says there's nothing to do here.
4. They feel _____. Everything in their life is great.
5. Sarah is really _____. She doesn't have much energy.
6. I'm _____. I want to cry.

6 In pairs, say how you feel right now. Use an adjective from the Vocabulary box.

> You don't understand, Mum. I like feeling unhappy!
>
> So maybe he's happy?

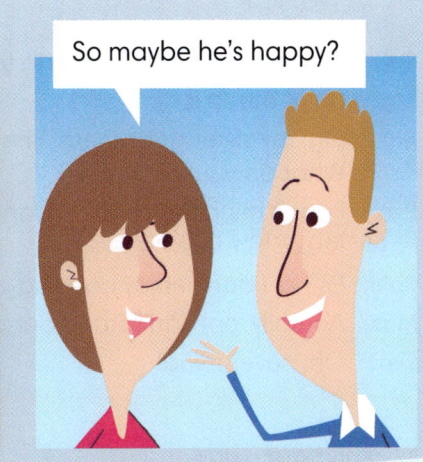

7 In pairs, talk about what you do when you're bored or unhappy. Use the ideas below and Exercise 3, or your own ideas.

> go for a walk   go to the shops   listen to music
> phone a friend   play with a pet

A: What do you do when you're bored?
B: I chat with friends online.

And YOU

Unit 3

3.6 SPEAKING Talking about likes and dislikes

I can talk about likes and dislikes.

AUDIO SOL, MEET EVA!

Max is skateboarding in the park with friends when, suddenly, he hears loud hip-hop music.

Eva: I'm Eva. What do you think of my dancing?
Max: I really like it. You're a great dancer! Good music too!
Eva: Oh, do you like hip-hop?
Max: I like it a lot. It's my favourite music.
Eva: Do you like dance as well?
Max: Yes, I do. I like capoeira a lot – but it's a bit hard for me. I prefer breakdance. Like this …
Eva: Wow, you're really good!
Max: Oh, it's my best friend, Sol. Hey, Sol! He's a great guy. Sol, meet Eva. Eva's an amazing dancer! She's half-Brazilian, half-English, but she lives here in Rye now. Unfortunately, she doesn't go to our school.
Sol: Oh. What school do you go to?
Eva: Saint Alfred's.
Sol: Oh, my sister goes there. She really likes it. What do you think of it?
Eva: I don't mind it. Are you a dance fanatic like Max?
Sol: Er, no. I don't enjoy dancing.
Max: Actually, Sol can't stand dancing.
Eva: Oh, never mind!

OUT of class
a bit hard   guy

1 Work in pairs. Is there a skateboard park in your town? Is it popular?

2 🔊 1.60 Read or listen and answer the questions.
1 Are both Eva's parents Brazilian?
2 What's her favourite music?
3 Does she go to Max and Sol's school?

3 Study the Speaking box. Find examples of the phrases in the dialogue.

Speaking Talking about likes and dislikes

What do you think of …? Do you like …?
What kind of … do you like?

🙂
It's my favourite (music).
I like … but I prefer …
I love/I really enjoy/I really like …
I like … (a lot).

😐
I quite like …
I don't mind …/It's OK.

☹
I don't like/I don't enjoy …
I hate/I can't stand …

Be careful!
We often use verbs of like/dislike with the -*ing* form.
I love/enjoy/don't mind/can't stand danc**ing**.

We also often use these phrases with pronouns (*it, him, her, them*, etc.).
A: Do you like dancing?
B: I love it!

4 Complete the dialogues with phrases from the Speaking box. In pairs, compare your answers.
1 A: What do you think of hip-hop?
   B: 😐 *I don't mind it.*
   C: 🙂 _____
2 A: Do you like cats?
   B: ☹ _____
   C: 🙂 _____
3 A: Do you like doing homework?
   B: 😐 _____
   C: ☹ _____

5 In groups of three, practise the dialogues in Exercise 4. Use new phrases from the Speaking box.

And YOU?

6 In pairs, take it in turns to ask and answer questions about the things below. Use phrases from the Speaking box.

Adele   Barcelona FC   Chinese food   chocolate
grammar exercises   guinea pigs   Justin Bieber
listening to jazz   opera   pizza   playing tennis
snow   techno   tidying your room
watching basketball

A: *What do you think of Adele?*
B: *I don't mind her. What about you?*

3.7 WRITING Describing daily routine

I can write about a daily routine.

Post by Erik, 19 November at 20.13
Hi, my name's Erik, I'm thirteen and I come from Tromsø in Norway. It's quite big (70,000 people) but it isn't a typical European city. We're 350 km north of the Arctic Circle, so from November to February it's dark, day and night. It's often very cold, even minus forty degrees. But we love winter – the sky is often a beautiful colour and we love skiing.

Post by Erik, 23 November at 21.12
My day
I wake up at seven o'clock, have a shower and then have breakfast: bread, cheese and yoghurt. After that I go to school.
School starts at eight thirty every day. We have lunch at eleven o'clock and at two o'clock we go home.
After school I do my homework – I'm in Grade 7, so there's a lot of homework now! My parents come home at four o'clock and then we have dinner – meat or fish and potatoes. After that I often meet my friends and we play computer games. In winter I usually stay at home because it's cold and dark. We read or we chat by the fire. I go to bed at ten o'clock.

1 Read Erik's first post quickly. In pairs, answer the questions.
 1 Which country is Erik from?
 2 In your opinion, is Tromsø a fun city to live in?

2 Read Erik's second post. In pairs, say what things are different in your lives.
In Norway school starts at eight thirty. In Poland it starts at eight o'clock.

3 Study the Writing box. In pairs, find the words in blue in Erik's second post. How do you say them in your language?

Writing | Writing about your daily routine

Use the Present Simple to describe your routine.
I wake up/get up at …
Then I …
After that I …
School starts/We go home at …
After school I …

Use conjunctions (e.g. *and, but, so, because*) to link sentences.
I don't have breakfast because I'm never hungry./
I'm never hungry, so I don't have breakfast.
I walk to school because it's very close./
I live near the school, so I walk.

---

4 Complete the sentences with *so* or *because*.
 1 We don't have a TV, **so** I watch DVDs on my computer.
 2 I often don't have breakfast _____ I don't have time.
 3 I wake up early _____ my cat wants something to eat.
 4 I often exercise, _____ I feel relaxed.
 5 I take the dog for a walk in the morning, _____ I get up early every day.
 6 I'm often tired in the evening, _____ I go to bed before 10 p.m.
 7 My mum drives me to school _____ it's too far to walk.

Writing Time

5 Write about your daily routine. Use Erik's second post, the vocabulary in Lesson 3.1 and the Writing box to help you.

WORDLIST Routine verbs | Verb collocations | Free time activities | Pets | Feelings

actor /ˈæktə/ n
afternoon /ˌɑːftəˈnuːn/ n
amazing /əˈmeɪzɪŋ/ adj
astronaut /ˈæstrənɔːt/ n
because /bɪˈkɒz, bɪˈkəz/ conj
bored /bɔːd/ adj
budgie /ˈbʌdʒi/ n
can't stand /kɑːnt stænd/ v
cat /kæt/ n
clean /kliːn/ adj
cold /kəʊld/ adj
cry /kraɪ/ v
DJ /ˌdiːˈdʒeɪ/ n
doctor /ˈdɒktə/ n
don't mind /dəʊnt maɪnd/ v
early /ˈɜːli/ adj
Earth /ɜːθ/ n
enjoy /ɪnˈdʒɔɪ/ v
evening /ˈiːvnɪŋ/ n
every (morning/day) /ˈevri ˈmɔːnɪŋ ˌdeɪ/ det
excited /ɪkˈsaɪtəd, ɪkˈsaɪtɪd/ adj
exercise /ˈeksəsaɪz/ n
favourite /ˈfeɪvərət, ˈfeɪvərɪt/ adj
(in your) free time /ɪn jə friː taɪm/ n
get up /ˈget ʌp/ v
guinea pig /ˈɡɪni pɪɡ/ n
(bad) habit /bæd ˈhæbət/ n
hamster /ˈhæmstə/ n
happy /ˈhæpi/ adj
hard (= difficult) /hɑːd/ adj
hate /heɪt/ v
have a party /hæv ə ˈpɑːti/ phr
have a shower /hæv ə ˈʃaʊə/ phr

hungry /ˈhʌŋɡri/ adj
ill /ɪl/ adj
instant /ˈɪnstənt/ adj
international /ˌɪntəˈnæʃənəl/ adj
kind (what kind of....?) /kaɪnd (wɒt kaɪnd əv)/ n
late /leɪt/ adj
like /laɪk/ v
love /lʌv/ v
morning /ˈmɔːnɪŋ/ n
never /ˈnevə/ adv
night /naɪt/ n
often /ˈɒfən, ˈɒftən/ adv
pet /pet/ n
pony /ˈpəʊni/ n
prefer /prɪˈfɜː/ v
relax /rɪˈlæks/ v
relaxed /rɪˈlækst/ adj
rich /rɪtʃ/ adj
sad /sæd/ adj
scientist /ˈsaɪəntəst, ˈsaɪəntɪst/ n
shout /ʃaʊt/ v
sleeping bag /ˈsliːpɪŋ bæɡ/ n
so /səʊ/ adv
sometimes /ˈsʌmtaɪmz/ adv
study (Medicine) /ˈstʌdi ˈmedsən/ v
teacher /ˈtiːtʃə/ n
thirsty /ˈθɜːsti/ adj
tidy /ˈtaɪdi/ adj
tired /taɪəd/ adj
tortoise /ˈtɔːtəs/ n
unfortunately /ʌnˈfɔːtʃənətli/ adv
unhappy /ʌnˈhæpi/ adj
wake up /weɪk ʌp/ v

wash /wɒʃ/ v
without /wɪðˈaʊt/ prep
work /wɜːk/ v
worried /ˈwʌrid/ adj

WORD FRIENDS
browse the internet
chat with friends online
check emails/Facebook
do experiments
do homework
do housework
do karate/Taekwondo/yoga
early bird
fall asleep
get the blues
get up
go home
go shopping/to the shops
go to bed
go to the cinema
go to work/school
have breakfast/lunch/dinner
listen to music
listen to the radio
meet friends
night owl
phone a friend
play cards
play with a pet
stay at home
take (a dog) for a walk
text friends
watch films

VOCABULARY IN ACTION

1 Use the wordlist to find:
1. six jobs *astronaut*, …
2. six pets
3. four times of the day
4. eight feelings or emotions

2 Replace the words in bold with the words below to make sentences with the opposite meaning. In pairs, say which sentences are true for you.

| bored   early   ~~hate~~   never
| unhappy   work   worried

1. I **enjoy** sleeping in a sleeping bag.
   I hate sleeping in a sleeping bag.
2. My dad **often** washes his car.
3. I'm always really **excited** at the start of the summer holidays.
4. I always arrive at school **late**.
5. I feel **relaxed** before I go to the dentist's.
6. My cat is always **happy** when I play with her.
7. Unfortunately, I've got too much **free time** at the moment!

3 Complete the Word Friends with one word in each gap. In pairs, say when you prefer to do these things.

1. *browse* the internet
2. go _____ the cinema
3. _____ a shower
4. listen _____ music
5. _____ homework

I usually … in the morning.

4 🔊 **1.61** **PRONUNCIATION** Listen to how we pronounce the /æ/ sound. Listen again and repeat.

| actor   astronaut   bag

5 🔊 **1.62** **PRONUNCIATION** In pairs, say the sentences. Listen, check and repeat.

1. Unhappy cats have bad habits.
2. Harry's hamster is always happy.
3. Do astronauts relax in their sleeping bags?
4. Pamela does karate when she's sad.
5. I can't stand that actor.

Revision

VOCABULARY

1 Complete the sentences with words from the Word Friends list.

1. I *text* friends all the time!
2. I never _____ breakfast – I don't have time!
3. My parents often _____ asleep in front of the TV.
4. I'm a night owl. I often _____ films or _____ to the radio late at night.
5. I _____ stand getting up on winter mornings.
6. I always _____ a party on my birthday.
7. I _____ mind dogs but I prefer cats.

2 Choose the correct option.

> It's the school holidays but I have jobs to do at home every day. Do your parents ask you to ¹make / *do* housework? I ²take / walk the dog for a walk every morning. In the afternoon I ³make / go shopping for my mum. After dinner I ⁴wake / wash up. And of course, Mum tells me to ⁵wash / tidy my room every day too!

3 Complete the sentences with the words below to make them true for you. In pairs, compare your answers.

> bored   cold   excited   happy   hungry   ill
> relaxed   sad   tired   thirsty   worried

1. I never feel _____ with my friends.
2. I often feel _____ after school.
3. I sometimes feel _____ on winter mornings.
4. I often feel _____ at school.
5. I often feel _____ in summer.

GRAMMAR

4 Choose the correct option.

> George is a photographer for *The Richmond Gazette*. He ¹get up / *gets up* at six o'clock. He tries to be quiet because he ²don't / doesn't want to wake up his wife, Ann. George and Ann ³live / lives in Richmond but they ⁴don't / doesn't have a car, so George walks to work. George usually ⁵has / have breakfast at a café near the office. Photographers at the Gazette ⁶start / starts work at 7 a.m. and they ⁷finish / finishes at 2 p.m. George doesn't usually ⁸go / goes home at 2 p.m. – he ⁹meet / meets Ann in town and they ¹⁰have / has lunch or go shopping.

5 Order the words to make questions. In pairs, answer the questions using the text in Exercise 4.

1. George / does / what time / get up / ?
   What time does George get up?
2. do / have / George and Ann / a car / ?
3. they / where / live / do / ?
4. have / does / breakfast / George / ?
5. start work / what time / does / George / ?
6. how many hours / work / the photographers / do / ?
7. in the afternoon / Ann and George / usually do / what / do / ?

SPEAKING

6 Work in pairs. How well do you know what your partner likes/doesn't like? Complete the sentences with the words below so they are true for your partner. Read your sentences to him/her to check.

> love   enjoy   quite like   don't mind
> don't like   can't stand

1. You *don't like* getting up early.
2. You _____ hamsters.
3. You _____ listening to music.
4. You _____ browsing the internet.
5. You _____ having a shower.
6. You _____ going shopping.
7. You _____ feeling hungry.

A: *You don't like getting up early.*
B: *It's true! I can't stand getting up early!*
A: *You love hamsters.*
B: *Yes, I do! But I prefer guinea pigs.*

DICTATION

7 🔊 **1.63** Listen. Then listen again and write down what you hear.

CULTURE

Do child actors go to school every day?

Child actors in London's West End

A lot of young people do the same things every day. They get up in the morning, go to school, play with friends, do homework and go to bed. But some children have a very different day.

Ezra Maye is eleven and he's a young actor. He acts in a show called *The Lion King*. He lives in London with his parents, but his day is often different from his friends. Every second Wednesday he finishes school at 12.00. His mum, dad or grandmother take him to the theatre. In the afternoon he acts in the matinée. He also acts in the show in the evening – two times every week. On those days he is at school all day. Then he eats dinner at a restaurant near the theatre. His favourite meal is burger and chips! After that he acts in the show. He's tired after school, but excited about the show. Sometimes he doesn't go to bed before midnight.

Some child actors don't live in London, but they are in shows there. They stay in London for the shows and then they go home for a few days. Then they come back to London again! They study with a special teacher in London. It's difficult and the children miss their friends and family at home. But they all think that they are very lucky because they love acting.

GLOSSARY
actor (n) sb who plays in films, television programmes or plays
matinée (n) an afternoon show of a play, film, etc.
show (n) sth you watch at the theatre or on TV
theatre (n) a building where you go to see plays

EXPLORE

1 In pairs, ask and answer the questions.
1. Write a list of the things you do every day. How many can you write in two minutes?
2. Which things are the same as your partner? Which are different?
3. What different things do you do at the weekend?

2 Read the article. Mark the sentences T (true) or F (false).
1. ☐ Ezra is a film star.
2. ☐ Ezra lives near the theatre.
3. ☐ Ezra goes to school every day.
4. ☐ Ezra's mum always takes him to the theatre.
5. ☐ Ezra always goes to bed after midnight.
6. ☐ Only children from London can act in a London show.
7. ☐ Being a child actor is sometimes difficult.

3 Would you enjoy a life like Ezra's? Why? / Why not?

EXPLORE MORE

4 You are going to watch part of a BBC programme about a typical day of schoolchildren in England, Japan, Wales and Papua New Guinea. Read the advert for the programme. Do you think they do the same things as you?

Your world

Life in different parts of the world is sometimes very different. Watch the programme and learn what children around the world do on a typical weekday.

5 Think of two countries on two different continents. How do you think life is different in these countries? Discuss in pairs.

6 ▶ 3.5 Watch the video and tick the things the children do not do.
1. ☐ get up
2. ☐ make breakfast
3. ☐ do the shopping
4. ☐ do the cleaning
5. ☐ put out the rubbish
6. ☐ go to school
7. ☐ go to clubs
8. ☐ do homework

7 ▶ 3.5 Watch again and write how the day of these children is different to each other's.
1. in the morning
   Some take the bus, some walk and some go to school by car.
2. during the day
3. in the afternoon
4. in the evening

8 Think of an ideal day. Write what you would like to do from morning to evening. Share it with the class.

YOU EXPLORE

9 CULTURE PROJECT In groups, write a presentation about a child (or children) with an unusual life in your country. You can write about a sports star, an actor, etc.
1. Use the internet to research the child/children.
2. Find some pictures or videos.
3. Write your presentation.
4. Share it with the class.

4 Love to learn

VOCABULARY
Classroom objects | School subjects
Making friends | Learning

GRAMMAR
Present Continuous | Present Continuous and Present Simple | Prepositions of place

Grammar: No school today

Speaking: The Maths exam

BBC Culture: Byron Court School

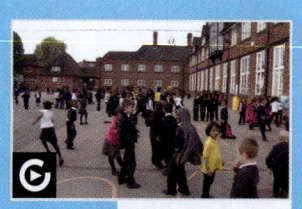

Workbook p. 53

BBC VOX POPS

KiDS Daily Times

Laura and Nik

Some of Laura's favourite erasers

Back to school blues? Not for Laura and Nik!

It's the end of August and for thousands of teenagers that means the end of the summer holidays. But for Laura Smith and her friend Nik Jones, it's their favourite time of year. The pair, who are in Year 8 at Newlands school, say they love buying pens, pencils, erasers and exercise books for the new school year. 'We're stationery* fanatics!' says Nik. Laura has more than 300 erasers. 'I buy new ones all the time. I can't stop!' she says.

* pens and materials for writing

4.1 VOCABULARY — School

I can talk about classroom objects and school subjects.

1 Read about Laura and Nik. Are you a big fan of pens and other writing materials?

2 **I KNOW!** Study the Vocabulary A box. In pairs, find four classroom objects in the text and add them to the list. How many more words can you think of in two minutes?

Vocabulary A	Classroom objects
calculator pencil case poster projector ruler sports bag textbook whiteboard	

3 🔊 2.01 Listen to five dialogues and write the classroom objects you hear.

4 Study the Vocabulary B box. In pairs, match the words with photos A–L on page 47. Which are your favourite subjects?

Vocabulary B — School subjects

☐ D Art ☐ Biology ☐ Chemistry ☐ English ☐ Geography
☐ History ☐ Maths ☐ Information Technology (IT) ☐ Music
☐ PE ☐ Physics ☐ Religious Education (RE)

46

A	B	C	D
E	F	G	H
I	J	K	L

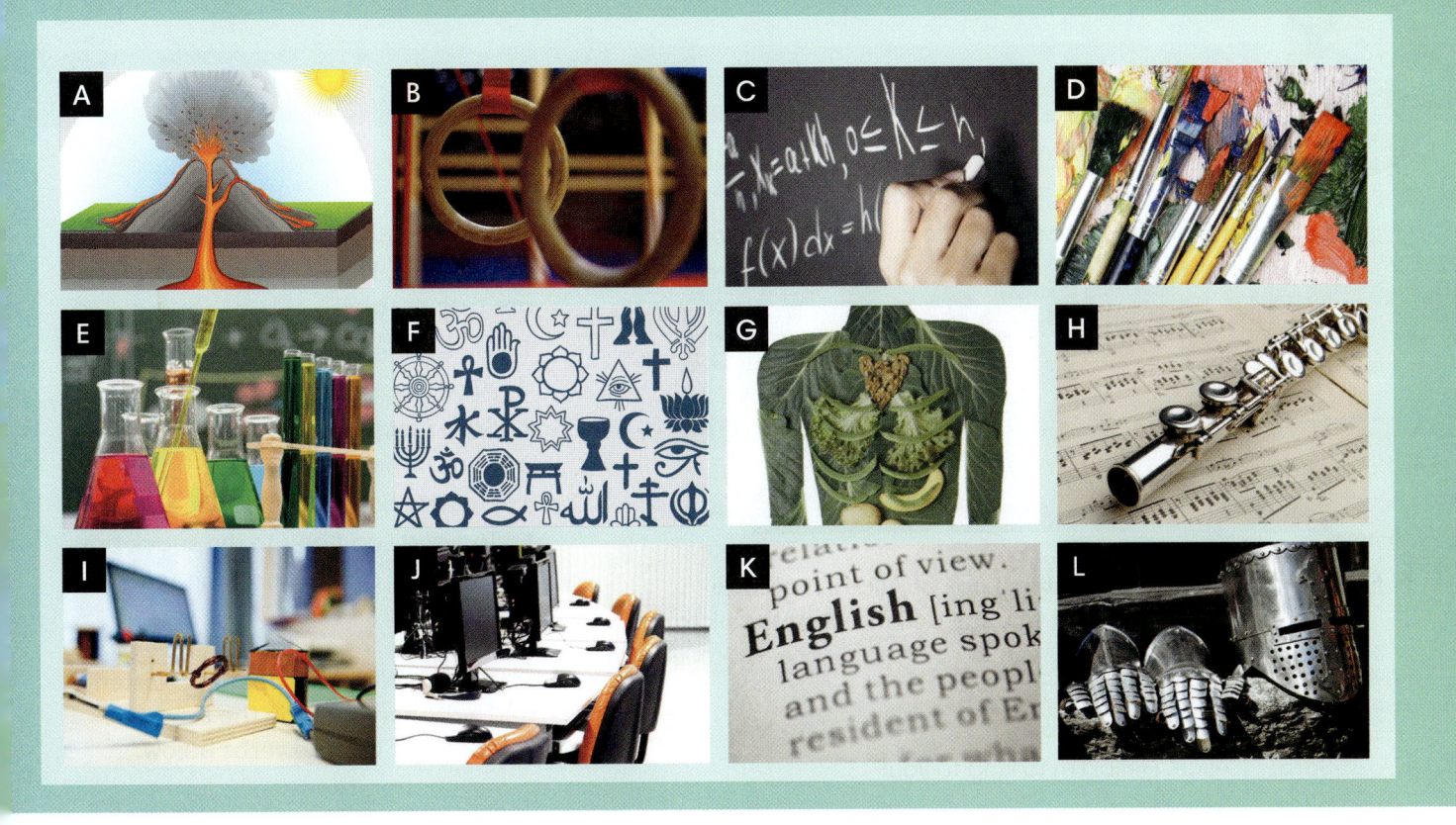

5 🔊 **2.01** Listen again and match dialogues 1–5 with school subjects a–e.

1 _____ 2 _____ 3 _____ 4 _____ 5 _____

a PE b English c Maths d History e Geography

6 In pairs, look at the timetable and complete the sentences about Newlands School and your school.

1 At Newlands School, they have *five* lessons every day. At our school, we have _____.
2 The first lesson starts at _____ o'clock. At our school, the first lesson _____.
3 Each lesson is _____ minutes long. At our school, lessons are _____ minutes long.
4 There are _____ breaks in a school day. At our school, there are _____.
5 There is a break of _____ minutes for lunch. At our school, _____.
6 At Newlands, French is the only foreign language. At our school you can learn _____.

Newlands School Class 8B Timetable

	Lesson 1 9.00–10.00	Lesson 2 10.00–11.00	11.00–11.20	Lesson 3 11.20–12.20	Lesson 4 12.20–13.20	13.20–14.10	Lesson 5 14.10–15.10
Mon	1 _____	Maths	Break	English	French	Lunch	2 _____
Tues	Art	3 _____		RE	Biology		French
Wed	Drama	English		History	4 _____		Geography
Thurs	French	Chemistry		Geography	English		History
Fri	English	Presentation skills		Maths	5 _____		PE

7 🔊 **2.02** Listen to Laura and Nik talking about their timetable for this year. Complete the table.

	Day she/he likes	Day she/he doesn't like
Laura		
Nik		

8 🔊 **2.02** Listen again and complete the timetable in Exercise 6 with the school subjects.

9 In pairs, talk about days you like/don't like at school. Say why.

I love Mondays because we have …
I don't like … because …

And YOU?

Unit 4 47

4.2 GRAMMAR Present Continuous

I can use the Present Continuous to talk about things happening now.

1 Look at the photo. Do you think the girls know each other?

2 🔊 **2.03** Read and listen. Look at Alice's message on page 128 to find out why she doesn't want to talk to her friends.

Sara: Hi, Alice. How's it going?
Alice: [silence]
Sara: Alice. Hello! I'm talking to you!
Alice: [silence]
Sara: You aren't speaking to me. Why?
Alice: [silence]
Sara: Are you feeling OK, Alice?
Alice: [silence]
Caitlin: Hi, you two! How's it going?
Sara: I'm fine, but Alice isn't speaking to me. Is she speaking to you?
Caitlin: I don't know. Are you speaking to me, Alice?
Alice: [silence]
Caitlin: No, she isn't! What's wrong, Alice? Are we irritating you?
Alice: [silence]
Sara: Yes, we are! We're wasting our time! Are you coming with me to the snack bar now, Caitlin? Ted and Leo are waiting.
Caitlin: Yes, I am. Wait a minute. Now she's writing something. And why is she smiling?

3 Study the Grammar box. Find more examples of the Present Continuous in the dialogue.

4 Make sentences in the Present Continuous. Decide if the sentences are true or false.
1. Alice / speak / to Sara
   Alice is speaking to Sara. It's false!
2. Sara / feel / fine
3. Sara / write / a note
4. Caitlin / not speak / to Alice
5. Ted and Leo / go / to the snack bar
6. Sara and Caitlin / not wait / at the snack bar

5 🔊 **2.04** What's happening? Listen and write sentences in the Present Continuous. Use the verbs below.

cry laugh rain run sleep type

It/Somebody is …
Some people are …

6 Complete the questions and short answers. Use the Present Continuous. In pairs, ask and answer the questions.
1. A: <u>Are you feeling</u> (you/feel) hungry?
   B: <u>No, we aren't.</u> Gran always gives us a big breakfast!
2. A: _____ (you/feel) tired?
   B: _____ I'm studying for a test!
3. A: _____ (it/rain) now?
   B: _____ I hope it stops soon!
4. A: _____ (your parents/watch) TV?
   B: _____ They're at work.
5. A: _____ (the teacher/wear) brown shoes today?
   B: _____ They're black.

Grammar	Present Continuous
+	**-**
I'm talking. You're talking. He's talking.	I'm not talking. They aren't talking. She isn't talking.
?	**Short answers**
Are they talking? Is she talking?	Yes, they are./No, they aren't. Yes, she is./No, she isn't.
How's it going? Why are they smiling?	

Time expressions: now, at the moment

GRAMMAR TIME > PAGE 121

7 In pairs, take it in turns to ask and answer about what people/animals in your life are doing now. Use the ideas below to help you.
- your best friend
- your brother/sister
- your grandparents
- your parents
- your pet
- your teacher

A: *What's your pet doing now?*
B: *My dog, Felek, is sleeping.*

Unit 4

4.3 READING and VOCABULARY School days

I can find specific detail in a short story and talk about making friends.

1 **CLASS VOTE** What memories do you have of your first day at your school?
- good
- bad
- good and bad

2 Check you understand the words below. Read the text. Does the story have a happy ending?

bell   classmates   form tutor   register

3 🔊 **2.05** Read the text again. Complete gaps 1–4 in the text with sentences a–e. There is one extra sentence.
a He's writing information about me in the register.
b He lives at the Children's Home.
c It's a very long walk.
d They've also got grey trousers and glasses.
e Some boys stop and look at me.

4 Read the text again. Mark the sentences ✓ (right), ✗ (wrong) or ? (doesn't say).
1 ☐ Mr Grey isn't friendly.
2 ☐ Maths is David's best subject.
3 ☐ The boys in David's class look the same.
4 ☐ David isn't happy to see the boy from the bus.
5 ☐ David doesn't like what Mr Grey says about him to the class.
6 ☐ David is smiling at Amrik.

5 **WORD FRIENDS** Which of the phrases can you find in the text? How do you say these phrases in your language?

best friend   get to know somebody
make friends with somebody
meet somebody for the first time

6 Complete the sentences with words from Exercise 5. In pairs, say which sentences are true for you.
1 I sometimes feel nervous when I meet people for the first *time*.
2 It's easy for me to make friends _____ people.
3 My _____ friend and I chat for hours every evening.
4 I'm shy. People say it's difficult to get to _____ me.

7 [VOX POPS ▶ 4.1] In pairs, say which things are important/not important to you when you make friends with someone. Use these ideas to help you.
- like the same fashion/style
- like the same music
- like the same football team
- live near me
- have a similar personality (funny, quiet etc.)

It's important/not important that my friends like the same music.

FIRST DAY

I'm meeting my form tutor for the first time – the two of us in a big classroom. Mr Grey has got glasses and he's wearing a grey jacket. ¹_____ I'm looking at the numbers on the board and thinking that he probably teaches Maths. I'm really bad at Maths.

The bell rings and boys are starting to come into the classroom. Tall, short, big, happy, sad. I'm standing at the front of the classroom with Mr Grey. ²_____ One of them is the tall boy from the bus this morning. Bad news!

Now Mr Grey is talking about me to my new classmates. 'This is David. Be nice to him. ³_____' Oh no! Why is he saying this? It's really difficult to make friends with people after that! I remember my first days at all the other schools.

'David, you can sit next to Amrik.' Now I'm walking to my new desk. ⁴_____ Amrik is looking at me with a small, brave smile. He's wearing an old Manchester City shirt. I already know we're best friends.

Unit 4 49

4.4 GRAMMAR Present Simple and Present Continuous

I can talk about what usually happens and what is happening now.

VIDEO NO SCHOOL TODAY

On Mondays Max, Sol and Eva usually have a long day at school. But it's a holiday today and they're having a day in the countryside with their bikes.

Supervisor: Welcome to the mountain bike course. You guys are really lucky – it always rains on Monday mornings but it isn't raining today! Are you ready to start?

Max, Sol and Eva are exploring the mountain bike course.

Max: Wow! Isn't this fantastic? Just think, Sol. Usually at this time on a Monday, Mrs Jones gives us a really difficult Physics test, but today we're riding our bikes in the beautiful countryside! Are you enjoying it, Eva?

Eva: Yeah! I don't usually enjoy adventure parks but I'm really enjoying myself today!

OUT of class
You're (really) lucky.
Are you ready? Wow!

1 🎥 4.2 🔊 2.06 Watch or listen. Where are Max, Sol and Eva spending the day?

2 Study the Grammar box. Find examples of the Present Simple and Present Continuous in the dialogue.

Grammar Present Simple and Present Continuous

We use the Present Simple for things we do regularly.
I usually **have** lunch at twelve o'clock.

We use the Present Continuous for something happening now/at the moment.
I'm on holiday. It's twelve o'clock and I**'m drinking** cola in a café.

GRAMMAR TIME > PAGE 121

3 Choose the correct option.
1 *Do they ride* / (*Are they riding*) their bikes now?
2 Usually it *doesn't rain* / *isn't raining* all summer.
3 Sol's sleeping. He *doesn't watch* / *isn't watching* TV.
4 Max's dad *goes* / *is going* to the supermarket on Saturdays.
5 Excuse me, *do you use* / *are you using* this computer?
6 My grandad *doesn't drive* / *isn't driving* – he can travel by bus for free.

4 Complete questions 1–6 with *is*, *are*, *do* or *does*. Match them with answers a–f.
1 [d] <u>Are</u> you wearing jeans now?
2 [ ] _____ you wear jeans at the weekend?
3 [ ] _____ it raining now?
4 [ ] _____ you have lunch at school?
5 [ ] _____ you checking your phone?
6 [ ] _____ your best friend often check his/her phone?

a Yes, he does. About every five minutes!
b No, I'm not. I'm listening to the teacher!
c Yes, I do. I bring sandwiches from home.
d No, I'm not. I'm wearing shorts.
e No, it isn't.
f No, I don't. I wear tracksuit trousers.

5 In pairs, ask and answer the questions in Exercise 4.

6 In pairs, talk about what you do on holiday and how it's different from now. Think about:
- the clothes you wear.
- what you do.
- what you eat or drink.
- the people you spend time with.

On holiday I … At the moment I …

And YOU

4.5 LISTENING and VOCABULARY Famous schools

I can identify specific detail in a radio programme and talk about boarding schools.

1 Are there any famous schools in your town/region/country?

2 🔊 **2.07** Listen to the first part of a radio programme about a famous boarding school. In pairs, answer the questions.

1. In which city is it?
2. Is it a new school?
3. Do all the pupils live in the school?
4. Are boarding schools popular in your country?

> **Watch OUT!**
> boarding school = a school where pupils live and study

3 🔊 **2.07** Listen again and complete the notes.

Broadboard School
- *private boarding school in the ^{1}_____ of London*
- *about ^{2}_____ years old*
- *costs £35,000 for one ^{3}_____*
- *has 750 pupils; about ^{4}_____ live at school seven days a week*

4 🔊 **2.08** Listen to the second part of the programme. Mark the sentences T (true) or F (false).

1. ☐ Pupils eat breakfast in their rooms.
2. ☐ Pupils don't have a long walk to their classrooms.
3. ☐ Classes finish at four o'clock, from Monday to Saturday.
4. ☐ Students study in the evenings from 7.15 p.m. to 9 p.m.
5. ☐ Students have an hour to relax before bed.

5 🔊 **2.09** **WORD FRIENDS** Listen and choose the correct option.

1. stop / (start) school
2. have / learn classes
3. go to / visit school
4. revise for / study exams
5. make / do homework

6 Complete the questions with words from Word Friends in Exercise 5. In pairs, ask and answer the questions.

1. Do you think it's a good idea to start *school* at ten o'clock every day?
2. What time do you usually _____ to school?
3. Do students at your school have _____ on Saturday mornings?
4. When do you usually do your _____?
5. Do you enjoy revising _____ exams?

7 **And YOU** What are the good things about going to a boarding school like Broadboard School? Read the sentences and tick the ones you agree with. In pairs, compare your ideas.

1. ☐ You live at school seven days a week.
2. ☐ You eat breakfast, lunch and dinner at school.
3. ☐ It's very expensive.
4. ☐ You have classes six days a week.
5. ☐ There's a lot of time to study.
6. ☐ It's not far to walk to school!
7. ☐ You're with your classmates all day.
8. ☐ You don't see you parents/sister/brother often.

A: It's good that you're with your classmates all day.
B: For me it's a bad thing.

Unit 4 51

4.6 SPEAKING Polite requests

I can make and respond to polite requests.

AUDIO THE MATHS EXAM

Teacher: Your Maths exam is starting now. You have three hours.
Max: Sol? Sol! Sol! Can I borrow your eraser?
Sol: Sure.
Max: Thanks, buddy! … Sol, can I borrow a pencil? This one's broken!
Sol: Yes, OK. Here you are.
Max: Sol, can I borrow your ruler?
Sol: I'm sorry, but I'm using it. You can have it in a minute, OK?
Max: OK, that's fine! Psst! Sol! Can you tell me the answer to question 3B? Is it 93?
Sol: Sorry, I can't! This is an exam! Can I have another piece of paper, please?
Teacher: Yes, of course.
Sol: Max, can you stop that?
Teacher: Sol Gardner! This is an exam! Why are you talking?

OUT of class
buddy
That's fine.

1 CLASS VOTE Do you often borrow school things (pens, pencils, etc.) from your classmates?

2 🔊 2.10 Read or listen. What three things does Sol ask to borrow?

3 Study the Speaking box. Find examples of polite requests and responses in the dialogue.

Speaking Polite requests

Request	☹	☺
Can I borrow your pen/phone?	Sorry, I'm using it.	Sure. Yes, OK. Yes, of course. Yes, no problem. OK, just a second.
Can I look at your exercise book?	Sorry, I need it. Sorry, you can't.	
Can I have a piece of paper/a glass of water?		
Can you help me with this exercise/box?	Sorry, I can't.	
Can you tell me the answer/the time?		

4 🔊 2.11 Complete the dialogues with one word in each gap. Listen and check. In pairs, practise reading the dialogues.

1 **A:** Excuse me, *can* you tell me the time, please?
   B: Yes, of _____. It's twenty to eight.
2 **A:** Sophie, can you help _____ with my homework?
   B: _____, I can't. I'm really busy.
3 **A:** Hi! Sorry, can _____ help me with this box?
   B: OK, _____ a second.
4 **A:** Can I _____ the keys to your car, Dad?
   B: Sorry, you _____. 'Never again' means 'never again'!

5 🔊 2.12 Listen and choose the correct response for each request. In pairs, compare your answers. Then listen again.

1 a Yes, OK.   b Sorry, I can't.
2 a Yes, of course.   b Sorry, you can't.
3 a Sorry, I can't.   b Sorry, I need it.
4 a Sorry, I can't.   b Sure.
5 a Sorry, you can't.   b Sorry, I can't.

6 In pairs, take it in turns to make and respond to requests. Use these ideas or your own. Don't be shy to say no!

And YOU?

Can I …?	Can you …?
• borrow your phone/dictionary/shoes	• tell me your address/the password on your phone
• have some of your water/your chair	• give me a piece of paper/£200/your watch
• look at your textbook/the texts on your phone	
• wear your glasses/jacket	

A: *Can you make me lunch?*   **B:** *Sorry, I can't!*

52 Unit 4

4.7 ENGLISH IN USE Prepositions of place

I can use prepositions of place to describe position.

1 In pairs, look at the picture. How many mice can you see?

Panic in the Biology class!

2 Study the Language box. How do you say the prepositions in your language?

Language	Prepositions of place		
🎒	behind	🗑️	next to
🪑	between	📚	on
🐭	in	🪑	under
📦	in front of		

3 In pairs, write sentences about the mice in the picture. Write one sentence for each preposition in the Language box. Ask your teacher for any new words. Compare your answers with another pair.

There's a mouse on the teacher's head.

4 Choose the correct option. Are any of the sentences true for you?

1. In Maths lessons I always sit *between* / *next* to my best friend.
2. There's a nice park *under* / *between* my house and my friend's house.
3. I always have a lot of papers *on* / *between* my desk.
4. Our teacher always stands *in front of* / *under* the class.
5. There's a bin *between* / *under* my desk at home.
6. I always have an extra pencil *in front of* / *in* my pencil case.

5 [VOX POPS ▶ 4.3] Choose three locations from the list. In pairs, tell your partner one object you keep there.

- in your pocket
- next to your bed
- on your desk
- under your bed
- in your pencil case
- in your school bag

I keep my keys in my pocket.

WORDLIST Classroom objects | School subjects | Learning | Prepositions of place

Art /ɑːt/ n
behind /bɪˈhaɪnd/ prep
(school) bell /(skuːl) bel/ n
between /bɪˈtwiːn/ adv
bin /bɪn/ n
Biology /baɪˈɒlədʒi/ n
blackboard /ˈblækbɔːd/ n
boarding school /ˈbɔːdɪŋ skuːl/ n
borrow /ˈbɒrəʊ/ v
box /bɒks/ n
break /breɪk/ v
broken /ˈbrəʊkən/ v
buddy /ˈbʌdi/ n
busy /ˈbɪzi/ adj
calculator /ˈkælkjəleɪtə, ˈkælkjʊleɪtə/ n
Chemistry /ˈkeməstri, ˈkemɪstri/ n
classmate /ˈklɑːsmeɪt/ n
classroom /ˈklɑːsrʊm, -ruːm/ n
countryside /ˈkʌntrisaɪd/ n
(mountain bike) course /(ˈmaʊntɪn baɪk) kɔːs/ n
desk /desk/ n
dictionary /ˈdɪkʃənəri/ n
difficult /ˈdɪfɪkəlt/ adj
English /ˈɪŋglɪʃ/ n
eraser /ɪˈreɪzə/ n
exam /ɪɡˈzæm/ n
exercise book /ˈeksəsaɪz bʊk/ n
ex-pupil /eks ˈpjuːpəl/ n
fantastic /fænˈtæstɪk/ adj
(for) free /(fə) friː/ adj
form tutor /fɔːm ˈtjuːtə/ n
Geography /dʒiˈɒɡrəfi, ˈdʒɒɡ-/ n
(hard) work /(hɑːd) wɜːk/ n
History /ˈhɪstəri/ n
hope /həʊp/ v
in /ɪn/ prep
in front of /ɪn frʌnt əv/ prep
Information Technology (IT) /ˌɪnfəˈmeɪʃən tekˈnɒlədʒi (aɪ tiː)/ n
irritate /ˈɪrəteɪt, ˈɪrɪteɪt/ v
laugh /lɑːf/ v
lesson /ˈlesən/ n
lucky /ˈlʌki/ adj
Maths /mæθs/ n
memories (of sth) /ˈmeməriz/ n
Music /ˈmjuːzɪk/ n
need /niːd/ v
next to /nekst tə/ prep
(classroom) object /(ˈklɑːsrʊm) ˈɒbdʒɪkt/ n
on /ɒn/ prep
pen /pen/ n
pencil /ˈpensəl/ n
pencil case /ˈpensəl keɪs/ n
Physical Education (PE) /ˈfɪzɪkəl ˌedjʊˈkeɪʃən (piː iː)/ n
Physics /ˈfɪzɪks/ n
piece of paper /piːs əv ˈpeɪpə/ n
pocket /ˈpɒkət, ˈpɒkɪt/ n
poster /ˈpəʊstə/ n
private (school) /ˈpraɪvət (skuːl)/ n
(school) project /(skuːl) ˈprɒdʒekt/ n
projector /prəˈdʒektə/ n
pupil /ˈpjuːpəl/ n
ready /ˈredi/ adj
register /ˈredʒəstə, ˈredʒɪstə/ n
Religious Education (RE) /rɪˈlɪdʒəs ˌedjʊˈkeɪʃən (ɑːr iː)/ n
ruler /ˈruːlə/ n
run /rʌn/ v
school bag /skuːl bæg/ n
school year /skuːl jɪə/ n
sports bag /spɔːts bæg/ n
(school) subject /(skuːl) ˈsʌbdʒɪkt/ n
teach /tiːtʃ/ v
test /test/ n
textbook /ˈtekstbʊk/ n
timetable /ˈtaɪmˌteɪbəl/ n
under /ˈʌndə/ prep
usually /ˈjuːʒuəli, ˈjuːʒəli/ adv
whiteboard /ˈwaɪtbɔːd/ n

WORD FRIENDS

best friend
do homework
get to know sb
go to school
have classes
make friends with sb
meet sb for the first time
revise for exams/tests
start school
wear school uniform
write a note

VOCABULARY IN ACTION

1 Use the wordlist to find:
1 ten school subjects *Art, …*
2 eight things that pupils take to school every day *calculator, …*
3 seven prepositions of place *behind, …*

2 In pairs, make five sentences about your classroom. Use the ideas below and the prepositions in Exercise 1.

> bin   blackboard   desk
> dictionary   exercise book   door
> pencil case   poster   projector
> school bag   our teacher   window
>
> *We're sitting next to/behind …*
> *There's a … on the …*
> *My school bag is …*

3 Complete the questions with one word in each gap. In pairs, answer the questions.
1 Who is your form *tutor* this year?
2 Where do you _____ for tests – at home, with friends or in the library?
3 Who is your best _____? Do you _____ to the same school?
4 Do you wear a school _____? Do you think it's a good idea?
5 Do you _____ classes at the weekend? How do you feel about it?

4 🔊 2.13 **PRONUNCIATION** Listen to how we pronounce the /j/ sound. Listen again and repeat.

> calc**u**lator   men**u**   m**u**sic   pop**u**lar

5 🔊 2.14 **PRONUNCIATION** In pairs, say the words. Listen, check and repeat.
1 exc**u**se me
2 t**u**tor
3 p**u**pil
4 st**u**dent
5 **u**niform
6 **u**sually

Revision

VOCABULARY

1 Complete the school subjects.
1 A_r_t
2 M _ t _ s
3 H _ _ t _ r _
4 G _ _ _ _ r _ p _ y
5 B _ _ l _ _ y
6 M _ si _

2 In pairs, ask and answer the questions.

Which subject:
1 do you enjoy?
2 do you think is easy?
3 do you think is difficult?

3 Match the words with the definitions.

> break   classmate   PE
> ~~register~~   timetable

1 a book with the names of all the pupils in a class _register_
2 a plan with all the lessons a class has in one week _____
3 a short time between lessons for pupils and teachers to relax _____
4 somebody who is in the same class as you _____
5 a school subject: you exercise or play sports _____

4 Complete the words in the sentences. In pairs, say who you are like.
1 Nina is always very quiet when she meets people for the **f**_irst_ time.
2 Charlie's got a lot of friends. It isn't a problem for him to make friends **w**_____ people.
3 Jake has very happy **m**_____ of his first school.
4 Trudi's mum always waits for her in her car in **f**_____ of the school.
5 Brett thinks that learning a language is hard **w**_____.
6 Lara usually sits **n**_____ to her **b**_____ friend.
7 Toni often asks if he can borrow a pen or a **p**_____ of paper.

I'm like Brett – I think languages are difficult.

GRAMMAR

5 Complete the text messages with the Present Continuous form of the verbs in brackets.

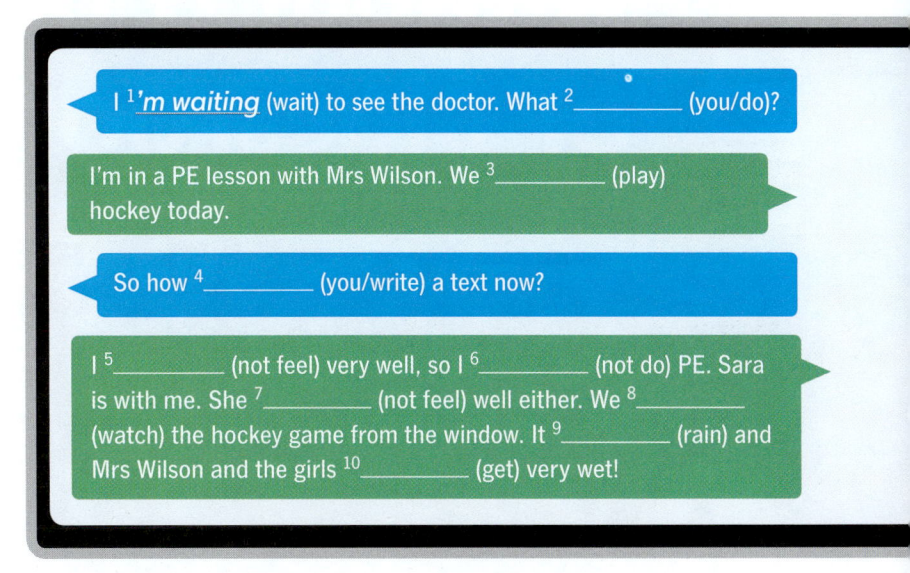

> I ¹'_m waiting_ (wait) to see the doctor. What ²_____ (you/do)?

> I'm in a PE lesson with Mrs Wilson. We ³_____ (play) hockey today.

> So how ⁴_____ (you/write) a text now?

> I ⁵_____ (not feel) very well, so I ⁶_____ (not do) PE. Sara is with me. She ⁷_____ (not feel) well either. We ⁸_____ (watch) the hockey game from the window. It ⁹_____ (rain) and Mrs Wilson and the girls ¹⁰_____ (get) very wet!

6 In pairs, complete the sentences with names of friends or classmates so that the sentences are true.
1 _Paolo_ is working hard at the moment.
2 _____ is wearing blue trainers today.
3 _____ always wears make-up.
4 _____ isn't feeling very well today.
5 _____ doesn't live far from the school.
6 _____ laughs a lot.
7 _____ is sitting next to the window.

7 Choose the correct option.
1 *Do you enjoy* / (*Are you enjoying*) this party?
2 Ella is a great student. She *works* / *is working* hard all year.
3 History is my favourite subject. We *learn* / *are learning* about Christopher Columbus at the moment.
4 Matt and Frank *aren't watching* / *don't watch* TV – they're revising for an exam.
5 My cat *usually sleeps* / *is usually sleeping* on my school bag!

SPEAKING

8 In pairs, make and respond to polite requests. Student A, follow the instructions below. Student B, go to page 128.
- Student A, you are in an English lesson. You don't have a pen. Ask Student B to lend you a pen. Thank Student B.
- Listen to Student B's problem. You have a dictionary but you're using it at the moment. Student B can borrow it in a minute.

DICTATION

9 🔊 2.15 Listen. Then listen again and write down what you hear.

BBC CULTURE

Can students learn without a timetable or classrooms?

Unusual schools

Every school has a timetable so students know what they are doing. Every school has classrooms so students know where to go. Every school gives the students homework and tests. Every school makes rules for its students. True or false? False! Some schools are very different.

1 Waldorf schools

There are primary and secondary Waldorf schools all over the world. These schools can decide about some of the things they teach, but they all teach art, social skills and critical thinking. Students do all sorts of creative play and practical activities, for example, painting, weaving and woodwork. Waldorf schools even have a special subject, Eurythmy. It is a very interesting drama and dance class. There are no tests in primary school, and secondary students take exams only if it is important for university. And there are no grades before students are fourteen or fifteen!

2 Vittra Telefonplan School, Stockholm

The Vittra Telefonplan School in Sweden wants children to learn languages, to learn to work together and to be creative. So in this school there are classrooms and spaces for different group, project and individual activities. The rooms are amazing, colourful places with wonderful furniture. And every student has a tablet or computer! Learning is fun here!

GLOSSARY
creative (adj) having a lot of new ideas or good at making new things
decide (v) choose what you are going to do after thinking about it
furniture (n) tables, desks, chairs, beds, etc.
practical (adj) about real things and situations, not about ideas, feelings, etc
rule (n) sth that tells you what you must or must not do
weave (v) make a basket

EXPLORE

1 In pairs, discuss the questions.
1 How many school subjects and activities can you name in two minutes?
2 Do you know someone who goes to an unusual school and does different things from you?
3 What's your perfect school?

2 Read the article. Match photos A–B with schools 1–2 from the article.

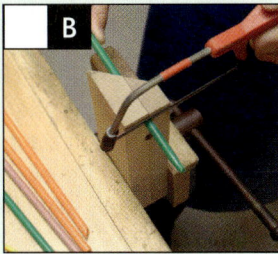

A

B

3 Read the text again. Choose WP (Waldorf primary) WS (Waldorf secondary) or VT (Vittra Telefonplan). Sometimes more than one answer is possible.

Which school:
1 does not have tests? *WP / WS / VT*
2 has a special subject? *WP / WS / VT*
3 teaches students to be creative? *WP / WS / VT*
4 doesn't have grades? *WP / WS / VT*
5 has interesting places for students to learn in? *WP / WS / VT*

4 Would you like to go to one of these schools? Why? / Why not?

EXPLORE MORE

5 You are going to watch part of a BBC programme about unusual schools. Read an advert for the programme and look at the photo. In pairs, try to guess the answers to these questions.
1 Where is this school?
3 How many different languages can you hear in this playground?
3 Which countries are the children from?

Byron Court School
This programme is about an unusual school. At Byron Court there are many nationalities and the children speak a lot of different languages.

6 ▶ 4.4 Watch the video and check your ideas from Exercise 5.

7 Watch again and tick the two countries which are *not* mentioned.

☐ Bulgaria ☐ China ☐ Iraq
☐ Poland ☐ Romania ☐ Somalia
☐ the Philippines

8 ▶ 4.4 Watch again and mark the sentences T (true) or F (false).
1 ☐ Children start this school when they are five.
2 ☐ There aren't any English children at the school.
3 ☐ The children's parents live in other countries.
4 ☐ All the children speak English when they start school.
5 ☐ The children learn about their classmates' countries.

9 Would you like to study at a school like Byron Court? Why? / Why not? Discuss in pairs.

Yes, because you have friends from different countries.
No, because some students don't understand.

YOU EXPLORE

10 **CULTURE PROJECT** In groups, write a presentation about an unusual school in your country.
1 Use the internet to research an unusual school.
2 Find some pictures or videos.
3 Write your presentation.
4 Share it with the class.

5 The music of life

VOCABULARY
Musical instruments | Types of music
Opinion adjectives | Live music

GRAMMAR
Comparatives | Superlatives

Grammar: The best dancer

Speaking: What do you suggest?

BBC Culture: National Youth Orchestra of Iraq

Workbook p. 65

BBC VOX POPS ▶
CLIL 3 > p. 138

Joe 90, Music Man

Joe Penna, or Mystery Guitar Man, is a Brazilian filmmaker and musician. He loves music. In one of his YouTube videos he visits the Musical Instrument Museum (MIM) in Phoenix, Arizona, USA. It's a museum with thousands of different instruments from all around the world. In the video, Joe plays ninety instruments from ninety countries in only ninety seconds!

5.1 VOCABULARY Music

I can talk about types of music and musical instruments.

1 Look at the photos and read the text. In pairs, answer the questions.
  1 Who is Joe Penna?
  2 What is the MIM?
  3 What does Joe do in the video?
  4 Do you like music?

2 Which instruments can you see in the photos?

Vocabulary A	Musical instruments		
☐ accordion	☐ drums	☐ harmonica	☐ saxophone
☐ bass guitar	☐ flute	☐ keyboards	☐ trumpet
☐ cello	☐ guitar	☐ piano	☐ violin

3 🔊 2.16 Listen and number the instruments in Vocabulary A in the order you hear them.

4 🔊 2.17 Listen and check your answers to Exercise 3.

5 Study the Vocabulary B box. In groups, write typical instruments for these types of music.
  1 classical: *cello, flute,* _____
  2 jazz: _____
  3 pop, reggae, rock: _____
  4 traditional: _____

Vocabulary B	Types of music
classical country hip-hop jazz pop rap reggae rock techno traditional	

6 Complete the information about musicians with words from Vocabulary A and B.

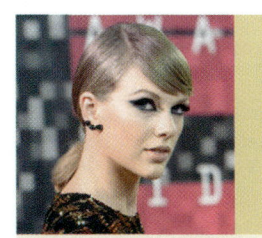

Taylor Swift is a ¹**c**ountry singer and a ²**p**_____ star. She can play the ³**g**_____ and the ⁴**p**_____.

Kanye West is a ⁵**h**_____-**h**_____ singer and songwriter. He can play the ⁶**k**_____ and the ⁷**d**_____.

Nicola Benedetti is a ⁸**c**_____ musician. She plays the ⁹**v**_____.

Mike Dirnt plays the ¹⁰**b**_____ **g**_____ in American ¹¹**r**_____ group Green Day.

Wynton Marsalis is a ¹²**j**_____ musician. He plays the ¹³**t**_____.

7 🔊 **2.18** Listen and complete the dialogue with one word in each gap. Who is Penny thinking of? Go to page 128 and check.

Mark: Is it a woman?
Penny: Yes, it is.
Mark: Does she play ¹_____ music?
Penny: No, she doesn't.
Mark: Does she play ²_____ music?
Penny: Yes, she does.
Mark: Can she play the ³_____?
Penny: Yes, she can. She can play the ⁴_____ and the bass guitar too.
Mark: Does she ⁵_____ in a group?
Penny: No, she doesn't. She's a solo artist.
Mark: Does she ⁶_____?
Penny: Yes, she does.
Mark: Is she ⁷_____?
Penny: Yes, she is.

8 In pairs, think of a famous musician. Ask *yes/no* questions to find who your partner is thinking of. Use the dialogue in Exercise 6 to help you.

9 🔊 **2.19** In groups, do the quiz. Listen and check.

The ABC of Music

1 Where is reggae music from?
 a Argentina   b Jamaica   c South Africa
2 Which of these instruments is typical in country music?
 a saxophone   b cello   c harmonica
3 What nationality are Sia Furler, Kylie Minogue and AC/DC?
 a Australian   b British   c Canadian
4 What's the name of Pharrell Williams' 2014 hit song?
 a *Happy*   b *Hello*   c *Sugar*
5 Which pop star is famous for the hit songs *Baby* and *Love yourself*?
 a Ed Sheeran   b Hozier   c Justin Bieber
6 How long is a standard violin?
 a 20.4 cm   b 35.6 cm   c 48.2 cm
7 Which pop star is famous for the hit songs *E.T.* and *Firework*?
 a Amy Winehouse   b Katy Perry   c Madonna
8 Listen to this piece of classical music. Who is the composer?
 a Beethoven   b Mozart   c Vivaldi

10 [VOX POPS ▶ 5.1] In pairs, ask and answer the questions.
1 What instruments can you play?
2 What instrument do you want to learn to play?
3 Can any of your friends or family play an instrument?
4 What kind of music do you listen to?
5 Do you follow any singers, musicians or groups on Twitter or Facebook?

A: *What instruments can you play?*
B: *I can play the flute but not very well. What about you?*

5.2 GRAMMAR Comparatives

I can make comparisons.

ALPHA BOYS

The number one fan page for the number one boy band!

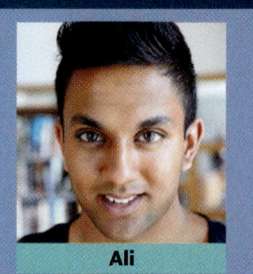

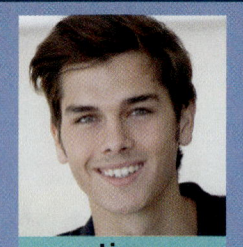

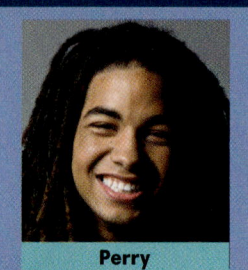

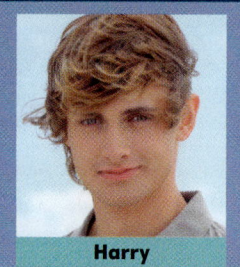

Ali | Liam | Perry | Harry | Akira

Fun facts about the Alpha Boys

	Age	Height	Personality
Ali	17	1.84	friendly
Liam	18	1.81	funny
Perry	19	1.81	cool
Harry	17	1.67	quiet
Akira	16	1.73	intelligent

Who's your favourite? Reply

Rico4	Ali's a great dancer.
bluesky	Ali's a good dancer, but Harry's better. Harry's cuter than Ali too.
trikimiki	I agree Harry's better than Ali, but I like Akira. He's really cool and intelligent.
bluesky	What? Harry's cooler than Akira! He's more intelligent too.
Rico4	Harry can't dance. He's worse than me! And he's really small. Ali's bigger and stronger than him. Ali's friendlier too. Harry never smiles.

1 Look at the Alpha Boys fan page. Which members of the band do Rico4, bluesky and trikimiki like?

2 Study the Grammar box. Find comparative adjectives in the message board.

Grammar — Comparative adjectives

Adjective	Comparative
quiet	quieter
brave	braver
sad	sadder
happy	happier
interesting	more interesting
good	better
bad	worse

Harry is quieter than Ali.

GRAMMAR TIME > PAGE 122

3 🔊 2.20 In pairs, complete the text with the comparative form of the adjectives in brackets. Which member of the Alpha Boys is it? Listen and check.

He's ¹*funnier* (funny) than Akira. He's got a ² _____ (good) sense of humour. He's ³ _____ (thin) than Akira and ⁴ _____ (tall) too but he's ⁵ _____ (short) than Ali. He's ⁶ _____ (old) than Ali but he's ⁷ _____ (young) than Perry.

4 Work in groups. How many comparative sentences can you write about the Alpha Boys? Use the adjectives below to help you.

> bad big cool cute friendly funny good
> intelligent nice old quiet strong tall thin young

Perry's taller than Akira.

5 Make comparative sentences.

1. Sam Smith / young / James Bay
   Sam Smith is younger than James Bay.
2. Taylor Swift / tall / Ed Sheeran
3. U2 / successful / AC/DC
4. Arcade Fire's music videos / good / Rebecca Black's
5. many pop songs / happy / rap songs
6. but some pop songs / sad / rap songs

6 In pairs, compare famous people and music groups. Use the Grammar box and the adjectives in Exercise 4 to help you.

A: Avril Lavigne is cuter than Adele.
B: Yes, but Adele is a better singer.

And YOU?

5.3 READING and VOCABULARY Musicals at the theatre

I can find specific detail in reviews and give opinions about musicals.

1 **CLASS VOTE** Answer the questions and count the votes.
1. Do you read reviews on the internet, e.g. before you go to see a film or concert?
2. In your opinion, which is better: the cinema or the theatre?
3. Do you like musicals – yes or no?

2 🔊 2.21 Read the reviews (1–2). Match them with these comments (a–b).

a 'I love this show! Go and see it!'
  ⬤⬤⬤⬤⬤

b 'This show isn't very good.'
  ⬤⬤⚪⚪⚪

3 Read the texts again and choose the correct answers.
1. *Emma Brown*
   a is a story about a doctor.
   b is a film and a theatre show.
   c has got old and new songs.
2. James likes the show because
   a he likes the film.
   b it's three hours long.
   c the acting, dancing and music are good.
3. Jo doesn't like the show because
   a it's long and not very interesting.
   b the acting and dancing are very bad.
   c it's longer than *The Music In You*.

4 Study the Vocabulary box. Find the adjectives in the texts and write them in the correct column in the table below. How do you say these adjectives in your language?

Vocabulary	Opinion adjectives
alright brilliant boring cool fantastic	
funny great interesting OK terrible	

+	+/-	-
brilliant	*alright*	

BetterCheckIt!

Reviews of
Emma Brown, The Musical
Regal Theatre, London

1 You probably know the story because it's a film. Emma is a girl from London. Her parents want her to be a doctor, but she wants to be a dancer. The film's OK, but the musical is better. It's wonderful! It's three hours long, but it never feels boring. The actors are brilliant and the dance routines are fantastic! The music's cool too – the songs are old but they're great. And it's funny! I recommend it 100 percent. In fact, I want to see it again!
James, Durham

2 I'm a big fan of musicals and I love dance shows, but this show really isn't much fun. The actors are talented and the dance routines are alright, but the story isn't very interesting and the music is terrible. The songs are really old – they're from the 1980s! The show is three hours long, but it seems longer. It's a bit boring, to be honest. *The Music In You* is better!
Jo, Watford

5 In pairs, compare these things. Use the adjectives in the Vocabulary box.
1. jazz music – rock music
2. classical music – techno
3. the cinema – the theatre
4. CDs – live streaming
5. your favourite music – your parents' favourite music

A: *I think rock music is boring. Jazz is better.*
B: *I prefer rock – it's cool. You can't dance to jazz music. I think it's terrible.*

6 Write a short review of your favourite film, theatre musical or music video. Use the reviews in Exercise 2 and the Vocabulary box to help you. In groups, compare your reviews.

And YOU

5.4 GRAMMAR Superlatives

I can use superlatives to compare more than two people or things.

VIDEO: THE BEST DANCER

Before the ceremony:

Max: The Steps are the most important prizes for dancers in the USA.

Sol: Max is my best friend. He's the nicest guy. I hope he wins.

Lily: Max trains hard. He's the fittest person in our family.

Eva: Max is sweet. He's the sweetest guy I know.

In the theatre:

Max: This is the worst moment! I'm really nervous!

Jenny: The prize for the best breakdancer goes to Max!

Max: Thank you! This is the happiest moment of my life. I want to thank my biggest fans: my dad and my sister Lily. And my best friends, Sol and Eva. Thank you, thank you!

Jenny: The prize for the most original dance routine goes to Max!

Max: Thank you! This is the most fantastic day!

Jenny: The coolest dance move … Max! The cutest hairstyle … Max! The greatest person in the world … Max!

Back home:

Dad: Max!

Max: What? What's going on?

Dad: It's time to get up! Really, Max, you're the laziest boy in England!

OUT of class

He's sweet. It's time to … What's going on?

1 Do you know these awards ceremonies? What are they for – cinema, music or TV?
- the Brits
- the Emmys
- the Grammys
- the Oscars

2 ▶ 5.2 🔊 2.22 Watch or listen and answer the questions.
1. Where are Max and the others?
2. Who thinks Max is fit? Sweet? Nice?
3. How many prizes does Max win?
4. Where is Max really?

3 Study the Grammar box. Find examples of superlatives in the dialogue.

Grammar	Superlatives	
Adjective	Comparative	Superlative
cool	cooler	the coolest
nice	nicer	the nicest
fit	fitter	the fittest
lazy	lazier	the laziest
original	more original	the most original
good	better	the best
bad	worse	the worst

GRAMMAR TIME > PAGE 122

4 In pairs, complete the sentences about the people in the photo with the comparative or the superlative form of the adjectives in brackets.
1. Eva is *younger than* Sol. Max is *the youngest*. (young)
2. Max is ____ Sol. Eva is ____. (fit)
3. Max is ____ Eva. Sol is ____. (funny)
4. Sol is a ____ dancer ____ Lily. Dad is ____ dancer. (bad)
5. Lily has ____ eyes ____ Jenny. Eva has ____ eyes. (beautiful)

5 Make similar sentences about the people in the photo with the words below.

good dancer   nice smile   old   small   tall

Lily is older …

6 In pairs, write superlative sentences for prizes in these categories.
1. long hair
2. short hair
3. fit boy/girl
4. tall boy/girl
5. nice smile
6. original ideas
7. funny stories
8. cool style

The prize for the longest hair goes to …

7 **And YOU?** In groups, decide on the prize winners from your class for the categories in Exercise 6.

A: I think the prize for the longest hair in our class goes to Isabel.
B: No, I think Ella has longer hair than Isabel.
C: OK, the prize for the longest hair goes to Ella.

Unit 5

5.5 LISTENING and VOCABULARY   World Music Day

I can identify specific detail in a radio programme and talk about live music.

1 Look at the poster for World Music Day. What instruments are the musicians playing? Where are they?

Fête de la Musique
World Music Day

2 Study the Vocabulary box. Check you understand the words.

Vocabulary	Live music
audience band concert group orchestra singer stage street musician	

3 🔊 2.23 Choose the correct option. Listen and check.

In a typical pop ¹*audience / concert* the singer and the band play on a ²*concert / stage*. They're higher up than the ³*audience / group*. It's different for the ⁴*band / orchestra* in a classical music concert, of course. And it's different for ⁵*singers / street musicians* too. They're right next to the audience.

4 🔊 2.24 Listen to a radio programme about World Music Day. Mark the sentences true (T) or false (F).

1 ☐ World Music day is a new festival from France.
2 ☐ World Music Day is only for professional musicians.
3 ☐ On World Music Day you can enjoy music in many different places.
4 ☐ On World Music Day you don't always pay to go to a concert.
5 ☐ People celebrate World Music Day in Dublin.

5 🔊 2.24 Listen again and complete the notes.

World Music Day (WMD)

Date: ¹_____
First WMD: Country: France
            Year: ²_____
People play music: in streets, in ³_____, at home
Takes place in: more than 700 cities in ⁴_____ countries
More information: visit wmddub.com or phone ⁵_____

6 In pairs, discuss the questions.
1 What do you like about World Music day?
2 What happens on World Music day in your country/city?

7 🔊 2.25 **WORD FRIENDS** Complete the questions with the verbs below. Listen and check.

buy ~~enjoy~~ go play see

1 What kind of live music do you *enjoy* the most?
2 How often do you _____ to concerts?
3 Do you ever _____ concert tickets online?
4 Which group or singer do you most want to _____ in a live concert?
5 Where do street musicians _____ music in your town?

8 [VOX POPS ▶ 5.3] In pairs, ask and answer the questions in Exercise 6.

A: What kind of live music do you enjoy the most?
B: I really enjoy classical music concerts.

Unit 5   63

5.6 SPEAKING Making suggestions

I can make and respond to suggestions.

AUDIO   WHAT DO YOU SUGGEST?

Lily: It's really hard to get a birthday present for Dad.
Eva: Can I make a suggestion?
Max: Sure.
Lily: Yes, of course.
Eva: Why don't you get him a musical instrument?
Max: Yeah, great idea! Why don't we get him a trumpet?
Lily: Yes, why not? Or what about a harmonica?
Eva: I don't get it. What's so funny?
Lily: Dad can't play music. He's worse than me and I'm terrible.
Max: Sorry, Eva. Have you got any other suggestions?
Eva: How about a karaoke system? … What?
Lily: That's not a good idea. Dad loves music, but he's the worst singer in the world!
Eva: Oh! Well, what do you suggest?
Lily: Let's get him a CD.
Max: No!
Eva: Why not?
Max: Because he only listens to punk rock. Listen!
Eva: Wow!
Max: I know. It's terrible!
Eva: I've got an idea. Why don't you …

OUT of class
I don't get it.   What's so funny?   Wow!   I've got an idea.

1 CLASS VOTE Is it harder to find a birthday present for your mother, father, grandparents, brother, sister or best friend? Why?

2 2.26 Read or listen and answer the questions.
1 What presents does Eva suggest?
2 Why do Max and Lily laugh?
3 Why does Max not like Lily's suggestion?

3 Study the Speaking box. Find examples of the phrases in the dialogue.

Speaking	Making suggestions
What do you suggest?	
Have you got any (other) suggestions?	
Can I make a suggestion?	Sure./Yes, of course.
Why don't you/we …?	Yes, why not?/Great idea!
How/What about …?	Maybe./I'm not sure.
Let's …	No, that's not a good idea.

4 2.27 Guess: what is Eva's final idea? Listen and check. Why is it a good present?

5 2.28 Complete the dialogue with phrases from the Speaking box. Listen and check.

Sol: I want to get my grandma a present. What ¹*do you suggest*?
Max: Why ²_____ get her a book?
Sol: I'm ³_____. Have you got ⁴_____?
Max: How ⁵_____ a CD?
Sol: Hmm, ⁶_____.
Max: Or ⁷_____ some chocolates?
Sol: Yeah, ⁸_____! ⁹_____ go to the shops.
Max: Can I ¹⁰_____?
Sol: ¹¹_____.
Max: ¹²_____ we look online? It's easier.

6 2.29 Listen to five suggestions. Respond with words or phrases from the Speaking box.

7 Work in pairs. Student A, follow the instructions below. Student B, go to page 128.   **And YOU**

1 Read these situations to Student B. Respond to his/her suggestions.
 • It's my father's/mother's birthday soon and I want to get him/her a present.
 • I'm a little bit hungry.
2 Listen to Student B's situations. Make suggestions. Use the ideas below if you need to.
 • go for a walk in the country/listen to music/read a book
 • study with a friend/play a game to relax/watch YouTube videos in English

64 Unit 5

5.7 WRITING Texts and tweets

I can write short messages (texts and tweets).

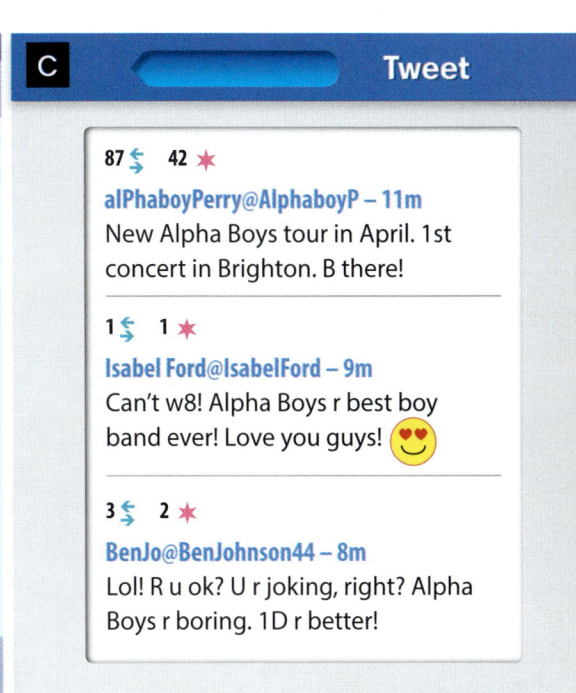

A

B 19.12 P.M. Messages

Gr8 news! 😊 Alpha Boys concert @ Brighton Centre on Fri 3 April @ 7.30. Tickets r £25. U can buy them online. Want 2 go?

Yes! Can u get tickets 4 me and my sister plz?

OK, I can get them l8r 2nite. bfn.

Thx, u r the best! Cu 2moro! 😘

C Tweet

87 42

alPhaboyPerry@AlphaboyP – 11m
New Alpha Boys tour in April. 1st concert in Brighton. B there!

1 1

Isabel Ford@IsabelFord – 9m
Can't w8! Alpha Boys r best boy band ever! Love you guys! 😍

3 2

BenJo@BenJohnson44 – 8m
Lol! R u ok? U r joking, right? Alpha Boys r boring. 1D r better!

1 Look at the pictures and answer the questions.
1. What's the person doing in picture A?
2. How are texts different from tweets?

2 CLASS VOTE Answer the questions.
1. Are you on Twitter?
2. How often do you write texts or tweets?
3. What's better, texting or tweeting? Why?

3 In pairs, read the texts and tweets in B and C and answer the questions.
1. When is the Alpha Boys concert in Brighton?
2. How much are the tickets?
3. Who likes/doesn't like Alpha Boys?

4 Study the Writing box. In pairs, write out the texts and tweets in pictures B and C with all the words.

Great news! There's an Alpha Boys concert …

Writing   Writing texts and tweets

To make texts and tweets short, you can:
- eliminate some words, e.g. *I, you, there; a/an, the, some; be, do, have*
- use symbols, abbreviations and acronyms, e.g.
  - @ = at; 2 = to/too; 4 = for
  - b = be; c = see; u = you; r = are; y = why
  - bfn = bye for now; lol = laughing out loud; plz = please; 2nite = tonight; 2moro = tomorrow
- use emojis
  1 😀 2 😘 3 😍 4 🙁 5 😮

5 Match emojis 1–5 in the Writing box with meanings a–e.
a ☐ I'm sad.
b ☐ Kisses!
c ☐ I'm shocked.
d ☐ I love it/you!
e ☐ I'm happy.

6 Make the sentences shorter. Use the Writing box to help you.
1. Do you want to come here later?
   Want 2 come here l8r?
2. I've got the tickets for the concert.
3. Wait for me at the bus stop, please.
4. Are you OK to see us tomorrow?
5. Great! Thanks. Bye for now.
6. See you tonight!
7. Why are you late?!

Writing Time

7 In groups, write texts or tweets to other groups about the ideas below. Use the Writing box to help you make the texts and tweets shorter. Reply to the messages you receive.
- school and homework
- plans with friends (TV, sport, shopping, music, cinema)

Maths homework difficult! Want 2 study 2gether 2nite? 🙁

Unit 5 65

WORDLIST   Musical instruments | Musical genres | Opinion adjectives | Live music

accordion /əˈkɔːdiən/ n
acting /ˈæktɪŋ/ adj
alright /ɔːlˈraɪt/ adj
audience /ˈɔːdiəns/ n
awards ceremony /əˈwɔːdz ˈserəməni/ n
ballet dancer /ˈbæleɪ ˈdɑːnsə/ n
band /bænd/ n
bass guitar /ˌbeɪs gɪˈtɑː/ n
boring /ˈbɔːrɪŋ/ adj
boy band /bɔɪ bænd/ n
break dancer /breɪk ˈdɑːnsə/ n
brilliant /ˈbrɪljənt/ adj
CD /ˌsiː ˈdiː/ n
cello /ˈtʃeləʊ/ n
cinema /ˈsɪnəmə, ˈsɪnɪmə/ n
classical music /ˈklæsɪkəl ˈmjuːzɪk/ n
composer /kəmˈpəʊzə/ n
concert /ˈkɒnsət/ n
cool /kuːl/ adj
country music /ˈkʌntri ˈmjuːzɪk/ n
cute /kjuːt/ adj
dance move /dɑːns muːv/ n
dance routine /dɑːns ruːˈtiːn/ n
dancer /ˈdɑːnsə/ n
dancing /ˈdɑːnsɪŋ/ n
drums /drʌmz/ n
fantastic /fænˈtæstɪk/ adj
film /fɪlm/ n
film-maker /ˈfɪlmˌmeɪkə/ n
fit /fɪt/ v
flute /fluːt/ n

fun /fʌn/ n
funny /ˈfʌni/ adj
great /greɪt/ adj
group /gruːp/ n
guitar /gɪˈtɑː/ n
harmonica /hɑːˈmɒnɪkə/ n
headphones /ˈhedfəʊnz/ n
hip-hop /ˈhɪp hɒp/ n
hit song /hɪt sɒŋ/ n
intelligent /ɪnˈtelədʒənt, ɪnˈtelɪdʒənt/ adj
interesting /ˈɪntrəstɪŋ, ˈɪntrɪstɪŋ/ adj
jazz /dʒæz/ n
keyboards /ˈkiːbɔːdz/ n
lazy /ˈleɪzi/ adj
live music /laɪv ˈmjuːzɪk/ n
message /ˈmesɪdʒ/ n
musical /ˈmjuːzɪkəl/ adj
musical instrument /ˈmjuːzɪkəl ˈɪnstrəmənt/ n
(street) musician /(ˈstriːt) mjuːˈzɪʃən/ n
OK /ˌəʊ ˈkeɪ/ interj
orchestra /ˈɔːkəstrə, ˈɔːkɪstrə/ n
original /əˈrɪdʒɪnəl, -dʒənəl/ adj
piano /piˈænəʊ/ n
pop music /pɒp ˈmjuːzɪk/ n
pop star /pɒp stɑː/ n
prize /praɪz/ v
punk rock /pʌŋk rɒk/ n
rap /ræp/ n
recommend /ˌrekəˈmend/ v
reggae /ˈregeɪ/ n

review /rɪˈvjuː/ n
rock music /rɒk ˈmjuːzɪk/ n
saxophone /ˈsæksəfəʊn/ n
sense of humour /sens əv ˈhjuːmə/ n
shocked /ʃɒkt/ adj
(dance) show /(dɑːns) ʃəʊ/ n
sing /sɪŋ/ v
singer /ˈsɪŋə/ n
solo artist /ˈsəʊləʊ ˈɑːtəst/ n
songwriter /ˈsɒŋˌraɪtə/ n
stage /steɪdʒ/ n
story /ˈstɔːri/ n
successful /səkˈsesfəl/ adj
talented /ˈtæləntəd, ˈtæləntɪd/ adj
techno /ˈteknəʊ/ n
terrible /ˈterəbəl, ˈterɪbəl/ adj
theatre /ˈθɪətə/ n
traditional /trəˈdɪʃənəl/ adj
trumpet /ˈtrʌmpət, ˈtrʌmpɪt/ n
typical /ˈtɪpɪkəl/ adj
violin /ˌvaɪəˈlɪn/ n
win /wɪn/ v
wonderful /ˈwʌndəfəl/ adj

WORD FRIENDS

be a big fan of something
buy tickets (online)
enjoy music
go to a concert
laugh at something
listen to music
look online

VOCABULARY IN ACTION

1 Use the wordlist to find:
1. eight musical instruments you play with your hands *accordion, …*
2. four musical instruments you play with your hands and mouth *flute, …*
3. ten people who work in music or dance *ballet dancer, …*

2 Complete the types of music.
1. p o p
2. r _ _
3. r _ c _
4. j _ _ z
5. h _ _ -h _ _
6. c _ u _ _ r _
7. t _ _ h _ _
8. r _ g g _ _
9. c _ _ s _ i _ a _
10. t _ _ d _ _ i _ _ a _

3 In pairs, complete the sentences with words from the Word Friends list. Say if the sentences are true for you.
1. My grandparents often *listen* to music at home. They have a piano in their living room.
2. I'm a big _____ of One Direction. I want to _____ them in concert one day.
3. My dad _____ rock music, especially AC/DC. He sometimes _____ to concerts.
4. My mum _____ to reggae every day in the car. She loves Bob Marley.
5. It's quicker and easier to _____ tickets for concerts online.

4 🔊 2.30 **PRONUNCIATION** Listen to how we pronounce the /æ/ and /ʌ/ sounds. Look at the underlined letters and decide which sound you hear. Write the words in the correct column.

| b<u>a</u>nd | dr<u>u</u>ms | f<u>a</u>n | p<u>u</u>nk | c<u>ou</u>ntry | j<u>a</u>zz | f<u>u</u>nny |
| r<u>a</u>p | b<u>a</u>llet | tr<u>u</u>mpet | cl<u>a</u>ssical | w<u>o</u>nderful |

/æ/	/ʌ/
band	drums

5 🔊 2.31 **PRONUNCIATION** Listen, check and repeat.

Revision

VOCABULARY

1 Complete the questions with the words below. There are two extra words. In pairs, ask and answer the questions.

> artist   award   ballet   classical   fan   hit
> instrument   moves   music   show   street

1 Do you like dancing? Have you got any good dance <u>moves</u>?
2 In your opinion, who's the best composer of _____ music?
3 Do you think it's more difficult to be a _____ dancer or a break dancer?
4 What's your favourite _____ song this year?
5 Where does the Oscar _____ ceremony take place?
6 Do your parents give money to _____ musicians?
7 What's the best place to listen to live _____ in your town?
8 Is your favourite singer a solo _____ or is he/she in a group?
9 Who in your family can play a musical _____?

2 Complete the words in the text.

> In a typical rock ¹g<u>roup</u> there is a
> ²s_____, a drummer, two
> ³g_____ players and a ⁴b_____
> guitarist. Sometimes there is a
> ⁵k_____ player too. In a rock
> ⁶c_____ the musicians stand on
> the ⁷s_____. The ⁸a_____ is
> in front of the group. If the concert
> is good, it's a lot of ⁹f_____ and
> everyone is ¹⁰d_____.

3 In pairs, use these adjectives to guess your partner's opinion about the people and things below.

> alright   boring   brilliant   cool   fantastic
> funny   great   interesting   OK   terrible

1 musicals
2 boy bands
3 hip-hop
4 dance shows
5 awards
6 ballet dancing
7 break dancing
8 punk rock
9 music lessons
10 classical music

A: *You think musicals are boring.*
B: *False – I think they're great.*

GRAMMAR

4 Study the fun facts and compare Stacey and Mo from the Go Girls.

Fun facts about the Go Girls

	Age	Height	Good musician?	Personality
Stacey	17	1.78	3 guitars	friendly, nice
Mo	18	1.60	5 guitars	intelligent, quiet

Stacey is younger than Mo.

5 Complete the questions with the superlative form of the adjectives in brackets. In pairs, ask and answer the questions.

1 Who is <u>the worst</u> (bad) singer in your family?
2 Who is _____ (funny) person in your school?
3 Who is _____ (talented) musician in your town?
4 Who has got _____ (nice) personality in your family?
5 Who is _____ (fit) person you know?
6 What is _____ (interesting) programme on TV right now?
7 What is _____ (good) pop group in the world?
8 Who is _____ (successful) singer your country?

A: *Who is the worst singer in your family?*
B: *My dad! No, my little sister – she's terrible!*

SPEAKING

6 Work in pairs. Student A, follow the instructions below. Student B, go to page 128.

- Student A, you have a ticket for a pop concert, but you can't go. You don't know what to do with the ticket. Ask Student B for suggestions.
- Listen and respond to Student B's suggestions. (Don't accept the first one!)
- Then listen to Student B's problem and make suggestions (e.g. throw the T-shirt away, wear it only in front of your grandmother, give it to a friend).

DICTATION

7 🔊 2.32 Listen. Then listen again and write down what you hear.

BBC CULTURE

Why do we play musical instruments?

Why learn an instrument?

Many children learn to play an instrument when they are young. In the UK today, seventy-six percent of children aged five to fourteen play an instrument. That's a lot more than in 1999, when it was only forty-one percent. Today, for the first time, the electric guitar is more popular than the violin! The most popular instrument to learn is the keyboards. And playing a musical instrument is good for us. Why?

A Scientists think that people who play an instrument can get cleverer. It changes their brains. They have better memories and get better marks in intelligence tests. They're good at Maths and Science too!

B Playing an instrument also helps with physical things. Your hearing gets better and you can do sports like running and swimming better too. That's because when we learn to play an instrument, we use different parts of our brains.

C It's good for relaxing. When we play an instrument, we can put our feelings into the music. If we're worried, music helps us. We also become more creative.

D We can play with other people. It's good for meeting new friends. It's also good to learn how to work together in a team. That's important for our future job.

E It's fun! It's exciting and it's rewarding. People listen to music and they're happy. It's a great feeling to make people happy with music.

So why are you waiting? Learn to play an instrument and change your life!

GLOSSARY
brain (n) the part inside your head that makes you think and feel
hearing (n) the ability to hear
physical (adj) connected with your body, not your mind
rewarding (adj) making you feel happy because you can do something difficult or important
team (n) a group of people who work together or play a sport/game together

EXPLORE

1 In pairs, ask and answer the questions.
   1 How many instruments can you name?
   2 What's your favourite instrument?

2 In pairs, try to guess the answers to these questions.
   1 What percentage of children in the UK play an instrument?
   2 What's more popular – the electric guitar or the violin?
   3 What's the most popular instrument for children to learn?

3 Read the article. Check your ideas from Exercise 2.

4 Read the text again. Mark the sentences T (true) or F (false).
   1 ☐ More children play instruments than before.
   2 ☐ People who play an instrument can remember more things.
   3 ☐ All good sports stars also play instruments.
   4 ☐ Worried people play better music.
   5 ☐ People who play an instrument find jobs quicker.
   6 ☐ Listening to music can help people feel better.

5 In pairs, order points A–E in the article (1 = most important, 5 = least important). Compare your ideas with another pair.

EXPLORE MORE

6 You are going to watch part of a BBC programme about an orchestra. Read an advert for the programme. Why do you think the orchestra is special?

National Youth Orchestra of Iraq
This programme is about a special orchestra of young people from Iraq. Why is it special? Watch and learn!

7 ▶ 5.4 Watch the video and match names 1–4 with photos A–D.
   1 ☐ Zuhal
   2 ☐ Chia Sultan
   3 ☐ Waleed Ahmed
   4 ☐ Tu'qa

8 ▶ 5.4 Watch again and answer the questions.
   1 Why is the orchestra in Scotland?
   2 Why can't they practise in their country?
   3 How do they learn to play instruments?
   4 How do they join the orchestra?
   5 What instrument does Waleed Ahmed play? Chia Sultan?

9 Would you like to go to a concert by this orchestra? Why? / Why not?

YOU EXPLORE

10 **CULTURE PROJECT** In groups, write a presentation about an interesting orchestra in your country.
   1 Use the internet to research an orchestra.
   2 Find some pictures, videos and audio.
   3 Write your presentation.
   4 Share it with the class.

6

A question of sport

VOCABULARY
Sports | Sportspeople
Collocations: *score a goal, win a match*, etc. | Sports competitions | Interests and hobbies: collocations with *go*, *do* and *play*

GRAMMAR
was/were | there was/there were | Past Simple affirmative (regular and irregular verbs) | *ago*

Grammar: A funny thing happened to me

Speaking: What do you do in your free time?

BBC Culture: Rugbynet

Workbook p. 77

BBC VOX POPS ▶

EXAM TIME 2 > p. 132

6.1 VOCABULARY Sports

I can talk about sports and sportspeople.

1 Study the Vocabulary A box. In pairs, ask and answer the questions.
  1 Which sports can you see in the photos?
  2 Which are team sports and which are usually individual sports?

Vocabulary A	Sports
archery baseball basketball cycling football ice hockey judo running swimming tennis	

2 **CLASS VOTE** What's your favourite sport to watch? To play?
My favourite sport to watch is …

3 Study the Vocabulary B box. Match the sportspeople with the right sports in the Vocabulary A box. Which word can go with more than one sport?

Vocabulary B	Sportspeople
cyclist player runner swimmer	

CRAZY FOR SPORTS

PART 1

1. In which city can you play a tennis match at Wimbledon?
   a London   b New York   c Paris
2. How many teams are there in the football World Cup finals?
   a 8   b 16   c 32
3. What sport do the Bulls, the Celtics and the Rockets play?
   a baseball   b basketball   c American football
4. To win this race, cyclists go about 3,500 km in July. In which country?
   a France   b Italy   c Spain
5. In the Olympics, what's the shortest race for a swimmer to win a gold medal?
   a 25m   b 50 m   c 100 m
6. 22 September 2015, Bayern Munich vs.* Wolfsburg. A Polish football player scores five goals in nine minutes! What's his surname?
   a Klose   b Lewandowski   c Podolski

*vs. = versus – it means 'against'

PART 2

7. The fastest _____ can cycle 1 kilometre in what time?
   a 1 minute   b 1 minute 30 seconds   c 2 minutes
8. US basketball _____ Steph Curry scores a lot of points and wins a lot of matches. How tall is he?
   a 1.61 m   b 1.91 m   c 2.21 m
9. The fastest marathon _____ usually come from two African countries. Ethiopia is one; what's the other?
   a Egypt   b Kenya   c Nigeria
10. Katie Ledecky is a fast _____. How far can she swim in 4 minutes?
    a 100 m   b 200 m   c 400 m

---

4 🔊 **2.33** In groups, do Part 1 of the quiz. Listen and check.

5 Complete the questions in Part 2 of the quiz. Use the correct form of the words in the Vocabulary B box.

6 🔊 **2.34** In the same groups as in Exercise 4, do Part 2 of the quiz. Listen and check. What's your group's score? Which group got the most points?

7 🔊 **2.35** WORD FRIENDS Find the words below in the quiz. Use them to complete the phrases. Listen and check.

| goal | ~~match~~ | medal |
| race | sport | |

play a *match* / _____
win a match / _____ / _____
score a _____ / point

8 In pairs, complete the sentences with the correct form of words from the Word Friends in Exercise 7. Identify the sports.

1. I play with my friends in the park. I <u>score</u> a lot of goals.
2. I don't think I can win the 100-metre _____, but I think I can _____ a medal.
3. We often play this _____ in PE. There are five players in each team. You score _____, not goals.
4. In my favourite sport, two or four players can _____ a match. To win a _____, you need to score more points than the other player(s).

1 football

9 [VOX POPS ▶ 6.1] In groups, ask and answer the questions. Who is the sportiest person in your group?

1. How often do you play/do your favourite sport? How often do you win?
2. What other sports do you play/do?
3. Do you play any sports video games? If so, which ones and how often?
4. Do you ever watch sports live? If so, which ones?

Unit 6

6.2 GRAMMAR was/were

I can use *was/were* to talk about events in the past.

1 🔊 **2.36** Read and listen to the interview. Find information about the things below.

> date   country   number of teams
> final match   crowd   champions

date – 1991

Leetown High School
School Magazine Issue 5

What do you know about women's football?

An interview with our PE teacher, Ms Schmidt by Heather Tremblay

Q: When was the first Women's Football World Cup?
A: It was in 1991.
Q: Was it in Europe?
A: No, it wasn't. It was in China.
Q: How many teams were there?
A: There were twelve teams.
Q: Which teams were in the final?
A: It was Norway vs. the USA.
Q: Was there a big crowd?
A: Yes, there was. There were 63,000 people in the stadium.
Q: What was the final score?
A: It was 2–1 to the USA.
Q: Were you there?
A: No, I wasn't! I was born in 1985. I was only six years old in 1991!

---

2 Study the Grammar box. Find examples of *was/were* and *there was/there were* in the interview.

Grammar	was/were
+	**-**
I was in China. We were happy.	She wasn't in Brazil. They weren't sad.
?	
Where was the match? Were you there? Yes, I was./No, I wasn't.	
there is/isn't → there was/wasn't	
there are/aren't → there were/weren't	

GRAMMAR TIME > PAGE 123

---

3 🔊 **2.37** Complete the second part of the interview with the correct form of *was* or *were*. Listen and check.

Q: Who's the best female footballer in the world?
A: The American Carli Lloyd. She ¹was the best player in the 2015 World Cup.
Q: ² _____ the 2015 World Cup in the USA?
A: No, it ³ _____ . It ⁴ _____ here in Canada.
Q: Which teams ⁵ _____ in the final?
A: The USA vs. Japan. The Japanese ⁶ _____ bad, but the Americans ⁷ _____ better. After sixteen minutes the score ⁸ _____ 4–0 to the USA! The final score ⁹ _____ 5–2.

4 Complete the dialogue between Lisa and her gran with the correct form of *there was* or *there were*.

Lisa: ¹Was there a girls' football team at your school, Gran?
Gran: No, ² _____ . But ³ _____ a hockey team.
Lisa: ⁴ _____ any boys in the hockey team?
Gran: No, ⁵ _____ . And ⁶ _____ any girls in the football team. But every year ⁷ _____ a hockey match – girls vs. boys.
Lisa: ⁸ _____ a football match with girls vs. boys too?
Gran: Yes, ⁹ _____ . It was great fun!

5 🔊 **2.38** In pairs, choose the correct option to complete the questions about a sports match. Listen and check.

1. What sport (was) / were it?
2. The match was / Was the match in a stadium?
3. How many players was / were there in each team?
4. There was / Was there a big crowd?
5. What was / wasn't the final score?
6. Was / Were you the best player?

6 In pairs, use the questions in Exercise 5 to talk about a time when you were a player in a sports match.

A: What sport was it?
B: It was volleyball.
A: Was the match in a stadium?
B: No, it wasn't. It was in a PE class at school.

And YOU?

72 Unit 6

6.3 READING and VOCABULARY — Young sports stars

I can find specific detail in a text and talk about places to play sport.

Young sports stars

A Adam Peaty was scared of water when he was a child, but now he loves the swimming pool. British swimmer Adam was born in October 1994. In 2015 he was the first man to win the 50 m and 100 m breaststroke in one world championship.

B Tennis player Garbiñe Muguruza was born in Caracas, Venezuela, in October 1993. Her mother is Venezuelan but her father is Spanish. So which country does she represent? It wasn't an easy decision. But now when she's on the tennis court, she's Spanish.

C When Dina Asher-Smith was eight, her dream was to run on the track in the Olympics. Now she's the fastest British female runner in history. Dina was born in December 1995. In July 2015 she was the first British woman to run 100 metres in under eleven seconds.

D Kristaps Porziņģis is was born in Latvia in August 1995. When he was fifteen years old, he was 2.03 m tall! Now he's 2.21 m tall. So where do you think he plays sport? On a basketball court, of course. Kristaps is one of the best players in the NBA.

1 CLASS VOTE Who is the most popular sports star in your country?

2 🔊 2.39 Read the texts and complete the table. If you can't find the information in the texts, try to guess the answers from the photos.

	Country	Sport	Age
Adam Peaty			
Garbiñe Muguruza			
Dina Asher-Smith			
Kristaps Porziņģis			

3 Read the texts again. Mark the sentences ✓ (right), ✗ (wrong) or ? (doesn't say).

1. ☐ Adam doesn't like water.
2. ☐ 2015 was a good year for him.
3. ☐ Garbiñe's father is from Madrid.
4. ☐ It wasn't easy for her to choose a country to play for.
5. ☐ Dina was in the Olympics when she was eight years old.
6. ☐ In 2015 she was the fastest woman in the world.
7. ☐ Kristaps was very tall when he was fifteen.
8. ☐ He's the tallest basketball player in the NBA.

4 Study the Vocabulary box. Which places can you see in the photos?

Vocabulary	Places to play sport
basketball court   tennis court   football field/pitch
swimming pool   running track

5 In pairs, complete the text with one word in each gap.

Our school is great for sport. There's a good football ¹*pitch* with a 400-metre-long running ²_____ around it. There are two outdoor tennis ³_____, there's a basketball ⁴_____ in the gymnasium and there's a small indoor swimming ⁵_____ too.

6 In pairs, ask and answer the questions. **And YOU**

1. When you were younger, what was your favourite sport? Who was your favourite sports star?
2. What's your favourite sport now? Who's your favourite sports star?
3. Do you want to be a professional sportsperson? Why? / Why not?

When I was younger, my favourite sport was … and my favourite star was …, but now …

Unit 6

6.4 GRAMMAR Past Simple affirmative (regular and irregular verbs)

I can use the Past Simple to talk about events in the past.

VIDEO — A FUNNY THING HAPPENED TO ME

Max: Good shot!
Eva: Thanks! I did archery at a sports camp last year. I had a great time. I won a medal!
Sol: Hi.
Max: Sol, what's wrong?
Sol: I went jogging yesterday.
Max: You went jogging?
Sol: Yes. It started well, but then I got something in my shoe, so I stopped. I took my shoe off and put it on a car. Then the car moved away. I tried to catch it. I ran after it but … I walked home – two miles with one shoe!
Eva: Wow! Poor you!
Max: A funny thing happened to me this morning. I wanted to do some skateboarding, so I came here. A reporter from South Radio saw me. She asked me lots of questions. It's for a show about young people and sport.
Eva: When's it on?
Max: Sunday.

OUT of class
Good shot!
What's wrong?   Poor you!
When's it on?

1 ▶ 6.2 🔊 2.40 Look at the photo. What sport is Sol doing? Watch or listen and check.

2 Study the Grammar A box. Write the Past Simple form of the verbs below. Find them in the dialogue and check.

ask   happen   move   start   stop
try   walk   want

Grammar A — Past Simple affirmative (regular verbs)

call – call**ed**   like – lik**ed**   jog – jog**ged**   carry – carr**ied**
I **called** you yesterday.

Time expressions: this morning, yesterday, last night, last week, last month, last year

GRAMMAR TIME > PAGE 123

3 🔊 2.41 Look at the table. Listen and repeat.

/d/	/t/	/ɪd/
called	watched	ended
jogged	danced	waited

4 🔊 2.42 Write the verbs from Exercise 2 in the correct column in the table above. Listen and check.

5 🔊 2.43 Find the Past Simple form of these verbs in the dialogue and complete the Grammar B box. Listen and check.

Grammar B — Past simple affirmative (irregular verbs)

come – *came*   put – _____
do – _____   run – _____
get – _____   see – _____
go – _____   take – _____
have – _____   win – _____

GRAMMAR TIME > PAGE 123

6 🔊 2.44 Complete Lily's story with the Past Simple form of the verbs in brackets. Listen and check.

'I ¹*went* (go) for a run yesterday. In the park I ² _____ (stop) to drink some water. There was a newspaper on a bench. I ³ _____ (start) to read it. I ⁴ _____ (find) two tickets for a tennis match! I was really happy. But then I ⁵ _____ (see) a young man. He ⁶ _____ (ask) me a question: 'Are they your tickets?' I ⁷ _____ (say) no and then ⁸ _____ (give) him the tickets. He ⁹ _____ (smile).'

7 Go to page 128. In pairs, take it in turns to make a sentence in the Past Simple. Your partner guesses if it's true or false.

A: *I went jogging in the park yesterday.*
B: *False!*
A: *No, it's true. One point for me!*

And YOU?

Unit 6

6.5 LISTENING and VOCABULARY — Sporting moments

I can identify specific details in a radio sports programme and talk about a sports match.

1 CLASS VOTE Are you more often happy or sad when you watch your favourite sports player or team?

2 Study the Vocabulary box. Check you understand the words. In pairs, answer the questions below.

Vocabulary	Sports competitions
cup league tournament	
final semi-final	

1 Is there an international tennis tournament in your country?
2 Who were the football league champions in your country last year? Who won the cup?

3 🔊 2.45 Listen to a radio phone-in and match the sentence halves to make true sentences about the speakers.

1 Keith   a ran in a race.
2 Emma   b is a sports fanatic.
3 Sam   c talks about 2016.
4 Jim   d tells a sad story.

4 🔊 2.45 Listen again and choose the correct answers.

1 Where was Keith when Andy Murray won Wimbledon?
   A   B   C

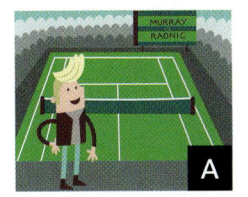

2 What was Emma's best time for ten kilometres before last Sunday?
   A 32:40   B 39:14   C 40:30

3 How much were the train tickets that Sam bought?
   A £45   B £57   C £75

4 What does Jim do every day?
   A   B   C

5 🔊 2.46 WORD FRIENDS Complete the sentences with the correct form of the verbs below. Listen and check.

do aerobics/exercise/judo
go cycling/jogging/running/swimming
play badminton/football/tennis
play for a team
win/lose a game/match/race/tournament

1 Andy Murray **won** the Wimbledon tennis tournament in 2016.
2 Emma often _____ running. Her friend _____ the race last Sunday.
3 Liverpool were in the cup final but they _____ the game 2–1.
4 Jim _____ jogging every morning. At weekends he _____ badminton and _____ judo. He _____ for the school football team.

6 🔊 2.47 Choose the correct option. Listen and check.

I love sport. I often ¹*do / go* cycling and I ²*do / play* gymnastics after school but my favourite sport is basketball. I ³*go / play* basketball a lot. I ⁴*play for / win* my school team. This year we ⁵*scored / won* our first three matches in the national tournament. In the semi-final I ⁶*lost / scored* twenty points! I was really happy. In the final we ⁷*played for / lost* the game by one point.

7 [VOX POPS ▶ 6.3]
In groups, talk about a sporting moment when you were really happy or sad. Use these ideas and the Word Friends in Exercise 5 to help you.

- I saw it on TV./I was there in the stadium.
- I played in a tournament.
- I scored a goal/won the match.
- The final score was …
- It was surprising/fantastic/great/crazy/terrible.
- I was really happy/sad.

Unit 6   75

6.6 SPEAKING — Talking about hobbies and interests

I can talk about hobbies and interests.

AUDIO — WHAT DO YOU DO IN YOUR FREE TIME?

Vicky: So, Greg, what do you do in your free time?
Max: I hang out with my friends and I do a lot … I dance. I mean, I do a lot of dancing.
Vicky: Dancers need to be fit. Do you do much sport? Do you go running, for example?
Max: No, I'm not very keen on running. It's boring.
Vicky: But you like sport, right?
Max: Not really. I play football sometimes but to be honest, I'm not really into sport. I love dancing.
Vicky: Do you play for a football team?
Max: No, I'm not interested in team sports. I go cycling with my friend Dad, I mean, Sol. I'm a big fan of skateboarding. Is that a sport?
Vicky: I don't think so, no. OK, thanks. That was twelve-year-old Greg Marks.

OUT of class: To be honest, …

1 Look at the photo and answer the questions. Go to page 129 and check.
1 Where is Max?
2 Who is he talking to?

2 🔊 2.48 Read or listen. Does Max do well or badly in the radio interview? Why?

3 Study the Speaking box. Find examples of the phrases in the dialogue.

> **Speaking — Talking about hobbies and interests**
>
> What are your hobbies and interests?
> What do you do in your free time?
> I go running/cycling.
> I do a lot of judo/sport/dancing.
> I play video games/football.
> I hang out with my friends.
> Are you into sport?
> I'm a big fan of skateboarding/mountain biking.
> I love/I'm interested in/I'm really into extreme sports.
> Not really./I'm not very keen on/I'm not really into sport.

4 In pairs, complete the text with one verb in each gap.

> Rob is a sports fanatic. He ¹*plays* basketball for a team. He ² _____ a lot of judo. He ³ _____ swimming every evening. He ⁴ _____ really into racket sports – he ⁵ _____ a big fan of squash. He always ⁶ _____ out with his friends at the sports centre.

5 🔊 2.49 Complete the dialogue with sentences a–h. There are three extra sentences. Listen and check.

Jay: What do you do in your free time?
Kay: ¹c
Jay: What sports do you do?
Kay: ² ___
Jay: Yes, mountain biking is cool.
Kay: ³ ___
Jay: I hang out with my friends.
Kay: ⁴ ___
Jay: Not really. I'm not very keen on sport. But I'm really into sports video games.
Kay: ⁵ ___

a Are you into sport?
b I did judo when I was younger.
c I do a lot of sport.
d I go swimming, I play football and I'm a big fan of cycling.
e I'm not into team sports.
f My sister's a great football player.
g Really? I'm not interested in video games. I prefer real-life sports.
h What about you? What are your hobbies?

6 In pairs, talk about your hobbies and interests. Tell the class about your partner.

And YOU

6.7 ENGLISH IN USE *ago*

I can use *ago* to talk about events in the past.

The history of sport

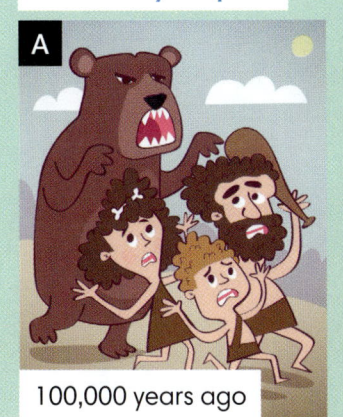

A 100,000 years ago
B 4,600 years ago
C 1,900 years ago
D 100 years ago

1 Match pictures A–D with captions 1–4.
1. ☐ The Ancient Romans loved team sports.
2. ☐ In the early years of the twentieth century, motor racing was a popular sport. It was very exciting.
3. ☐ In prehistoric times, people were big sports fans. Sometimes they ran very fast.
4. ☐ The Ancient Egyptians were keen on sport. They did a lot of weight training.

2 Study the Language box. How do you say the phrases in your language?

Language	*ago*

To talk about when something happened, we use a time expression + *ago*.

ten seconds ago — twenty minutes ago
an hour ago — a few days ago
three weeks ago — six months ago
many years ago — a long time ago

3 In pairs, work out how long ago these things happened.
1. The first Tour de France was in 1903 – _____ ago.
2. Women first swam in the Olympic Games in 1912 – _____ ago.
3. Basketball legend Michael Jordan was born in 1963 – _____ ago.
4. Serena Williams won Wimbledon for the first time in 2002 – _____ ago.
5. Spain won the Football World Cup in South Africa in 2010 – _____ ago.
6. The Olympic Games were in Rio do Janeiro in 2016 – _____ ago.

4 In groups of three, look back at this unit and work out how long ago these things happened.
1. Robert Lewandowski scored five goals in nine minutes _____ .
2. The first Women's Football World Cup was _____ .
3. Garbiñe Muguruza was born _____ .
4. Dina Asher-Smith ran 100 metres in under eleven seconds _____ .
5. Andy Murray won Wimbledon _____ .

5 🔊 2.50 Complete the text with one word in each gap. Listen and check.

I'm very keen ¹**on** sport. I ² _____ a lot of exercise. Two weeks ³ _____ I ran in a ten-kilometre race and I won a gold ⁴ _____ ! ⁵ _____ week I played tennis on a beautiful tennis ⁶ _____ at Wimbledon. I lost, but it ⁷ _____ a great game. Yesterday I played ⁸ _____ England in the football World Cup. We won the ⁹ _____ 4–2 and I scored all four ¹⁰ _____ . Yes, I'm a big fan ¹¹ _____ sports video games!

6 In pairs, say how long ago you did these things.
- go swimming
- have a PE lesson
- look at your phone
- play basketball
- watch sport on TV
- win a video game
- play in a tournament
- do aerobics

I went swimming three months ago. How about you?

And YOU?

Unit 6 77

WORDLIST Sports | Sportspeople | Places to play sports | Sports competitions

archery /ˈɑːtʃəri/ n
badminton /ˈbædmɪntən/ n
baseball /ˈbeɪsbɔːl/ n
basketball /ˈbɑːskətbɔːl, ˈbɑːskɪtbɔːl/ n
basketball court /ˈbɑːskətbɔːl kɔːt/ n
breaststroke /ˈbreststrəʊk/ n
champion /ˈtʃæmpiən/ n
the Champions' League /ðə ˈtʃæmpiənz liːɡ/ n
crowd /kraʊd/ n
cup /kʌp/ n
cycle /ˈsaɪkəl/ n
cycling /ˈsaɪklɪŋ/ n
cyclist /ˈsaɪkləst, ˈsaɪklɪst/ n
dream /driːm/ n
exciting /ɪkˈsaɪtɪŋ/ adj
final /ˈfaɪnəl/ adj
fit /fɪt/ v
football /ˈfʊtbɔːl/ n
football field (pitch) /ˈfʊtbɔːl fiːld (pɪtʃ)/ n
footballer /ˈfʊtbɔːlə/ n
gymnasium /dʒɪmˈneɪziəm/ n
hobby /ˈhɒbi/ n
hockey /ˈhɒki/ n
ice hockey /aɪs ˈhɒki/ n
individual sport /ˌɪndəˈvɪdʒuəl spɔːt/ n
indoor /ˈɪndɔː/ adj
interests /ˈɪntrəsts/ n
interview /ˈɪntəvjuː/ n
jog /dʒɒɡ/ v
jogging /ˈdʒɒɡɪŋ/ n

judo /ˈdʒuːdəʊ/ n
league /liːɡ/ n
marathon /ˈmærəθən/ n
(gold) medal /(ɡəʊld) ˈmedl/ n
motor racing /ˈməʊtə ˌreɪsɪŋ/ n
mountain biking /ˈmaʊntən ˌbaɪk ɪŋ/ n
the NBA /ðɪ ˌen biː ˈeɪ/ n
the Olympics /ði əˈlɪmpɪks/ n
outdoor /ˌaʊtˈdɔː/ adj
player /ˈpleɪə/ n
professional /prəˈfeʃənəl/ adj
racket sports /ˈrækət spɔːts/ n
reporter /rɪˈpɔːtə/ n
runner /ˈrʌnə/ n
running /ˈrʌnɪŋ/ n
running track /ˈrʌnɪŋ træk/ n
(final) score /(ˈfaɪnəl) skɔː/ n
semi-final /ˌsemiˈfaɪnl/ n
sports centre /ˈspɔːts ˌsentə/ n
sports fan /ˈspɔːts fæn/ n
sports fanatic /ˈspɔːts fəˈnætɪk/ n
sports star /ˈspɔːts stɑː/ n
sportsman/woman /ˈspɔːtsmən, ˈspɔːtsˌwʊmən/ n
squash /skwɒʃ/ v
stadium /ˈsteɪdiəm/ n
swimmer /ˈswɪmə/ n
swimming /ˈswɪmɪŋ/ n
swimming pool /ˈswɪmɪŋ puːl/ n
table tennis /ˈteɪbəl ˌtenəs/ n
team /tiːm/ n
team sport /ˈtiːm spɔːt/ n

tennis /ˈtenəs, ˈtenɪs/ n
tennis court /ˈtenəs kɔːt/ n
ticket /ˈtɪkət, ˈtɪkɪt/ n
tournament /ˈtʊənəmənt/ n
video game /ˈvɪdiəʊ ɡeɪm/ n
volleyball /ˈvɒlibɔːl/ n
weight training /weɪt ˈtreɪnɪŋ/ n
world championship /wɜːld ˈtʃæmpiənʃɪp/ n
the World Cup /ðə wɜːld kʌp/ n

WORD FRIENDS

be interested in sth
be into something
be keen on sth
be scared of sth
do aerobics/archery/exercise/ judo/ skateboarding
go cycling/jogging/running/swimming
great fun
hang out with friends
have a great time
lose a game/match/tournament
play a match / a sport
play badminton/football/tennis
play for a team
run in a race
run on the track
score a goal/point
watch sports live
win a cup/game/match/ (gold) medal/ race/tournament

VOCABULARY IN ACTION

1 Use the wordlist to find:
1 eleven people *champion, …*
2 eight places *basketball court, …*
3 eight ball sports *baseball, …*
4 five sports with races *cycling, …*

2 Match pictures 1–8 with words from the wordlist.

1 *team*   2 _____   3 _____
4 _____ 5 _____   6 _____
7 _____ 8 _____

3 In pairs, complete the sentences with words from the Word Friends list. Say if the sentences are true for you. If not, change them to make them true.

1 I'm not interested *in* football.
2 My mum runs _____ marathons.
3 My brother's really keen _____ mountain biking.
4 I don't like swimming. I'm scared _____ water.
5 I often _____ cycling with my friends.
6 My grandma _____ aerobics every morning.
7 My friend plays hockey _____ a team.
8 My football team won their _____ 6–2 last week.

1 *I am interested in football. It's my favourite sport.*

4 🔊 **2.51** **PRONUNCIATION** In pairs, listen and find one word in each group with a different pronunciation from the others. Use the underlined letters to help you.

1 f<u>i</u>nal   f<u>i</u>t   l<u>i</u>ve (adj)   t<u>i</u>me
2 c<u>y</u>cling exc<u>i</u>ting <u>i</u>ce hockey the Ol<u>y</u>mpics
3 badm<u>i</u>nton b<u>i</u>king sw<u>i</u>mming w<u>i</u>n

5 🔊 **2.52** **PRONUNCIATION** Listen, check and repeat.

Revision

VOCABULARY

1 In pairs, match events 1–4 with definitions a–d. Do you find these events boring, OK or exciting?

1 ☐ the Champions' League
2 ☐ the NBA
3 ☐ the Olympics
4 ☐ the World Cup

a An international football tournament that happens every four years.
b The best football teams in Europe try to win this every year.
c It happens every four years; there are lots of different sports.
d A basketball competition in North America.

A: *What do you think of the World Cup?*
B: *It's exciting. I love it.*

2 Choose the correct option.

1 My uncle Jim is a sports (fanatic) / *player* / *star* – he watches sports on TV all day long.
2 There was a big *crowd* / *team* / *ticket* at the match – 60,000 people.
3 Volleyball is a(n) *individual* / *racket* / *team* sport.
4 Let's go to the swimming *court* / *pool* / *track*.
5 Did you see the match? What was the final *champion* / *goal* / *score*?
6 I was first in the race. I *lost* / *scored* / *won* the gold medal!
7 Do you want to *do* / *go* / *play* tennis on Saturday?
8 On sports day I ran in the 100-metre *goal* / *point* / *race*.

GRAMMAR

3 Choose the correct option.

A: Where ¹(was) / *were* the final of the football World Cup in 1950?
B: It ²*was* / *were* in the Maracana stadium in Rio de Janeiro, Brazil.
A: Which teams ³*was* / *were* in the final?
B: Brazil and Uruguay.
A: How many people ⁴*there were* / *were there* in the stadium?
B: ⁵*There were* / *Were* almost 200,000 people!
A: ⁶*Was* / *Were* there a surprise?
B: Yes, ⁷*there* / *it* was. On paper, the Uruguayan team ⁸*wasn't* / *weren't* so good. The Brazilian players ⁹*was* / *were* better. But the final score ¹⁰*there was* / *was* Uruguay 2, Brazil 1.
A: Oh! The Brazilian fans ¹¹*wasn't* / *weren't* very happy!

4 Make sentences in the Past Simple. In pairs, guess if your partner's sentences are true or false.

1 get up / five hours ago
2 watch / TV / this morning
3 run / five kilometres / yesterday
4 call / a friend / last night
5 find / some money / a few days ago
6 see / a good film / last week

A: *I got up five hours ago.*
B: *True.*
A: *No, it's false. I got up about three hours ago.*

5 Complete the text with the Past Simple form of the verbs in brackets.

My family ¹**had** (have) a really sporty weekend. My mum ²_____ (take) part in a race. My dad ³_____ (win) a tennis tournament. My sister ⁴_____ (do) something new: she ⁵_____ (try) ice hockey for the first time and she ⁶_____ (love) it! My little six-year-old brother ⁷_____ (jog) two miles and ⁸_____ (play) football in the park. My grandparents ⁹_____ (come) for lunch on Sunday – they ¹⁰_____ (walk) six miles from their house! And me? Well, I ¹¹_____ (make) a cake and then we all ¹²_____ (eat) it. I don't like sport!

SPEAKING

6 Work in pairs. How well do you know what your partner does in his/her free time? Complete the sentences so they are true for him/her. Read your sentences to him/her to check.

1 You often go *cycling*.
2 You do a lot of _____.
3 You play _____.
4 You often hang out with your friends in _____.
5 You're a big fan of _____.
6 You're interested in _____.
7 You're really into _____.
8 You're not very keen on _____.

A: *In your free time you often go cycling.*
B: *That's right – I'm really into cycling.*

DICTATION

7 🔊 **2.53** Listen. Then listen again and write down what you hear.

When did football begin?

The UK's national sport

1. How many people in the world play football? Over 270 million. And there are about 3.5 billion fans! That's a lot of people! In the UK there are about 8 million players and it's the national sport. Every Saturday people play in matches or support their teams. But where did football start and when? Where was the first game?

2. Some people think it started in China two or three thousand years ago. Others think it was in Greece, Italy or Japan. But it probably started in England, many hundreds of years ago. In 1170 some young men went to a field 'for a game of ball'. They made a ball from an animal bladder with air inside! The game got more and more popular. The King was worried because too many people played football and stopped doing archery. And at that time archery was important for wars! There was a football ban!

3. But football continued. At first, football was a game for working people. It was fun, but there weren't many rules. Players had lots of fights. Sometimes there were 1,000 players on the pitch! In the eighteenth century boys at expensive schools (public schools) started to play football too. In 1848 there was a meeting to make better rules for the game. We still use a lot of those rules today.

4. The British took modern football to other countries. The first game outside Europe was in Argentina in 1867. Some Englishmen worked there and took the game with them. Now it's in every country, in every town and nearly every street!

GLOSSARY
ban (n) a rule that someone must not do something
bladder (n) a part inside your body that is like a bag and keeps water that your body does not need
fight (n) when people try to hurt each other because they disagree
support (v) to think that sb or sth is the best
war (n) when two or more countries fight

EXPLORE

1 In pairs, ask and answer the questions.
1. How many sports can you name in two minutes?
2. What's the national sport in your country?
3. What do you think is the most popular sport in the world?

2 Read the article. Match paragraphs 1–4 with photos A–D.

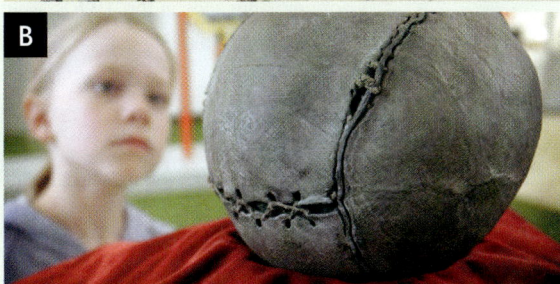

A

B

C

D

3 Read the text again. What do these numbers refer to?
1. 270 million _____
2. 8 million _____
3. 1170 _____
4. 1,000 _____
5. 1848 _____
6. 1867 _____

4 Is it better to watch football on TV or live at the stadium? Why?

EXPLORE MORE

5 You are going to watch part of a BBC programme about a new sport. Read an advert for the programme. What do you think happens in this sport?

> **Rugbynet**
>
> Do you want to try an interesting, exciting sport? Perhaps this is the answer! Watch the next programme in the BBC series about new sports.

6 ▶ **6.4** Watch the video and check your ideas from Exercise 5. Tick the sports you hear about.
1. ☐ badminton
2. ☐ football
3. ☐ netball
4. ☐ rugby
5. ☐ tennis

7 ▶ **6.4** Watch again and mark the sentences T (true) or F (false).
1. ☐ In rugbynet the players can throw the ball.
2. ☐ The game started ten years ago.
3. ☐ Real rugby players don't play this game.
4. ☐ Rugbynet doesn't have many rules.
5. ☐ The presenter can run fast.
6. ☐ The players don't like the game because it's dangerous.

8 Would you like to play rugbynet? Why? / Why not?

YOU EXPLORE

9 **CULTURE PROJECT** In groups, write a presentation about a new or unusual sport in your country.
1. Use the internet to research a new or unusual sport.
2. Find some pictures or videos.
3. Write your presentation.
4. Share it with the class.

7 The time machine

VOCABULARY
Talking about history
Technology, internet and computers
Everyday technology

GRAMMAR
Past Simple negative (regular and irregular verbs) | Past Simple questions and short answers (regular and irregular verbs)

Grammar: When I was your age, …

Speaking: The picnic

BBC Culture: The Black Museum

Workbook p. 89

BBC VOX POPS

CLIL 4 > p. 139

The Great Ideas Competition

Last week we asked you to choose one great idea and say how it changed our lives for the better. Here are the first of your suggestions.

1 Laura, 15, Bristol
Before the invention of the bicycle in the nineteenth century, most people never travelled more than fifty kilometres all their lives. Thanks to the bicycle, it became easier for people to change where they lived or worked.

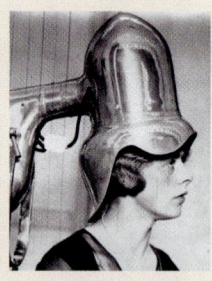

2 Ed, 16, Stoke-on-Trent
Today's hairdryers aren't very different from the first ones from 100 years ago. Thanks to the hairdryer, people began to wash their hair more often (a good thing!). There was also an explosion of new hairstyles in the 1920s, which continues to this day.

7.1 VOCABULARY History and technology

I can talk about technology and important moments in the past.

1 CLASS VOTE Are you interested in history?

2 Study the Vocabulary A box. How do you say the phrases in your language? Order the phrases (1 = the oldest, 6 = the most recent).

Vocabulary A	Talking about history
☐ in 2012 ☐ in the 1700s ☐ in the 1970s **1** in the Middle Ages
☐ in the nineteenth century ☐ seventy years ago

3 Read the texts on the website and put the ideas on this timeline. In pairs, say which idea you think was the most important.

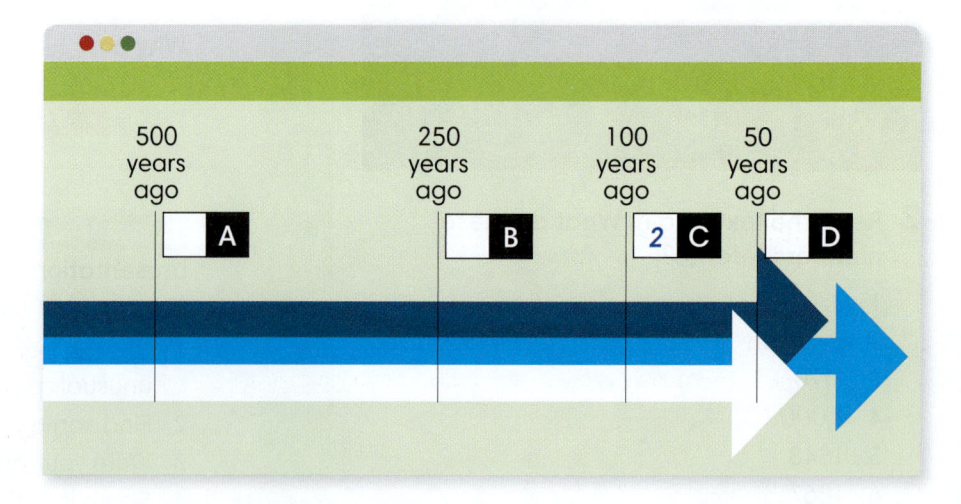

500 years ago — A
250 years ago — B
100 years ago — **2** C
50 years ago — D

4 In pairs, find regular verbs in the Past Simple in the texts.

3 Elly, 16, London
Before the 1500s, people thought that the Earth was the centre of the universe. Then Copernicus wrote his theory that the Earth goes around the Sun. It completely changed how we understood our world.

4 Amadip, 16, Birmingham
When IBM sold its first personal computer, it was a revolution! After this computers were for everyone, not just computer programmers. Millions of people bought their first computers in the 1980s.

Remember to vote here. Four more of your ideas next week!

5 Look at the highlighted irregular Past Simple forms in the texts. Match them with the infinitives below. How do you say the verbs in your language?

become   begin   buy   sell   think
understand   write

become – became

6 Complete the blog post with the Past Simple form of the verbs in brackets. Which of the dates was most important in your opinion?

Randolph's guide to internet history

1990 British scientist Sir Timothy Berners-Lee ¹thought (think) of the first internet web browser, the World Wide Web.

1993 Scientists at Cambridge University connected a camera to the internet. They wanted to check when their coffee was ready. It ² _____ (become) the first webcam.

1998 The birth of the Google search engine. It quickly ³ _____ (become) one of the most popular websites on the internet.

2001 The Wikipedia website ⁴ _____ (begin). Jimmy Wales ⁵ _____ (write) the first words: 'Hello, world!'

2006 Anyone with an email address ⁶ _____ (can) join the social networking site Facebook.

2007 The first iPhones. Apple ⁷ _____ (sell) 1 million in seventy-four days!

2008 Millions of people ⁸ _____ (buy) their first smartphone. People ⁹ _____ (can) use their phones to get on the web, play games, take photos and watch videos. Smartphones changed millions of lives.

7 Study the Vocabulary B box. How do you say the words in your language? Use the highlighted words in Exercise 6 to help you.

Vocabulary B	Computers and Information Technology

search engine   smartphone
social networking site   web browser
webcam   website

8 In groups, think of as many examples of these things as you can.
- search engine: *Google, ...*
- web browser: *Firefox, ...*
- social networking sites: *Pinterest, ...*

9 In pairs, ask and answer the questions.
1 Which three websites do you visit most?
2 Which web browser do you use?
3 Is there a webcam that you often check?
4 What's your favourite search engine?
5 Have you got a smartphone? Do you get on the internet with it?
6 Are you a member of a social networking site?

7.2 GRAMMAR Past Simple (negative)

I can use the Past Simple negative to talk about events in the past.

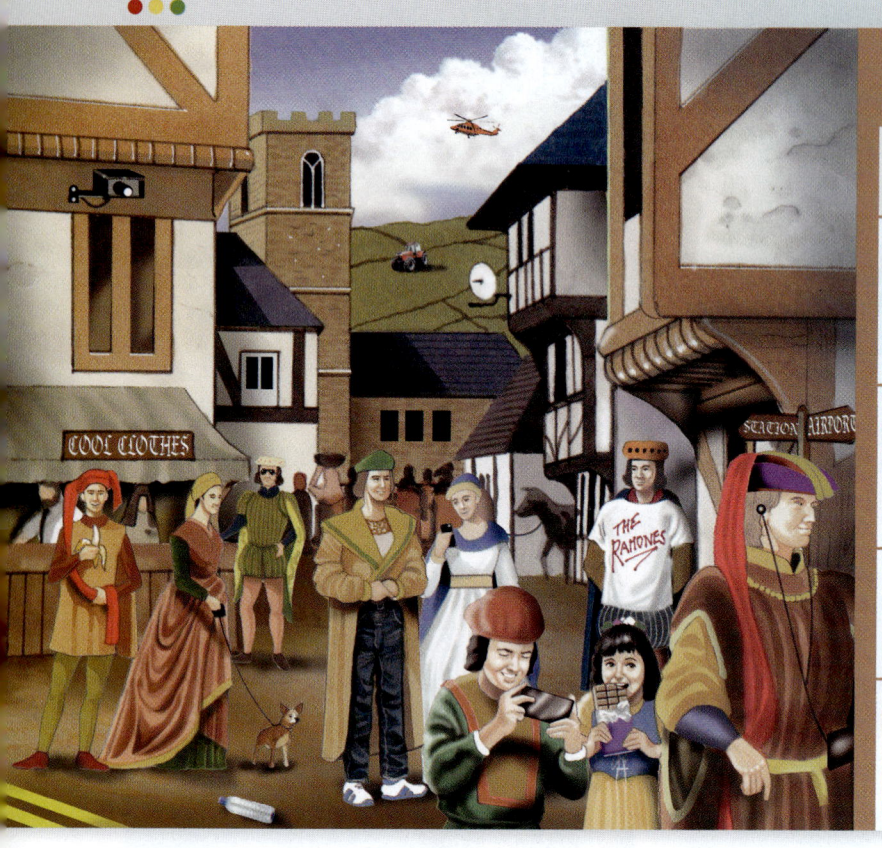

Peoplechat
Nottingham in the fourteenth century
Posts | Photos | Discussions | Reviews

Ivor: OMG! Guys, look at this picture from a website about the history of Nottingham! Nottingham had a castle in the Middle ages but it didn't have a station! 😮

Bea: Also people wore shoes or boots in the Middle Ages but they didn't wear trainers. And people didn't say 'cool' in the Middle Ages! 🙂

Nathan: Children ate cakes in the fourteenth century but they didn't eat chocolate bars!

Smiffy: LOL! You saw dogs and pigs in towns in the fourteenth century but you didn't see Chihuahuas.

1 In pairs, talk about the oldest buildings in your town. What are they? When do they date from?

The Old Town dates from the Middle Ages.
I think the castle dates from the fourteenth century.

2 In pairs, look at the picture above. What is strange about it? Read the comments and check.

3 Study the Grammar box. Find more examples of Past Simple negatives in the comments.

Grammar	Past Simple (negative)

They **didn't wear** jeans.
They **didn't watch** satellite TV.
People **wore** boots but they **didn't wear** trainers.
They **played** football but they **didn't play** basketball.

GRAMMAR TIME > PAGE 124

4 In pairs, make more sentences about the mistakes in the picture. Use the ideas below to help you.

> bananas   buses   cameras   computer games
> helicopters   MP3 players   phones   plastic bottles
> sunglasses   tractors   trainers   T-shirts   TVs

People didn't wear/eat/use/play … in the Middle Ages.
You didn't have … in the fourteenth century.

5 Complete the sentences with the Past Simple form of the verbs in brackets.

1. I _walked_ (walk) to the shops but I _____ (not buy) anything.
2. Ola _____ (have) a shower this morning but she _____ (not wash) her hair.
3. Last night Dan _____ (go) to bed early but he _____ (not sleep) well.
4. We _____ (work) hard yesterday but we _____ (not feel) tired.
5. They _____ (come) to the party on Saturday but they _____ (not stay) long.
6. Marion _____ (tell) me what to do but I _____ (not understand).
7. I _____ (want) to go to the concert but I _____ (not have) enough money for a ticket.

6 [VOX POPS ▶ 7.1] In pairs, talk about what you did/didn't do last night. Use the ideas below or your own.

> do homework   go to bed early
> have a cup of coffee   have a shower
> listen to music   see a film   stay at home
> talk to friends   watch TV

Last night I did homework. I didn't see a film …

And YOU

Unit 7

7.3 READING and VOCABULARY Living without technology

I can find specific detail in an article and talk about everyday technology.

1 In pairs, look at the photo in the article. Do you think the girls are having a good time?

2 🔊 3.01 Check you understand the words below. Then read the article and choose the best title.

> candle   experiment   take part

A The worst month of my life
B A schoolgirl's dream comes true
C We don't know how lucky we are!

3 Read the text again. Mark the sentences ✓ (right), ✗ (wrong) or ? (doesn't say).
1 ☐ Only people from Birmingham took part in The Big Switch Off.
2 ☐ Becky plays a musical instrument.
3 ☐ It was quite difficult for Becky to live without the internet.
4 ☐ The Carters often ate at the table before the experiment.
5 ☐ The Carters couldn't cook during The Big Switch Off.

4 Study the Vocabulary box. In pairs, say which of the things in the box:
1 Becky talks about in the article.
2 you usually find in the kitchen/bathroom.
3 you think are most useful.

Vocabulary	Everyday technology 1

charger   cooker   electric toothbrush   fridge   kettle   washing machine

The Birmingham Mail

Last month Birmingham schoolgirl Becky Carter and her family took part in The Big Switch Off, an experiment to live without electricity for a month. Becky talked to us about the experiment.

Q: Was it difficult to live without electricity?
A: No, not really – it was fun! Sometimes we all played cards. My sister and I gave little concerts – we played guitars. Often we just sat with candles and read or talked. We also went to the cinema a lot! But it was a bit hard without the internet at home. At the beginning I used my phone but then the battery died and I couldn't use my charger!

Q: What were the best things?
A: It was cool to eat together at the table every day. Before The Big Switch Off we always had dinner in front of the TV.

Q: What were the lessons you learned from the experiment?
A: First, it's great we have a gas cooker! Most important, I learned that electricity is awesome! Man lived for hundreds of thousands of years without electricity – we're lucky to have it.

5 In pairs, talk about the last time you/your family were without electricity. How was it?

Last winter we had no electricity for twenty-four hours after some bad weather. It was exciting/boring/fun!

And YOU?

7.4 GRAMMAR Past Simple (questions and short answers)

I can use the Past Simple to ask and answer questions about the past.

VIDEO WHEN I WAS YOUR AGE, …

Dad: Twelve o'clock and you're having breakfast! When I was your age, I got up at five o'clock!
Max: Seriously? Did you really get up at five o'clock every day?
Dad: Yes, I did.
Lily: Why did you get up so early?
Dad: I had a job. Did I never tell you about it?
Max: No, you didn't. What did you do?
Dad: I worked at a gas station. I got pocket money for washing cars!
Lily: So, did you leave school when you were thirteen?
Dad: No, I didn't. Of course not! I worked before school every morning.
Max: Did Grandma drive you to school?
Dad: No, she didn't. I cycled ten miles to school – and it always rained in 1995! And I was busy after school.
Lily: What did you do after school?
Dad: Well, I helped Grandpa in his shop for four hours. Then I took Daisy for a walk – another hour.
Max: Half past four, half past eight, half past nine …
Dad: And I helped in the kitchen for an hour. And I had three or four hours of homework.
Max: Half past ten, half past two … Dad, did you have longer days in 1995? Dad?

OUT of class
Seriously?   Of course not!

1 In pairs, look at the photo. What do you think Max's dad is saying?

2 ▶ 7.2 🔊 3.02 Watch or listen. Why did Max's dad get up early when he was a teenager?

3 Study the Grammar box. Find examples of Past Simple questions and short answers in the dialogue.

Grammar	Past Simple (questions and short answers)

Did you **get up** early?   Yes, I **did**./No, I **didn't**.
Did they **cycle** to school?   Yes, they **did**./No, they **didn't**.
Where **did** he **work**?

GRAMMAR TIME > PAGE 124

4 In pairs, order the words to make questions. Ask and answer questions about your morning.
1 you / have / a good sleep / did / ?
2 get up early / you / did / ?
3 did / you / for breakfast / have / what / ?
4 have / did / a shower / you / ?
5 walk / you / did / to school / ?
6 arrive / what time / you / at school / did / ?

A: *Did you have a good sleep?*
B: *No, I didn't! I …*

5 Complete the questions with the Past Simple form of the verbs below.

come   do   go   have   ~~learn~~   live

1 *Did* you *learn* English at primary school?
2 Which primary school ____ you ____ to?
3 ____ your mum ____ a job when you were little?
4 ____ your family ____ in a different town when you were little?
5 What ____ your grandad ____ ?
6 Where ____ your grandparents ____ from?

6 Match questions 1–6 in Exercise 5 with answers a–f.
a ☐ I went to the primary school in Aston.
b ☐ 1 No, we didn't. But we learned Spanish.
c ☐ Yes, she did. She worked as an engineer.
d ☐ I think they came from Portugal.
e ☐ Yes, we did. We lived in London.
f ☐ He was a teacher.

7 In pairs, ask and answer the questions in Exercise 5. Tell the class about your partner.

Jacob's grandparents came from the Lake District. …

And YOU

7.5 LISTENING and VOCABULARY   The noughties

I can identify specific detail in a radio interview and talk about my childhood.

Noughties nostalgia
The best website about growing up in the first decade of the twenty-first century!

Did you enjoy being young in the noughties*? Share your memories here!

A Who didn't love Clifford, 'the big red dog'?

B LOL small!

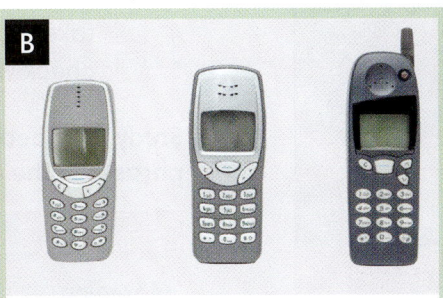

C With a fingerboard, the fun never ended! 😃

D Harry, our hero!

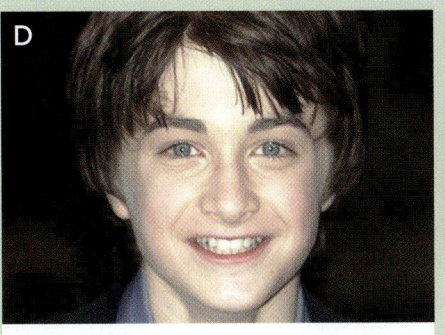

E Ah, these boots! I wanted some but Mum always said no! ☹

F Hannah Montana was the best!

*a popular name for the years 2000–2009

1 In pairs, look at the webpage. How many of the things/people from the noughties do you know?

2 🔊 3.03 Listen and match the speakers (1–3) with the questions they are answering (a–f). There are two questions for each speaker.
   a ☐ Who was your idol when you were seven or eight?
   b ☐ Did you have a favourite singer or group when you were little?
   c ☐ Which cartoons did you like?
   d ☐ What was your first phone like?
   e ☐ What toys did you like best?
   f ☐ Do you remember any fashion from when you were younger?

3 🔊 3.03 Listen again and write down the speakers' answers to the questions in Exercise 2.

4 Study the Vocabulary box. How do you say the words in your language?

Vocabulary	Everyday technology 2

CDs   DVDs   earphones   games console
MP3 player   ringtone   tracks (songs)

5 Complete the questions with words from the Vocabulary box. In pairs, ask and answer the questions.
   1 How many music *tracks* do you have on your phone or _____?
   2 Does your family have any film _____? If yes, which ones?
   3 Who has the biggest collection of music _____ in your family?
   4 Do you listen to music on _____? What colour are they?
   5 How often do you change the _____ on your phone?
   6 Do you have a _____? What's your favourite game?

6 [VOX POPS ▶ 7.3] In pairs, talk about when you were younger. Ask and answer the questions in Exercise 2.
My idol when I was six was Spiderman!
My favourite singer was Jennifer Lopez. I had all her CDs!

Unit 7   87

7.6 SPEAKING — Agreeing and disagreeing

I can agree and disagree with statements.

AUDIO — THE PICNIC

Max, Dad and Eva are having a picnic. Dad is telling funny stories.

Dad: You're not listening to me – you're checking your phones! People don't talk or listen any more – they just check their phones.

Eva: That's not fair! We are listening. You can have a conversation and check your phone at the same time.

Dad: Sorry, but I disagree. It's rude. Smartphones are terrible. They're bad for your eyes and the microwaves can't be good for your brain.

Max: Maybe you're right, but smartphones are really useful for checking information. Train times, for example. Remember when you could only get information at the station? It was a pain in the neck!

Eva: I agree. Smartphones are great. And a phone is more than a phone. It's an alarm clock, an MP3 player, an address book, a camera …

Dad: That's true, but I still think smartphones are dangerous. People don't look where they're going because they look at their smartphones all the time. Max! You're looking at your phone again!

OUT of class
That's not fair!
a pain in the neck

1 CLASS VOTE How often do you check your phone?
☐ sometimes ☐ often ☐ very often

2 🔊 3.04 Read or listen to Part 1. Who is/isn't a fan of smartphones?

3 🔊 3.05 Listen to Part 2. Tick the things Max and Eva do with their smartphones.
1 ☐ phone the police
2 ☐ phone for an ambulance
3 ☐ take a selfie with a police officer
4 ☐ take a photo of the car
5 ☐ check where they are on a map

4 Study the Speaking box. Find examples of the phrases in the dialogue.

Speaking	Agreeing and disagreeing
Agreeing	**Maybe**
I agree.	Maybe you're right, but …
I think so too.	Perhaps that's true, but …
That's right.	I'm not sure.
Disagreeing	
(Sorry, but) I don't agree/I disagree.	

5 🔊 3.06 Complete the dialogue with one word in each gap. Use the Speaking box to help you. Listen and check.

A: History is a really interesting subject.
B: I think ¹<u>so</u> too.
A: We're lucky to have Mrs Brown this year. She's a great teacher.
B: Yes, I ²_____. But she gives us too much homework.
A: Maybe you're ³_____, but homework is a great way to learn.
B: Sorry, ⁴_____ I don't agree. The best way to learn is to have fun!
A: Perhaps that's ⁵_____.

6 In pairs, take it in turns to read these statements to your partner. Does he/she agree with you? **And YOU**

- The computer is the most important invention of the last 150 years.
- Smartphones are very useful.
- People don't have conversations anymore because of smartphones.
- Homework is a bad idea.

A: *The computer is the most important invention of the last 150 years.*
B: *I'm not sure. Perhaps the car is the most important invention.*

7.7 WRITING An email

I can write a personal email with news.

1 In pairs, ask and answer the questions.
1 Do you often send emails? Who do you write to?
2 Who do you get emails from?

I sometimes write thank-you emails to aunts and uncles after Christmas.
Most of the emails I get are spam!

2 In pairs, read the email and answer the questions.
1 Who wrote the email?
2 Who did he write to? Why?
3 Who is staying with Max and his dad at the moment?

Hi Lily,

How are you? I tried to phone but there was no answer. Did your first exam go OK?

Grandma came to stay yesterday. This morning we went to Rochester Castle. Then we had lunch in a restaurant next to the river. The castle was boring but lunch was nice! After that Grandma bought me two T-shirts for my birthday. Lucky me!

Guess what! I asked Grandma about Dad's job at the gas station. She said that he lost his job after only three days because he was late for work every morning! 🙂

Phone me!

Lots of love,

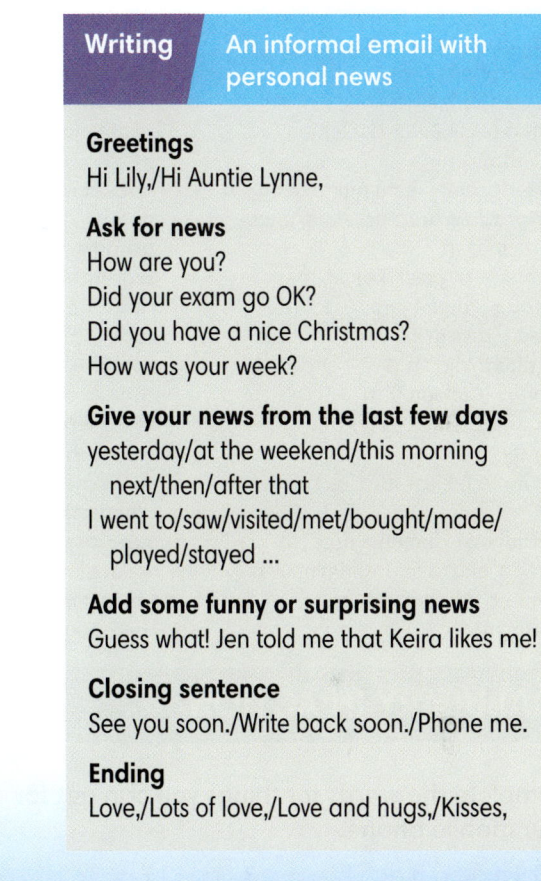

Max
xxx

---

3 In pairs, tick the things Max writes about in his email.
1 ☐ what he did yesterday/today
2 ☐ plans for the future
3 ☐ funny or surprising news

4 Study the Writing box. Find examples of the phrases in Max's email.

> **Writing An informal email with personal news**
>
> **Greetings**
> Hi Lily,/Hi Auntie Lynne,
>
> **Ask for news**
> How are you?
> Did your exam go OK?
> Did you have a nice Christmas?
> How was your week?
>
> **Give your news from the last few days**
> yesterday/at the weekend/this morning
>   next/then/after that
> I went to/saw/visited/met/bought/made/
>   played/stayed …
>
> **Add some funny or surprising news**
> Guess what! Jen told me that Keira likes me!
>
> **Closing sentence**
> See you soon./Write back soon./Phone me.
>
> **Ending**
> Love,/Lots of love,/Love and hugs,/Kisses,

5 In pairs, find examples of the Past Simple in Max's email.

Writing Time

6 Write an email to a good friend with your news from last week. Use Max's email and the Writing box to help you. In your email, you should:
- include a greeting.
- ask for news.
- give your news.
- add some funny or surprising news.
- include a closing sentence and an ending.

Unit 7

WORDLIST History | Internet and computers | Everyday technology

address book /əˈdres bʊk/ n
(seventy years) ago /(ˈsevənti jɪəz) əˈgəʊ/ adv
agree /əˈgriː/ v
at the same time /ət ðə seɪm taɪm/
bathroom /ˈbɑːθrʊm, -ruːm/ n
battery /ˈbætəri/ n
become /bɪˈkʌm/ v
begin /bɪˈgɪn/ v
buy /baɪ/ v
candle /ˈkændl/ n
cartoon /kɑːˈtuːn/ n
CD /ˌsiː ˈdiː/ n
(in the nineteenth) century /(ɪn ðə ˌnaɪnˈtiːnθ) ˈsentʃəri/ n
change /tʃeɪndʒ/ v
charger /ˈtʃɑːdʒə/ n
collection (of DVDs) /kəˈlekʃən (əv ˌdiː viː ˈdiːz)/ n
computer game /kəmˈpjuːtə geɪm/ n
computer programmer /kəmˈpjuːtə ˈprəʊgræmə/ n
(gas) cooker /(gæs) ˈkʊkə/ n
dangerous /ˈdeɪndʒərəs/ adj
disagree /ˌdɪsəˈgriː/ v
DVD /ˌdiː viː ˈdiː/ n
earphones /ˈɪəfəʊnz/ n
electric toothbrush /ɪˈlektrɪk ˈtuːθbrʌʃ/ n
electricity /ɪˌlekˈtrɪsəti, ɪˌlekˈtrɪsɪti, ˌelɪk-/ n
email address /ˈiːmeɪl əˈdres/ n
engineer /ˌendʒəˈnɪə, ˌendʒɪˈnɪə/ n
experiment /ɪkˈsperəmənt, ɪkˈsperɪmənt/ n

fridge /frɪdʒ/ n
games console /geɪmz kənˈsəʊl/ n
gas station /gæs ˈsteɪʃən/ n (US)
grandparents /ˈgrænd ˌpeərənts/ n
hairdryer /ˈheəˌdraɪə/ n
helicopter /ˈhelɪkɒptə, ˈhelɪkɒptə/ n
idol /ˈaɪdl/ n
invention /ɪnˈvenʃən/ n
kettle /ˈketl/ n
kitchen /ˈkɪtʃən, ˈkɪtʃɪn/ n
little (=young) /ˈlɪtl/ adj
map /mæp/ n
member (of a site) /ˈmembə (əv ə saɪt)/ n
MP3 player /ˌem piː ˈθriː ˈpleɪə/ n
Old Town /ˌəʊld taʊn/ n
personal computer (PC) /ˈpɜːsənəl kəmˈpjuːtə (piː siː)/ n
plastic bottle /ˈplæstɪk ˈbɒtl/ n
pocket money /ˈpɒkət ˈmʌni/ n
police /pəˈliːs/ n
primary school /ˈpraɪməri skuːl/ n
remember /rɪˈmembə/ v
ringtone /ˈrɪŋtəʊn/ n
rude /ruːd/ adj
satellite /ˈsætəlaɪt, ˈsætɪlaɪt/ n
search engine /sɜːtʃ ˈendʒən/ n
sell /sel/ v
smartphone /ˈsmɑːtfəʊn/ n
social networking site /ˈsəʊʃəl ˈnetwɜːkɪŋ saɪt/ n
sunglasses /ˈsʌnˌglɑːsəz, ˈsʌnˌglɑːsɪz/ n
tech deck /ˈtek dek/ n
the noughties /ðə ˈnɔːtɪz/ n

theory /ˈθɪəri/ n
think /θɪŋk/ v
toy /tɔɪ/ n
track (=song) /træk/ n
tractor /ˈtræktə/ n
travel /ˈtrævəl/ v
TV /ˌtiː ˈviː/ n
understand /ˌʌndəˈstænd/ v
universe /ˈjuːnəvɜːs, ˈjuːnɪvɜːs/ n
useful /ˈjuːsfəl/ adj
washing machine /ˈwɒʃɪŋ məˈʃiːn/ n
web browser /web ˈbraʊzə/ n
webcam /ˈwebkæm/ n
website /ˈwebsaɪt/ n
World Wide Web /ˌwɜːld waɪd web/ n
write back /raɪt bæk/ v

WORD FRIENDS

check your phone/information/location
date from
get on the web/internet
have a conversation
have a cup of coffee
have a good sleep
have a job
have fun
in the Middle Ages/1970s/1700s
join a website
lose your job
phone for (an ambulance)
take a photo/selfie
take part in (an experiment)
work as (a doctor)

VOCABULARY IN ACTION

1 Complete the words for things you can get for your mobile phone.

1 r i ng t o n e
2 b _ _ t _ r _
3 c _ _ r _ _ r
4 e _ _ p _ _ n _ s

2 Match pictures 1–5 with words from the wordlist. In pairs, say which you think was the most important invention.

1 *fridge*    2  _____   3 _____
4  _____   5 _____ 

3 Match words 1–6 with words a–f. In pairs, choose three word pairs and make sentences with them.

1 [f] pocket   a bottle
2 [ ] web   b engine
3 [ ] primary   c browser
4 [ ] search   d cooker
5 [ ] plastic   e school
6 [ ] gas   f money

4 🔊 3.07 **PRONUNCIATION** Listen to the words below and write them in the correct group according to the word stress.

> address   agree   become   begin
> cartoon   coffee   email   kitchen   photo
> police   smartphone   website

1 Oo *coffee, …*
2 oO *address, …*

5 🔊 3.08 **PRONUNCIATION** Listen, check and repeat.

90 Wordlist

Revision

VOCABULARY

1 Replace the words in bold with the words below to make sentences with the opposite meaning.

> begin   disagree   join   lose   ~~remember~~
> rude   sell

1 I never **forget** my email address.
   I never remember my email address.
2 Last year I decided to **leave** a popular social networking site.
3 The people who work in that phone shop are very **friendly**.
4 It was a good idea to **buy** that smartphone.
5 Piotr and I always **agree** about which computer games we like.
6 When did she **get** her job?
7 What time did the race **end**?

2 Complete the words in the sentences. Use the wordlist to help you.

1 Leonardo da Vinci lived in the fifteenth c_____ .
2 I wrote her an email but she never wrote b_____ .
3 The first satellite d_____ from the 1950s.
4 My dad has got a very big c_____ of CDs.
5 My dad always has a c_____ of coffee at breakfast.
6 I don't use social n_____ sites very often.

3 In pairs, say when you/your family first got these things.

1 your first smartphone
2 your first PC
3 your first colour TV

I got my first smartphone four years ago.
I think we got our first PC in the noughties.
I'm not sure, but I think we got our first colour TV in the 1970s.

GRAMMAR

4 Think about your life when you were ten years old. Make sentences about what you did/didn't do using the Past Simple form of the verbs below. In pairs, compare your answers.

> buy   eat   have   like   listen to   play

I bought lots of computer games when I was ten.
I didn't …

5 Complete the dialogue with the Past Simple form of the verbs in brackets.

Where ¹*were you* (you/be) yesterday? I ²_____ (not see) you online.

My phone ³_____ (stop) working and I couldn't get on the web.

Oh! What ⁴_____ (you/do)?

I ⁵_____ (go) for a walk with my brother.

Really? Where ⁶_____ (you/go)?

We ⁷_____ (visit) the old town. And we ⁸_____ (have) dinner at a lovely restaurant.

Nice! ⁹_____ (your brother/enjoy) it?

Yes, he ¹⁰_____ ! He ¹¹_____ (take) a lot of photos – he ¹²_____ (not want) to go home! We're planning to have another day without the internet tomorrow! 😅

Cool!

SPEAKING

6 In pairs, follow the instructions below. Then swap roles.

- Student A, make a sentence that is true for you using the ideas below.

  I think the noughties were cool.

- Student B, do you agree with Student A's opinion?

electric toothbrushes		useful
plastic bottles		dangerous
social networking sites	is	brilliant
the noughties	are	cool
games consoles	were	expensive
smartphones		boring
the World Wide Web		exciting
the twenty-first century		

DICTATION

7 🔊 3.09 Listen. Then listen again and write down what you hear.

SELF-ASSESSMENT Think about this unit. What did you learn? What do you need help with?

BBC CULTURE

Are museums boring?

Are museums boring? I don't think so!

Museums are often very boring places to visit, but a few years ago some big museums started to get more visitors, especially young people. Why? There was a series of three very funny Hollywood films called *Night at the Museum*. In the films, the exhibits at the museums come alive at night! People started to get more interested in history. They wanted to visit the museums from the films.

1 American Museum of Natural History, New York

This is where they made the first film. The year after the film, twenty percent more people visited the museum. There were more than five million visitors. They wanted to see exhibits like the statue of Theodore Roosevelt, the US president from the film. The museum first opened in 1869. Roosevelt's father started it. It's a wonderful place. They've got the skeleton of a very old woman – she's over three million years old! And there are very big African elephants, lots of dinosaurs and a blue whale that is more than twenty-eight metres long!

2 British Museum, London

They filmed the third film in London. This museum opened in 1759. It was the first free museum in the UK and it's still free today. It's got more than seven million things to see. There are sculptures from Egypt and Italy, like in the film, and the oldest exhibit is nearly two million years old. It's a stone – one of the first human tools. More than six million people visit this museum every year. Because of the film, they are hoping to get more and more visitors.

Maybe the exhibits don't come alive, but they're certainly not boring!

GLOSSARY
come alive (phr) start to move, speak, etc., like you are a real person or animal
exhibit (n) sth you can see in a museum
sculpture (n) a model of a person or animal made from stone, wood, etc.
skeleton (n) all the bones of a dead person or animal
tool (n) a thing that you can hold and use to do a particular job
whale (n) a very large animal that lives in the sea

EXPLORE

1 In pairs, ask and answer the questions.
1. Can you name any famous museums in the world?
2. Do you like going to museums? Why? / Why not?
3. Do you know the *Night at the Museum* films? What are they about?

2 Read the article. Match photos A–B with museums 1–2 from the article.

A

B

3 Read the text again. Choose AM (American Museum of Natural History) or BM (British Museum).

Which museum:
1. is the oldest? AM / BM
2. has the most exhibits? AM / BM
3. has the oldest exhibit? AM / BM
4. is free to visit? AM / BM
5. has the most visitors? AM / BM

4 In pairs, ask and answer the questions.
1. Why are more people visiting these museums?
2. Which museum would you like to visit? Why?

EXPLORE MORE

5 You are going to watch part of a BBC programme about a special museum in London. Read an advert for the programme. Have you ever watched a TV programme about a museum?

The Black Museum

There is a museum in London that you can't visit! Some people call it The Black Museum. Why? Watch this amazing programme to find out.

6 ▶ 7.4 Watch the video and answer the question in the advert in Exercise 5.

7 ▶ 7.4 Watch again and complete the sentences with the numbers below.

200   600   1875   1963   1996
2000   2007

1. The Crime Museum opened in _____.
2. There are _____ exhibits at the Museum of London.
3. The Great Train Robbery was in _____.
4. The police car is from _____.
5. The airport fire was in _____.
6. The cost of the diamond was _____ million pounds.
7. People tried to take the diamond in _____.

8 In pairs, ask and answer the questions.
1. Which exhibit do you think is the most interesting? Why?
2. Is it a good idea to have exhibits from crimes like this? Why? / Why not?

YOU EXPLORE

9 CULTURE PROJECT In groups, write a presentation about an interesting museum in your country.
1. Use the internet to research a museum.
2. Find some pictures or videos.
3. Write your presentation.
4. Share it with the class.

8 Talking to the world

VOCABULARY
Geography | Learning languages
Communicating | Verb + preposition collocations

GRAMMAR
Modal verbs: *have to/don't have to*, *mustn't* | Articles: first and second mention

Grammar: A mystery prize

Speaking: What do you mean?

BBC Culture: The Penguin Post Office

Workbook p. 101

BBC VOX POPS ▶

8.1 VOCABULARY Geography

I can talk about different countries.

What's special about ...?

Young people around the world tell us what's special about their countries.

Jessica, 21 years old

#1 New Zealand

'New Zealand isn't the most important country in the world but it's one of the most beautiful. It's a land of islands and mountains, lakes and rivers. The highest mountains are on the South Island. That's where they filmed *Lord of the Rings*. Aoraki/Mount Cook is 3,724 metres high! Most people live on the North Island, especially in Auckland, the biggest city. The longest river, the Waikato, is on the North Island too. It's 425 kilometres long.

What's special about New Zealand? Well, it's very far away from other countries. It's in the South Pacific Ocean, about 10,000 kilometres west of South America. And it's 1,500 kilometres east of Australia across the Tasman Sea.

Another special thing is that there are only 4.6 million people but there are about 30 million sheep!

New Zealand has spectacular mountains and beautiful rivers and lakes.

Fact box

Population: 4.6 million
Languages: English/Maori
Capital city: Wellington
Money: New Zealand dollar
Flag:

Did you know?

- In 1893 New Zealand became the first country in the world where women could vote.
- Film-maker Peter Jackson, actor Russell Crowe and opera singer Kiri Te Kanawa are from New Zealand.
- The national sport of New Zealand is rugby.

1 🔊 **3.10** CLASS VOTE What do you know about New Zealand? Are these sentences true or false? Count your votes. Read the text on page 94 and check.

1 They filmed *Lord of the Rings* there.
2 It's in the Atlantic Ocean.
3 It's 10,000 kilometres from South America.
4 6 million people live there.

2 Read the text again. What two special things about her country does Jessica mention?

3 Study the Vocabulary box. Which of the words can you find in the text? How do you say them in your language?

Vocabulary	Geography

Compass points
east   north   south   west

Continents
Africa   Antarctica   Asia   Australia
Europe   North America   South America

Countries
capital city   flag   language   money
population

Nature
island   lake   mountain   ocean   river   sea

4 In pairs, take it in turns to ask and answer the questions about New Zealand. Check what your partner knew.

1 What's the population?
2 What are the colours of its flag?
3 Where is it?
4 What is the capital city? Is it the biggest city?
5 What's the name of its highest mountain? How high is it?
6 What's the name of its longest river? How long is it?
7 What languages do the people speak?
8 What money do they use?
9 What famous people come from there?
10 What's the most popular sport?

A: *What's the population of New Zealand?*
B: *Four point six million.*
A: *Did you know that?*
B: *Yes, I did./No, I didn't.*

5 🔊 **3.11** In pairs, use the Vocabulary box to complete Brendan's text about Ireland. What are the two special things he mentions? Listen and check.

Brendan, 17 years old — Ireland

'Ireland's a beautiful country in the west of ¹E u r o p e. It's an ²i _ _ _ _ _ _ between the North Atlantic ³O _ _ _ _ _ and the Irish ⁴S _ _ _. Our nearest neighbours are Northern Ireland to the ⁵n _ _ _ _ and Wales to the ⁶e _ _ _ _. It's a small country – the ⁷p _ _ _ _ _ _ _ _ _ _ is 6.4 million. There are two official ⁸l _ _ _ _ _ _ _ _ _ , Irish and English, but most people speak English. The ⁹c _ _ _ _ _ _ _ city is Dublin and the ¹⁰f _ _ _ is green, white and orange. But what's special about Ireland?

1 It's very green because it rains a lot.
2 Irish people are crazy about music!'

6 In groups, do the quiz. Go to page 129 and check. Did you get all the answers right?

What do you know about the world?

1 The capital city of Japan is *Beijing / Cairo / Tokyo*.
2 The country to the south of France is *Belgium / Italy / Spain*.
3 China is in *Africa / Asia / Europe*.
4 The population of *China / Egypt / France* is ninety million.
5 The *Chinese / French / Italian* flag is green, white and red.
6 The *Amazon / Danube / Nile* river starts in Peru.
7 The money in Canada is the Canadian *dollar / franc / pound*.
8 Mont Blanc is a *mountain / river / sea* between France and Italy.
9 In Switzerland there are *two / three / four* official languages.
10 Madagascar is a(n) *island / lake / ocean* to the east of Africa.

7 🔊 **3.12** Listen to a girl talking about her country. Where is she from?

8 [VOX POPS ▶ 8.1] In pairs, ask and answer the questions in Exercise 4 about your country or another country you know well.

A: *What's the population of your country?*
B: *… million. What are the colours of its flag?*

And YOU

Unit 8

8.2 GRAMMAR Modal verbs: *have to/don't have to, mustn't*

I can use *have to/don't have to* and *mustn't* to talk about cultural rules.

1 🔊 **3.13** Check you understand the phrases below. Read paragraph A of the text. Which country has the most surprising rule?

> accept a present   jump the queue   wait in a queue

Culture shock

A When you travel, you have to know about the cultural rules in the countries you visit. For example, in China you have to take a present with two hands, but in the USA you don't have to use two hands to accept a present – one is fine. In Spain, in the summer, you mustn't be noisy after lunch. You don't have to sleep a siesta, but you have to be quiet. And in Britain you have to wait in a queue for everything and you mustn't jump the queue.

B In Japan you ¹*have to / mustn't* take off your shoes when you visit someone's home. But in France you ²*have to / don't have to* take off your shoes – you can keep them on. Austrians are very punctual, so you ³*don't have to / mustn't* be late for a meeting in Vienna. In Germany you ⁴*have to / don't have to* wait for the green light to walk across the street, but in Egypt you ⁵*have to / don't have to* wait – you can cross any time! And in Singapore you ⁶*have to / mustn't* chew gum in public.

2 Study the Grammar box. Find examples of *have to*, *don't have to* and *mustn't* in paragraph A of the text.

Grammar	Modal verbs: *have to/don't have to, mustn't*

You **have to** be quiet. = It's necessary.
You **don't have to** sleep a siesta. = It isn't necessary.
You **mustn't** be noisy. = Don't do it!

GRAMMAR TIME > PAGE 125

3 🔊 **3.14** Read paragraph B of the text and choose the correct option. Listen and check.

4 🔊 **3.15** In pairs, complete the sentences with *have to*, *don't have to* or *mustn't*. Listen and check.

In Britain:
1 you _____ queue at the bus stop when you're the only person there.
2 you _____ say 'please' and 'thank you' a lot.
3 you _____ forget to say 'thank you' when someone opens a door for you.

In Spain:
4 you _____ say 'please' or 'thank you' in a café.
5 you _____ give a friend two kisses when you meet.
6 you _____ forget to kiss everyone goodbye.

5 Match sentences 1–5 with notices A–E.
1 You have to walk here.
2 You don't have to eat here, but you can if you want.
3 You mustn't use your phones in class.
4 You have to talk in English all the time.
5 You mustn't say anything at this time.

A Don't use Spanish in the English class!
B NO RUNNING IN THE CORRIDORS!
C Why not try the school cafeteria today?
D Turn off your mobiles!
E DO NOT TALK DURING THE EXAM.

And YOU

6 Complete the sentences with *have to*, *don't have to* or *mustn't* so they are true for you. In pairs, compare your answers.

1 I _____ get up at 6 a.m. every day.
2 I _____ forget to do my homework.
3 I _____ do my homework before I go to bed.
4 I _____ do housework every day.

I don't have to get up at 6 a.m. every day. What about you?

Unit 8

8.3 READING and VOCABULARY Esperanto

I can find specific detail in an article and talk about learning languages.

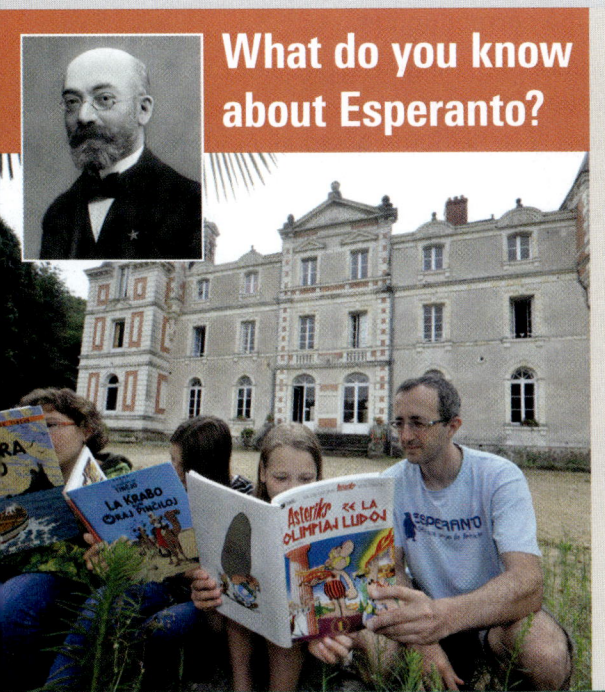

What do you know about Esperanto?

In 1873 a fourteen-year-old schoolboy in Warsaw began to invent a language. Ludwik Zamenhof was born in Bialystok, Poland. He was bilingual: his native languages were Russian and Yiddish. He spoke French and Hebrew fluently too. He had to learn two other foreign languages, Polish and German, to understand the different ethnic groups in his home town.

Esperanto: Mondo sen milito*

Ludwik believed that there were conflicts in the world because people spoke different languages. He wanted a world without war. So he decided to invent a universal language. In 1887 he published the book *Unua Libro* under the pseudonym Doktoro Esperanto. He called his new language Lingvo Internacia, but people preferred the name Esperanto.

After Ludwik's death in 1917, Esperanto became more popular. In some countries children had to study it at school. In the 1920s and 1930s many people shared Ludwik's dream of a peaceful world with a universal language. Unfortunately, the Second World War started. Ludwik's children died in the Holocaust and so did Ludwik's dream of a world without war. Esperanto, however, didn't die. Perhaps it is not the world language, but it survived.

*a world without war

1 In pairs, decide if these sentences about Esperanto are true or false. Go to page 129 and check.
1. ☐ Esperanto is an invented language with simple grammar and vocabulary.
2. ☐ Esperanto is more difficult to learn than English.
3. ☐ Esperanto is the language of a country called Esperanti.
4. ☐ There are more than a million native speakers of Esperanto in the world.
5. ☐ You can read articles on Wikipedia in Esperanto.

2 🔊 3.16 Read the text quickly. Who was Ludwik Zamenhof?

3 Read the text again. In pairs, answer the questions.
1. How many languages did Ludwik Zamenhof speak?
2. Why did he invent a language?
3. Who was Doktoro Esperanto?
4. What name did Zamenhof give to his language?
5. When did Zamenhof die?
6. When was Esperanto very popular?

4 Study the Vocabulary box. Which words/phrases can you find in the text? How do you say them in your language?

Vocabulary	Learning languages

bilingual   foreign language   grammar   native language
native speaker   speak fluently   understand   vocabulary

5 Complete the sentences with the correct form of words and phrases from the Vocabulary box.
1. Your _____ is the language you learn at home when a child.
2. She can speak two languages fluently; she's _____.
3. There are about 360 million _____ of English in the world.
4. French is the most popular _____ in Britain.
5. For me it's easier to speak English than to _____ English people.
6. I like learning vocabulary but I don't like learning _____.
7. You don't have to _____ to have a conversation in a foreign language.

6 [VOX POPS ▶ 8.2] In pairs, ask and answer the questions.
1. What's your native language?
2. Are you bilingual? Do you know any bilingual people?
3. How many native speakers of your language are there?
4. What are the two most popular foreign languages in your country?
5. Do you think English is easy? Is it easier to speak or to understand?

8.4 GRAMMAR   Articles: first and second mention

I can use *a/an* and *the* to talk about places in town.

VIDEO   A MYSTERY PRIZE (Part 2)

Sol: Read that clue again.
Max: 'Look for a woman with wings.'
Eva: Is there a statue of **an angel** here?
Max: Look, under the angel's feet! There's **a note**!
Eva: Take a photo of the note. Has your camera got **a zoom**? Use the zoom. What does it say?
Max: 'William entered here B4!'
Eva: I don't get it.
Max: 'William entered here before.' Is it a door? Or **a gate**?
Sol: Got it! William is King William IV! Let's go to the Pavilion!

Later:

Sol: Here's the gate – the William IV gate!
Max: And there's the clue: 'Iri al la bibilioteko'? Is that French?
Eva: No, and it isn't Spanish. I think it's Esperanto.
Max: What does it mean?
Eva: *Biblioteca* is library in Spanish. Is there **a library** near here? Let's go to the library.

OUT of class   Got it!   What does it mean?

1 🔊 3.17 In pairs, check you understand the words below. Use a dictionary if necessary. Listen to Part 1 and complete the advert.

charity   clue   mystery prize   treasure hunt

Charity Treasure Hunt
Where and when: Brighton, ¹_____ 10 May, 10 a.m.
Prize: You can win a ²_____ !
Entry fee: ³£_____ per person
Make money for ⁴_____ in the World!

2 ▶ 8.3 🔊 3.18 Watch or listen to Part 2 and choose the correct option.
1 'A woman with wings' is *a pop star* / *a statue of an angel*.
2 William IV is the name of *a gate* / *the Pavilion in Brighton*.
3 In Esperanto, 'bibilioteko' means *'book'* / *'library'*.
4 The prize is *a dictionary* / *a language course*.

3 Study the Grammar box. Look at the words in bold in the dialogue. Find and underline the second time these things are mentioned in the dialogue.

Grammar	Articles: first and second mention
The first time we mention something, we use *a* or *an*. You have to find *a* place. Is there *an* island here?	The second time we mention something, we use *the*. Then you go to *the* place. Let's go to *the* island.

GRAMMAR TIME > PAGE 125

4 Complete the sentences with *a/an* or *the*.
1 There's *a* dance studio in Max's garage. He dances in _____ studio every day. Mr Gregg has got _____ car, but he never puts _____ car in _____ garage.
2 Sol has got _____ smartphone and tablet. He uses _____ phone more than _____ tablet. He bought _____ phone from _____ shop in London. _____ shop is really big.
3 There's _____ interesting city in the south of England. _____ city is called Brighton. There's _____ palace there. _____ palace is fantastic.

And YOU

5 Complete the questions with *a/an* or *the*. In pairs, ask and answer the questions.
1 Have you got _____ smartphone? Where did you buy _____ phone? What do you use _____ phone for?
2 Is there _____ statue of _____ famous person in your city? Where is _____ statue? Who's _____ famous person?
3 Think of _____ interesting city. What is the name of _____ city? Where is _____ city? Is there _____ palace in _____ city? How old is _____ palace?
4 Think of _____ country. Where is _____ country? Do you know _____ famous person from this country? Who is _____ famous person?

Unit 8

8.5 LISTENING and VOCABULARY Communication

I can identify specific detail in a conversation and talk about communication.

1 Study the Vocabulary box. What types of communication can you see in the photos? Write the words from the Vocabulary box in the correct column in the table below.

Vocabulary	Types of communication
conversation email (Facebook) post letter phone call postcard Skype call text message tweet	

Speaking	Writing
conversation	email

2 CLASS VOTE Which three types of communication do you use the most with your friends?

3 3.19 Listen to a class of English language students in the UK. What is the class about?
- a how to write emails and messages
- b communication problems
- c foreign languages

4 3.19 Listen again and choose the correct answers.
1 The teacher tells a story about
  a a phone call.   b a Facebook post.
  c a Skype call.
2 The teacher's surname is
  a What.   b Watt.   c Wedd.
3 Sonia wanted to eat
  a a jam sandwich.   b some strawberries.
  c a ham sandwich.
4 Mario
  a lives in the US.   b made a mistake.
  c did something brave.
5 Ania's
  a dog is noisy.   b father is noisy.
  c father sleeps in the garden.

5 3.20 WORD FRIENDS Complete the Word Friends with the verbs below. Listen and check.

ask   call   chat   have   make   post   send

1 _____ a conversation
2 _____ a phone call
3 _____ someone
4 _____ someone a question
5 _____ online
6 _____ a message on Facebook
7 _____ a text

6 Complete the sentences with one word in each gap.
1 I _____ a good conversation at breakfast this morning.
2 My mum asks me a lot of _____ about school. I don't always answer her.
3 My best friend lives in New Zealand. We often _____ online.
4 I _____ a message on Facebook last night.
5 I _____ a friend on the phone last night. We talked for hours.
6 I don't like making _____ calls. It's quicker and cheaper to send a _____.

7 In pairs, say if the sentences in Exercise 6 are true for you.

A: I had a good conversation about music at breakfast this morning. What about you?
B: No, I didn't have a good conversation. I never talk to anyone at breakfast!

Unit 8 99

8.6 SPEAKING Understanding

I can check if people understand me and say if I understand.

AUDIO — WHAT DO YOU MEAN? (Part 1)

Grandma:	Hey, sweetie, can I use the phone to call Marta in Miami?
Dad:	Sure, Mom.
Max:	Why don't you use my tablet?
Grandma:	Skypee. What's that?
Max:	It's not 'Skypee', it's 'Skype'. It's an application for video chats.
Grandma:	I don't understand. What do you mean?
Max:	You can make free video calls.
Grandma:	Oh, I see!
Max:	To join, you have to fill in your profile, right?
Grandma:	I'm not sure I understand. Do you mean my name?
Max:	Yeah, personal details. Your name, date of birth – know what I mean? Have you got an email address?
Grandma:	Sure, I use email a lot.
Max:	OK, then you have to choose a Skype name. Do you understand?
Grandma:	No. I'm sorry, I don't get it.
Max:	It's a name to identify you on Skype. Look, that's my name – you see?
Grandma:	Oh, right. Now I get it.

OUT of class

Hey, sweetie!

1 🔊 3.21 Look at the photo. What is Max explaining? Does his grandma understand? Read or listen to Part 1 and check.

2 Study the Speaking box. Find the phrases in the dialogue.

Speaking — Understanding

Check people understand
(Do you) know what I mean?   (Do) you see?
(Do you) get it/understand?   …, right?

Say you don't understand
I'm sorry, I don't get it/understand.
I'm not sure I get it/understand.

Ask for clarification
What do you mean?   Do you mean …?

Say you understand
Now I get it/understand.   I see.   Oh, right!

---

3 🔊 3.22 Listen to Part 2. Why is Dad surprised? Who does Grandma call in the end?

4 🔊 3.23 Complete the dialogue with one word in each gap. Listen and check.

Grandad:	What are you doing, Kirsty?
Kirsty:	I'm writing a tweet on Twitter.
Grandad:	I'm not ^{1}sure I understand. What's Twitter?
Kirsty:	It's a social networking service.
Grandad:	I'm ^{2}_____, I don't ^{3}_____. What do you ^{4}_____?
Kirsty:	Tweets are like texts, but you can only use 140 characters.
Grandad:	^{5}_____ you mean 140 words?
Kirsty:	No, 140 characters – letters or numbers, ^{6}_____? Look.
Grandad:	Oh, right. Now I see.

And YOU?

5 Work in pairs. Student A, follow the instructions below. Student B, go to page 129.

1. Explain how to connect to wi-fi with a smartphone. Use the Speaking box to help you.

> switch on your phone → go to settings → check that the wi-fi is on → go into wi-fi and choose a network → write in the password

OK, to connect to wi-fi with your phone, first you have to switch on your phone, right? Then you have to …

2. When Student B explains, say you understand or don't understand and ask for clarification if necessary. Use the Speaking box to help you.

I'm sorry. I don't get it. What's …?

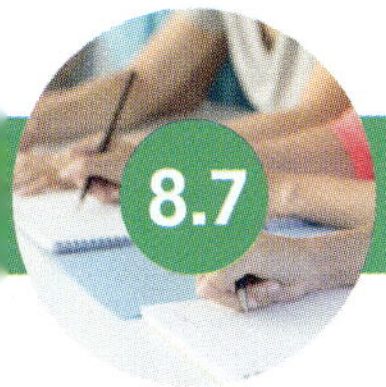

8.7 ENGLISH IN USE Verbs and prepositions

I can use verb + preposition collocations to talk about successful vlogging.

How to make a vlog

A — Prepare well.
You don't have to be original, but you have to talk about something interesting. Learn about your subject. Look for fascinating facts. And find a good name for your vlog.

B — Look good.
Think about your clothes, your hair, the room and the lighting. Ask your friends and family for help. And don't forget to edit your videos.

C — Be happy.
Look at the camera and smile at your audience. You mustn't shout at your viewers – talk to them.

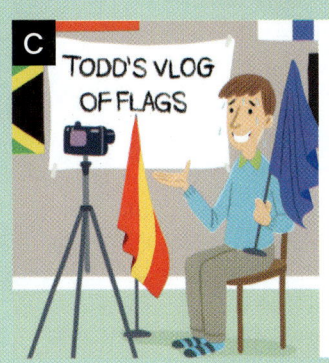

TODD'S VLOG OF FLAGS

D — Don't worry.
Not an instant internet success? Don't worry about it. Believe in yourself!

"Four."
"How many viewers have you got, son?"

---

1 In pairs, ask and answer the questions.
1. What kind of video blogs (vlogs) do you watch?
2. Do you know any vloggers?
3. Have you got a vlog? Would you like to make one?
4. Do you think it's easy or difficult to make a vlog?

2 Look at the cartoon and answer the questions.
1. What is Todd's vlog about?
2. Has he got a lot of viewers?
3. What is the best suggestion in the cartoon?

3 Study the Language box. Find the verbs and prepositions in the cartoon.

Language	Verbs and prepositions	
learn about	look at	ask for
talk about	shout at	look for
think about	smile at	talk to
worry about	believe in	

4 In pairs, complete the sentences with prepositions. Are the sentences true for you?
1. I never worry *about* exams.
2. My dad never shouts _____ me.
3. My mum smiles _____ me every day.
4. It's difficult to learn _____ vlogging.
5. I believe _____ life on other planets.

5 Complete the text with one word in each gap.

My favourite vlogger ¹*is* Tyrannosauruslexxx. Her real name is Lex Croucher and she comes ² _____ the UK. On her vlog she talks ³ _____ beauty. But she's ⁴ _____ in politics too. She believes ⁵ _____ social media and says it can change the world. She never shouts ⁶ _____ her viewers. She looks ⁷ _____ the camera, talks ⁸ _____ you and tells you what she thinks ⁹ _____ things. If you're looking ¹⁰ _____ an interesting vlogger to follow, check her out.

6 Complete the questions with a verb in each gap. In pairs, ask and answer the questions. *And YOU*
1. Do you *talk* about school with your parents?
2. Do you _____ at your school books at the weekend?
3. Do you ever _____ for help with your homework? Who do you ask?
4. Does your mum/dad have to _____ for the car keys every morning?
5. How often do you _____ about your appearance?

Unit 8

WORDLIST
Geography | Learning languages | Types of communication | Verbs and prepositions

Africa /ˈæfrɪkə/ n
Antarctica /ænˈtɑːktɪkə/ n
Asia /ˈeɪʃə, -ʒə/ n
ask for /ˈɑːsk fə/ v
Australia /ɒˈstreɪliə/ n
believe in /bəˈliːv ɪn/ v
bilingual /baɪˈlɪŋɡwəl/ adj
camera /ˈkæmərə/ n
capital city /ˈkæpətl ˈsɪti/ n
charity /ˈtʃærəti, ˈtʃærɪti/ n
clue /kluː/ n
communication /kəˌmjuːnəˈkeɪʃən, kəˌmjuːnɪˈkeɪʃən/ n
communication problem /kəˌmjuːnəˈkeɪʃən ˈprɒbləm/ n
compass point /ˈkʌmpəs pɔɪnt/ n
conflict /ˈkɒnflɪkt/ n
continent /ˈkɒntənənt, ˈkɒntɪnənt/ n
conversation /ˌkɒnvəˈseɪʃən/ n
country /ˈkʌntri/ n
culture shock /ˈkʌltʃə ʃɒk/ n
east /iːst/ n
email /ˈiːmeɪl/ n
Europe /ˈjʊərəp/ n
flag /flæɡ/ n
foreign language /ˈfɒrən ˈlæŋɡwɪdʒ/ n
forget /fəˈɡet/ v
free /friː/ adj
funny sketch /ˈfʌni sketʃ/ n
gate /ɡeɪt/ n
geography /dʒiˈɒɡrəfi/ n
grammar /ˈɡræmə/ n
intensive course /ɪnˈtensɪv kɔːs/ n
invented language /ɪnˈventɪd ˈlæŋɡwɪdʒ/ n
island /ˈaɪlənd/ n
join /dʒɔɪn/ v
lake /leɪk/ n

language /ˈlæŋɡwɪdʒ/ n
language course /ˈlæŋɡwɪdʒ kɔːs/ n
learn about /ˈlɜːn əˈbaʊt/ v
letter /ˈletə/ n
library /ˈlaɪbrəri, -bri/ n
look at /lʊk ət/ v
look for /lʊk fə/ v
money /ˈmʌni/ n
mountain /ˈmaʊntən, ˈmaʊntɪn/ n
mystery prize /ˈmɪstəri praɪz/ n
native language /ˈneɪtɪv ˈlæŋɡwɪdʒ/ n
native speaker /ˈneɪtɪv ˈspiːkə/ n
nature /ˈneɪtʃə/ n
north /nɔːθ/ n
North America /nɔːθ əˈmerəkə/ n
ocean /ˈəʊʃən/ n
official /əˈfɪʃəl/ n
original /əˈrɪdʒɪnəl, -dʒənəl/ adj
palace /ˈpæləs, ˈpælɪs/ n
password /ˈpɑːswɜːd/ n
personal details /ˈpɜːsənəl ˈdiːtəɪəlz/ n
phone call /ˈfəʊn kɔːl/ n
population /ˌpɒpjəˈleɪʃən, ˌpɒpjʊˈleɪʃən/ n
(Facebook) post /(ˈfeɪsbʊk) pəʊst/ n
postcard /ˈpəʊstkɑːd/ n
queue /kjuː/ n
river /ˈrɪvə/ n
sea /siː/ n
shout at /ʃaʊt ət/ v
Skype call /skaɪp kɔːl/ n
smile at /smaɪl ət/ v
south /saʊθ/ n
South America /saʊθ əˈmerəkə/ n
speak (fluently) /spiːk (ˈfluːəntli)/ v
statue /ˈstætʃuː/ n
survive /səˈvaɪv/ v
talk about /tɔːk əˈbaʊt/ v
talk to /tɔːk tə/ v

text message /tekst ˈmesɪdʒ/ n
think about /θɪŋk əˈbaʊt/ v
travel /ˈtrævəl/ v
treasure hunt /ˈtreʒə hʌnt/ n
tweet /twiːt/ v
understand /ˌʌndəˈstænd/ v
video blog/vlog /ˈvɪdiəʊ blɒɡ vlɒɡ/ n
vlogger /ˈvlɒɡə/ n
video call /ˈvɪdiəʊ kɔːl/ n
video chat /ˈvɪdiəʊ tʃæt/ n
viewer /ˈvjuːə/ n
vocabulary /vəˈkæbjələri, vəˈkæbjʊləri, vəʊ-/ n
war /wɔː/ n
west /west/ n
wi-fi /ˈwaɪ faɪ/ n
world /wɜːld/ n
worry about /ˈwʌri əˈbaʊt/ v
zoom /zuːm/ v

WORD FRIENDS
accept a present
ask sb a question
call sb
chat online
edit a video
fill in your profile
have a conversation
jump the queue
learn a language
make a phone call/video call
post a message on Facebook
send a text
sleep a siesta
take off your shoes
visit someone's home
wait in a queue

VOCABULARY IN ACTION

1 Write the correct word for each definition.
1 The opposite of south. **n o r t h**
2 The opposite of east. **w** _ _ _ _
3 Every country has one. **f** _ _ _ _
4 You need this to buy things. **m** _ _ _ _ _
5 The continent to the east of Europe. **A** _ _ _

2 Complete the questions with words from the Word Friends list.
1 Do you believe *in* love at first sight?
2 Do you know how to edit a _____?
3 When was the last time you shouted _____ your computer?
4 When did you last _____ online with a friend? What did you talk _____?
5 How often do you think _____ your future?
6 What foreign _____ would you most like to learn?

3 In pairs, ask and answer the questions in Exercise 2.

4 🔊 3.24 **PRONUNCIATION** Listen to how we pronounce the /ʃ/ and /tʃ/ sounds. In pairs, say the words.

/ʃ/: **sh**oe, conversa**ti**on, o**c**ean, _____, _____, _____, _____

/tʃ/: **ch**at, na**tu**re, ques**ti**on, _____, _____

5 🔊 3.25 **PRONUNCIATION** Write the words below in the correct group in Exercise 4. Use the underlined letters to help you. Listen, check and repeat.

charity   offi**c**ial   popula**ti**on
shock   **sh**out   sket**ch**   sta**tu**e

Revision

VOCABULARY

1 Look at the map. Complete the text about Peru with one word in each gap.

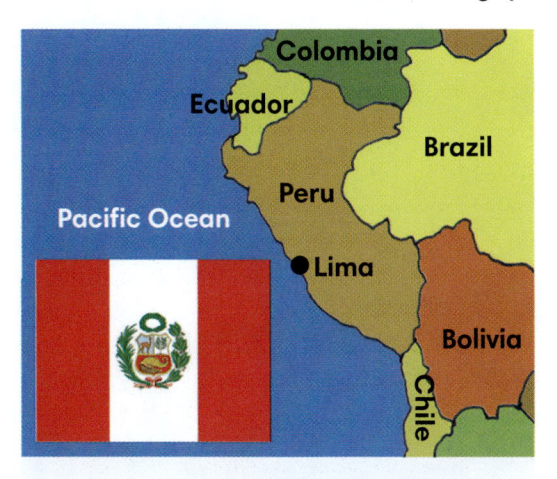

Peru is in ¹*South* America. It has five neighbours: Ecuador and Colombia to the ² _____ , Brazil and Bolivia to the ³ _____ and Chile to the ⁴ _____ . To the west is the Pacific ⁵ _____ . The highest ⁶ _____ , Huascarán Sur, is 6,768 metres high. Peru has a ⁷ _____ of thirty-one million people. Its ⁸ _____ is red and white. The ⁹ _____ is Lima. There are three official ¹⁰ _____ : Spanish, Quechua and Aymara.

2 Write about your country. Use the text in Exercise 1 to help you.

3 Complete the sentences with the words below. In pairs, say if you agree.

> bilingual   call   fluently   ~~foreign~~
> grammar   vocabulary

1 To get a good job in this country, you have to speak two *foreign* languages.
2 English _____ is easy – except for the irregular verbs.
3 It's a good idea to study new _____ just before you go to sleep.
4 You can learn to speak a language _____ in two years.
5 _____ people speak two languages fluently.
6 It's easier to write a letter in English than to make a phone _____ .

4 Choose the correct option.
1 I *asked* / (*had*) an interesting conversation with Joe.
2 You don't have to take *off* / *on* your shoes in the kitchen.
3 You have to put your hand up to *ask* / *make* the teacher a question.
4 You mustn't worry *about* / *for* the exam – it's next week.
5 You have to *fill* / *look* in your profile to join this group.

GRAMMAR

5 Complete the sentences with the correct form of *have to*, *don't have to* or *mustn't*. Write two similar sentences about your country.
1 In many African countries you *have to* use your right hand to eat – you _____ eat with your left hand.
2 In some countries, like Germany, you _____ cross the road when the light is red. You _____ wait for the green light. In other places you can cross the road when you like – you _____ wait for the green light.
3 In Switzerland you _____ throw things on the street – you _____ put them in a bin.

6 Complete the questions with *a*, *an* or *the*. In pairs, ask and answer the questions.
1 Have your parents got *a* car? What colour is ___ car? Is there ___ computer in ___ car?
2 Did you get ___ postcard from ___ friend last summer? Where was ___ postcard from? Who was ___ friend?
3 Is there ___ river in your town? What's the name of ___ river? Does ___ river go into ___ lake? What's the name of ___ lake?

SPEAKING

7 Work in pairs. Student A, follow the instructions below. Student B, go to page 129.

- Student A, explain to Student B how to send a text message from your phone. Use these phrases to make sure Student B understands you.

  > (Do you) know what I mean?   Do you get it?   You see?

- Swap roles. Student B tries to explain something to you. Use at least three of these phrases to say you understand/don't understand and ask for clarification.

  > I'm sorry, I don't get it.   I'm not sure I understand.
  > What do you mean?   Now I get it.   I see.   Oh right!

DICTATION

8 🔊 3.26 Listen. Then listen again and write down what you hear.

CULTURE

Can you send postcards from Antarctica?

Writing to the World

1 We love to visit different countries for holidays and to learn about different cultures. In the past, people often sent picture postcards of the places on their holidays to friends back home. These were very popular and showed different parts of the world. In the 1880s the most popular picture postcard was the Eiffel Tower in Paris.

2 Now we have email and social media, and postcards are rare. But there is one young boy from the UK, Toby Little, who had the idea for a brilliant project. When he was five, he decided to write to someone in every country in the world! He wanted people to write to him, send him postcards and tell him about their cultures. He called his project Writing to the World. At first, he sent letters to his mum's friends. The first letter was to a woman in Hawaii. She lived in a town called Volcano. His first question was, 'Do you really live in a town called Volcano?' She sent him a reply.

3 Today Toby gets messages from people all over the world who want him to write to them. He completed his project. He wrote to every country and he's got replies from nearly all of them. Last year he got one from Antarctica. It told him about life for the scientists there. But Toby is continuing. Every week he writes about ten more letters! He usually asks, 'How are you?' 'What's your favourite place?' and 'Can you send me a recipe?' Toby's dream is to visit some of those countries. He wants to start with Gambia!

GLOSSARY
complete (v) finish
rare (adj) if sth is rare, you don't see it or it doesn't happen very often
reply (n) answer
volcano (n) a mountain that sometimes explodes and sends out fire and hot rocks

EXPLORE

1 In pairs, ask and answer the questions.

1. Do you write and send postcards when you're on holiday? Why? / Why not?
2. Imagine you are writing to a new friend in any country. You can ask three questions about the country. Which country do you choose? What questions do you ask?

2 Read the article. Compare your questions from Exercise 1 with Toby's.

3 Read the text again. Match photos A–C with paragraphs 1–3.

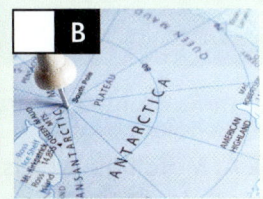

A

B

C

4 Read the article again and answer the questions.

1. Why don't people send many postcards today?
2. What was Toby's project?
3. Where did he send his first letter?
4. What does he want to do in the future?

5 Which country would you like to visit? Why?

EXPLORE MORE

6 You are going to watch part of a BBC programme from a series called *The Natural World*. Read an advert for the programme. Answer the question in the advert.

The Penguin Post Office

Where is the Penguin Post Office? The answer is in the next programme in the series *The Natural World*.

7 **8.4** Watch the video and check your ideas from Exercise 6. Tick the things the visitors do.

1. ☐ go swimming
2. ☐ take photos
3. ☐ go shopping
4. ☐ have coffee
5. ☐ write postcards
6. ☐ send postcards
7. ☐ go skiing

8 **8.4** Watch again and choose the correct option.

1. Antarctica is *700 / 7000* miles from Argentina.
2. There are a lot of *Gentoo / Emperor* penguins here.
3. *18,000 / 3,000* penguins live here.
4. The visitors can buy *coats / T-shirts*.
5. They send postcards of *penguins / mountains*.
6. The postcards go to *the UK only / all countries*.

9 Would you like to buy something from the Penguin Post Office?

10 Imagine you are visiting the Penguin Post Office. Write a postcard to a friend.

YOU EXPLORE

11 **CULTURE PROJECT** In groups, prepare a digital presentation about an unusual and interesting place in your country.

1. Use the internet to research the unusual place.
2. Find some pictures or videos.
3. Write a short script and record your presentation.
4. Share it with the class.

9
Getting around

VOCABULARY
Transport | Travel | Holiday activities | Weather

GRAMMAR
Present Continuous for future arrangements | *going to* for plans

Grammar: Here comes the summer

Speaking: Twenty minutes before Max's audition

BBC Culture: Travelling on the Tube

Workbook p. 113

BBC VOX POPS ▶
EXAM TIME 3 > p. 134
CLIL 5 > p. 140

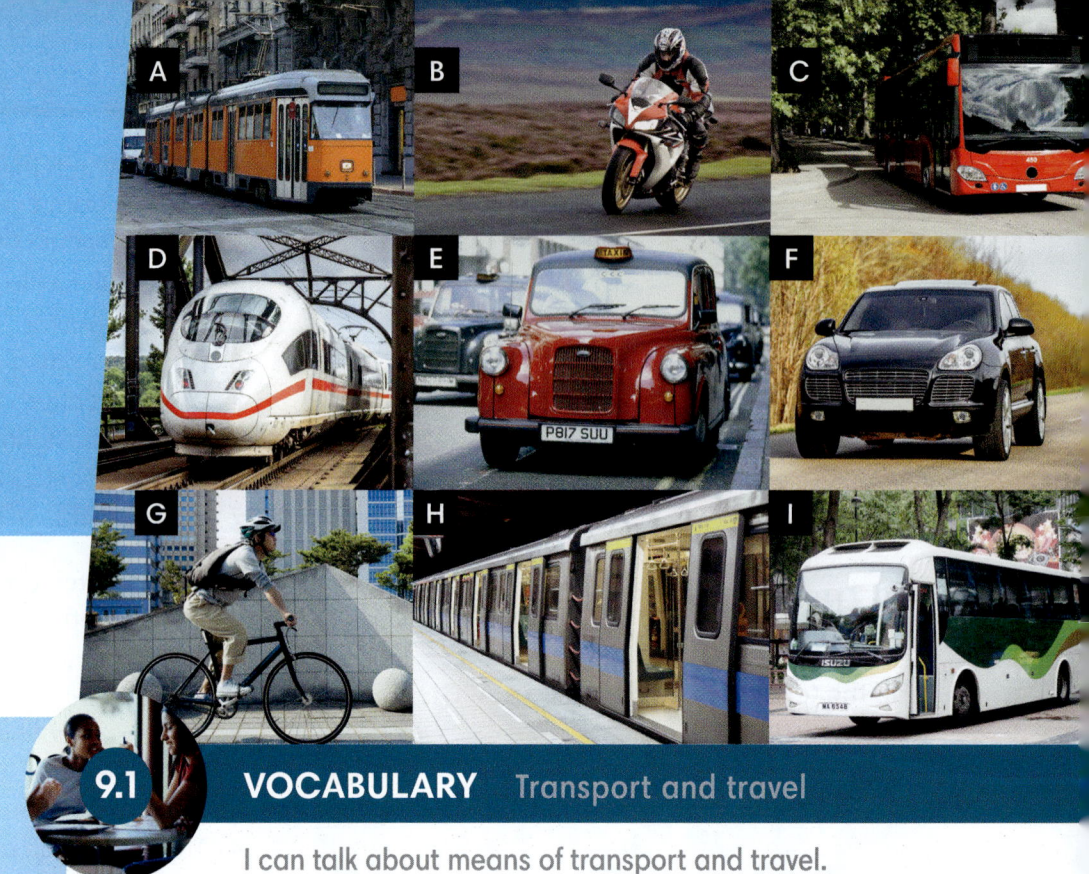

9.1 VOCABULARY   Transport and travel

I can talk about means of transport and travel.

1 Study Vocabulary box A. Match the words with photos A–I. Which of these means of transport do you use?

Vocabulary A	Means of transport
bicycle/bike bus car coach motorbike taxi train tram underground/metro	

2 🔊 3.27 Read the article. What is a commuter challenge?
a   a sports event
b   a plan for better public transport
c   a way to compare different forms of transport

LIFESTYLE   BUSINESS DIRECTORY   LOCAL INFO   BUY/SELL   REGISTER | SIGN IN

The Newtown Herald

Lifestyle > Travel

Traffic is a big problem in Newtown. There are too many cars. Not enough people ride bikes or walk to get to the city centre. Sue and Scott Stewart wanted to do something about it. So these two students from Newtown High School organised a commuter challenge. Our reporter Dev White talked to them.

Dev: What is a <u>commuter challenge</u>?
Sue: It's a race between commuters using different means of transport. We've got a pedestrian, a bike, a motorbike, a car and a bus. Each commuter has to go across town from the train station to the university.
Scott: We want to show the best way to get around town.
Dev: You mean the fastest form of transport?
Scott: Yes, but also the cheapest and most enjoyable.
Sue: The healthiest and the most ecological too.

106

3 🔊 **3.28** Study the Vocabulary B box. Listen to Part 2 of the interview and complete the notes below.

Vocabulary B	Places in town
bike lane bus station bus stop	
car park train station university	

Newtown Commuter Challenge
- 5 participants
- Pedestrian: Sue Stewart
- ¹_____: Scott
- Motorbike: their cousin ²_____
- Distance: ³_____ km
- Stop at the ⁴_____ on the way – more realistic
- Car: Mrs Harris (Scott's ⁵_____)
- ⁶_____: Mr Stewart (Sue and Scott's dad)

4 🔊 **3.28** WORD FRIENDS Listen again and complete the phrases with the verbs below.

drive   get (x2)   go (x2)   park   ride   take   wait (x2)

1 *go* on foot
2 _____ a bike/a motorbike
3 _____ by bus/car/motorbike
4 _____ a car
5 _____ a car/a motorbike (in a car park)
6 _____ into/out of a car/a taxi
7 _____ a bus/a train/your car
8 _____ at the bus stop
9 _____ on/off a bus/train/bike
10 _____ for a bus

5 🔊 **3.29** Read the text about the results of the commuter challenge and choose the correct option. Listen and check. Are you surprised by the results?

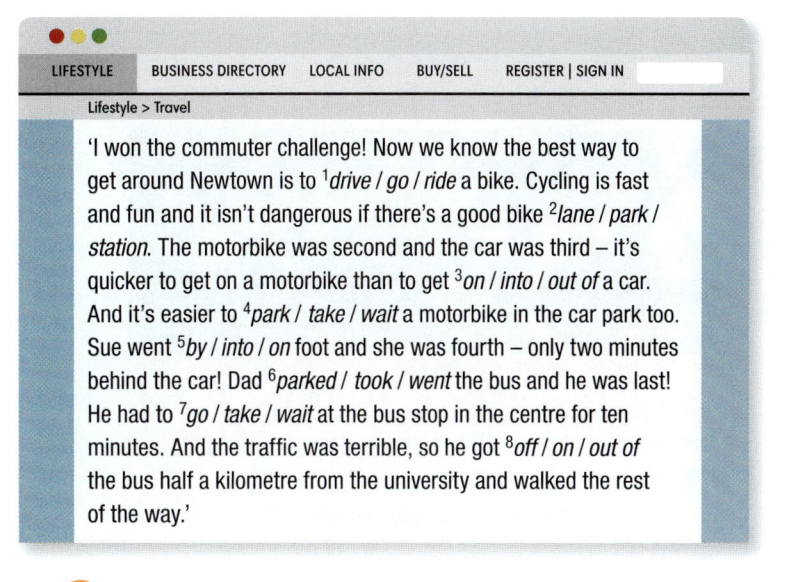

'I won the commuter challenge! Now we know the best way to get around Newtown is to ¹*drive / go / ride* a bike. Cycling is fast and fun and it isn't dangerous if there's a good bike ²*lane / park / station*. The motorbike was second and the car was third – it's quicker to get on a motorbike than to get ³*on / into / out of* a car. And it's easier to ⁴*park / take / wait* a motorbike in the car park too. Sue went ⁵*by / into / on* foot and she was fourth – only two minutes behind the car! Dad ⁶*parked / took / went* the bus and he was last! He had to ⁷*go / take / wait* at the bus stop in the centre for ten minutes. And the traffic was terrible, so he got ⁸*off / on / out of* the bus half a kilometre from the university and walked the rest of the way.'

6 🔊 **3.30** Complete the comments with one word in each gap. Listen and check.

How do you get to school?

Briony: I go to school ¹*by* bus. I get ²_____ the bus at the bus stop near my house. I never have to wait long ³_____ a bus – only a minute or two. I ⁴_____ off the bus at the bus stop near the school.

Jeff: I ⁵_____ the bus from my house to the train ⁶_____. Then, I go to Middleford by train. When I ⁷_____ off the train, I walk to school. It isn't far.

Millie: My dad ⁸_____ us a lift to school every morning by car. We get ⁹_____ of the car at the big car ¹⁰_____ near the school. We're sometimes late when the traffic is bad.

Mohammed: I usually ride my ¹¹_____ to school but sometimes I ¹²_____ on foot. It isn't far but it's quicker to go ¹³_____ bike. I'm never late for school.

7 [VOX POPS ▶ 9.1] In groups, talk about how you get to school. Use Exercise 6 to help you. Who has the easiest/most difficult trip to school? Who has the most fun/most boring trip?

A: How do you get to school?
B: I usually go on foot but in bad weather I sometimes get a lift.

9.2 GRAMMAR   Present Continuous for future arrangements

I can use the Present Continuous to talk about future arrangements.

1 Do you know the person in the photo? Read the posts and check.

Fanpages
Ed Sheeran in Bristol!
Posts | Latest photos | Discussions | Reviews

edfan1: Wow! Ed Sheeran is playing in Bristol on 22 June! Are you guys going?

Jimbo: I'm not going. We're going on holiday that day.

Cara: Yes, I am! 😊 I'm going with Pablo. His mum is giving us a lift from Cardiff. What about you, edfan1?

edfan1: Yes, I'm going too. I live in Bristol, so I'm taking the bus. You're lucky you're going with Pablo – I don't know any fans in Bristol! 🙁

Pablo: Why don't we meet before the concert? We're going to Perfect Pizza on Broad Street first – my mum's got us a table for seven o'clock. You're welcome to join us.

edfan1: Great! Thanks, Pablo! BTW, what are you guys wearing to the concert?

Pablo: We're wearing our new Ed-Sheeran-With-Cat T-shirts, of course! 😄

2 Read the posts again. In pairs, answer the questions.
1. When is the Bristol concert?
2. Who plans to go to the concert by car?
3. Where do they agree to meet? What time?

3 Study the Grammar box. Find examples of the Present Continuous in the posts.

Grammar	Present Continuous for arrangements

We're going to the Bristol concert on 22 June.
He isn't going. He's going on holiday.
Are you coming with us tomorrow?   Yes, we are.

GRAMMAR TIME > PAGE 126

4 Complete the text with the Present Continuous form of the verbs in brackets.

Fanpages
Ed Sheeran – December concerts!
Posts | Latest photos | Discussions | Reviews

edfan1: Ed Sheeran ¹*is giving* (give) a Christmas concert in Bristol on Thursday. I ²_____ (go) – I've got a ticket already. Anybody else?

Cara: I can't go. My sister and I ³_____ (sing) in the school Christmas concert that evening. 🙁 What about you, Pablo?

Pablo: I ⁴_____ (not go) but my mum is. She ⁵_____ (see) Ed in Bristol on Thursday. And she ⁶_____ (go) to his Birmingham concert on Saturday. On Sunday he ⁷_____ (play) in Manchester – she's buying a ticket for that too! She's crazy about him! I'm sorry, but I don't like Ed Sheeran now! 🙁

5 In pairs, plan an afternoon in town. Student A, follow the instructions below. Student B, go to page 129.

Student A
- Start the conversation. Ask Student B if he/she is doing anything on Friday.
- On Saturday you and your family are travelling to the capital city to see a musical. Ask Student B if he/she is doing anything on Sunday evening.
- Suggest going to the cinema at 6 p.m. on Sunday.

6 In pairs, talk about what's in your diary for the next few weeks. Say at least three things. Use these ideas or your own.

I / My family and I / My friend(s) and I	meet / visit / watch / have lunch with / go to (the dentist/doctor) / see (a film) / take the train/bus to / have a party

My family and I are having lunch with my grandparents on Sunday.
I'm meeting Adrian to play tennis next week.

Unit 9

9.3 READING and VOCABULARY Holidays

I can find specific detail in a text and talk about holidays.

1 **CLASS VOTE** Where do you prefer to spend your holidays?
- in the mountains
- in a quiet village
- visiting a city
- on the beach
- by a lake
- at home

2 🔊 **3.31** Read the descriptions of people looking for a holiday. What do they like?

1 ☐
Kirsty, fourteen, and her brother Evan, thirteen, like trying new things. This year their parents don't have time to take them on holiday, so Kirsty and Evan are looking for other options.

2 ☐
Damon and his girlfriend Julia are eighteen and from London. They love the sea but Julia doesn't like flying.

3 ☐
The Darlings are a couple with two teenage children. They love nature but don't like staying in one place on holiday.

3 🔊 **3.32** Read the holiday adverts (A–D) and match them with the people in Exercise 2 (1–3). There is one extra advert. In pairs, say which holiday sounds most interesting to you.

4 Study the Vocabulary box. In pairs, find the words in the adverts. How do you say them in your language? In your opinion, which holiday activities are most fun?

Vocabulary	Holiday activities

hiking sailing shopping sightseeing skiing
sunbathing surfing swimming walking

5 In groups, suggest a city, town or region in your country for people who want to try the activities in the Vocabulary box.

Naples is a good place for sightseeing.
The Alps are good for skiing.

6 Work in groups. You're going on holiday together for four days. Choose your location and plan your holiday. Tell the class. Decide:
- where you are going.
- how you are getting there.
- which activities you are doing each day.

This week's TOP HOLIDAY TIPS

A Go hiking through the beautiful mountains of the Mercantour National Park in the south of France – with a donkey! A family holiday to remember! Don't worry, we teach you how to make friends with your donkey!

B Intensive three-week Esperanto courses in beautiful Switzerland. Learn a new language and make friends with people your own age from across the world. There is also lots of time to go skiing or sailing on Lake Geneva! The price includes accommodation and all meals. Our next course for teens is starting on 19 June.

C Rockaway Beach is great for sunbathing, swimming and surfing. At the same time, you're only forty-five minutes away from central New York – just take the A train to go shopping or sightseeing in Manhattan. We recommend the fun, inexpensive Freeland Hotel near the beach.

D Are you looking for an unusual place to stay? The 180-year-old West Usk Lighthouse has dramatic views of the Bristol Channel but is only two hours by car from London. Great for walking – the sunsets over the sea are spectacular. Ideal for families or perhaps a special weekend for two?

9.4 GRAMMAR *going to* for plans

I can use *going to* to talk about future plans.

VIDEO — HERE COMES THE SUMMER!

Eva: It's the end of school year soon. Any plans for the summer?
Sol: I'm not going to do anything for a week! I'm really tired!
Eva: Yeah, tell me about it! What are you going to do, Max?
Max: Well, I've got that big audition at the National Youth Theatre in London.
Eva: How are you going to get there?
Max: Believe it or not, Dad's going to take me!
Sol: Your dad? But he hates driving in London.
Max: I know. But we're going to leave really early, just to be safe. What about you, Eva? Any plans?
Eva: We're going to spend most of the summer in Brazil, with my grandparents. So I'm not going to be here much.
Max: Lucky you!

A text arrives on Sol's phone.

Sol: That's my mum. It's time to go – we promised to be back at eight thirty.

OUT of class
Tell me about it!
Believe it or not, …
Lucky you!

1 In pairs, look at the photo. What do you think Max, Sol and Eva are thinking about? How do you think they are feeling?

2 9.2 3.33 Watch or listen. Why is Max planning to go to London this summer?

3 Study the Grammar box. Find examples of *going to* in the dialogue.

Grammar	*going to* for plans
I**'m going to get up** late every morning! They**'re not going to tell** anyone. What **are** you **going to do** after you leave school? **Are** you **going to live** abroad in the future? Yes, I **am**./No, I**'m not**.	

GRAMMAR TIME > PAGE 126

4 3.34 Complete the sentences with the correct form of *going to* and the verbs in brackets. Listen and check.
1 I'm tired. I **'m going to go** (go) to bed early.
2 Your exam results are terrible. You _____ (work) harder next year, son.
3 Nadia says she _____ (not go) to university.
4 I'm worried about you. When _____ (you/go) to the doctor's?
5 Next year we _____ (travel) around Europe by train.
6 I _____ (not buy) him a birthday present – he never buys one for me!

5 Look at the table and make five sentences about the people's plans for the summer. Use *going to*.

	get up early	help in the garden	visit family
Sol	✗	✗	✗
Max and Lily	✓	✓	✗
Eva	✓	✗	✓

6 In pairs, ask and answer about your plans for the near future.

A: What are you going to do this evening/this weekend/this summer/this Christmas?
B: I'm/My family is/My friends and I are (not) going to …

7 In pairs, take it in turns to talk about your plans for the next ten years. Use these ideas or your own.
- learn to drive
- get married
- move to another country
- start a business
- study at university
- write a novel/make a film
- be a famous musician/actor/sports star

I'm going to be a famous actor but I'm not going to move to another country.

Unit 9

9.5 LISTENING and VOCABULARY   World weather

I can identify specific detail in conversations and talk about the weather.

1 Study the Vocabulary box. Match the underlined words with the photos. How do you say these words in your language?

Vocabulary	Weather	
☐ cloudy	☐ hot	☐ sunny
cold	☐ rainy	☐ warm
☐ foggy	☐ snowy	windy

2 🔊 3.35 Listen to three people talking about today's weather in their city. Write the names of the cities and match them with the photos.

Speaker	Name of city	Photo
1		
2		
3		

3 🔊 3.36 Listen to three recordings and answer the questions.
1. How high are the passengers flying at the moment?
2. What is Kitty doing after lunch?
3. Where is Struan going with his grandfather?

4 🔊 3.36 Listen again and choose the correct answers.
1. The weather in London is
   a cloudy.
   b cold.
   c windy.
2. The weather in Athens at the moment is
   a great.
   b foggy.
   c cold.
3. Struan's grandfather thinks that in Scotland
   a the weather never changes.
   b it's never warm.
   c it often rains.

5 [VOX POPS ▶ 9.3] In pairs, ask and answer the questions.
1. What's the weather like today?
2. What was the weather like yesterday?
3. What's your favourite month for the weather?

I like May because it's often warm and sunny.

Unit 9   111

9.6 SPEAKING Directions

I can ask for and give directions.

AUDIO
TWENTY MINUTES BEFORE MAX'S AUDITION (Part 2)

Max: There's one problem with this plan. We don't know where to go.

Sol: Just a sec! I've got a map app on my phone. Oh no, the GPS on my phone isn't working!

Eva: It's probably all these tall buildings. Why don't we ask somebody for directions?

Max: Good thinking! Excuse me. Where's the National Youth Theatre, please?

Woman: Go to the end of the road. Then turn left at the traffic lights into Holloway Road. Go past the Odeon Cinema. Then take the first turning on the left. That's Windsor Road. The theatre's on the right. You can't miss it! It's not far.

Max: Great, thank you. So, go straight on, turn left, then take the first turning on the right …

Sol/Eva: Left!

OUT of class
Just a sec!   Good thinking!

1 🔊 **3.37** Listen to Part 1. Why do Max, Eva and Sol decide to get out of the car?

2 🔊 **3.38** Read or listen to Part 2. Are they far from the theatre?

3 Study the Speaking box. Find examples of the phrases in the dialogue.

Speaking | Asking for and giving directions

Excuse me. Where's the …?/How do I get to …?/
Is there a … near here?

There's a … in Windsor Street.
Go to the end of the road.
Go straight on.
Go past the cinema/station.
Turn left/right.
Turn left at the crossroads/traffic lights, into …
Take the first/second turning on the left.

It's next to/opposite the …
It's on the left/right.
It's not far.
You can't miss it.

4 🔊 **3.39** Complete the dialogue with words from the Speaking box. Listen and check.

Eva: Excuse me, Mr Gregg. Where's the car? I left my phone there.

Dad: Go to the ¹*end* of the road. ²_____ left into Holloway Road. Go ³_____ the library. ⁴_____ the third turning on the left. My car's ⁵_____ the left. It's ⁶_____ far. Here's the key!

5 🔊 **3.39** You're outside the National Youth Theatre. Find it on the map. Listen again. Where did Dad park his car?

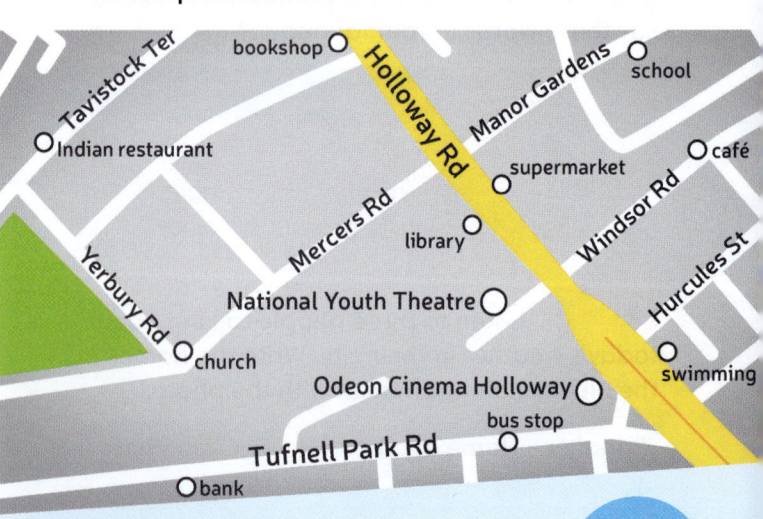

6 In pairs, look at the map in Exercise 5. You're at the school on Manor Gardens. Ask for and give directions. Use the Speaking box to help you.

Student A, ask for directions from the school to:
- the swimming pool.
- the Indian restaurant.

Student B, ask for directions from the school to:
- the bookshop.
- the bank.

And YOU

112 Unit 9

9.7 WRITING An invitation

I can write an invitation email.

1 In pairs, talk about the last good news you celebrated. How did you celebrate?

2 In pairs, read the email quickly and answer the questions.
1. Who wrote the email?
2. What is the good news?
3. Who is she going to invite?
4. What time is Eva planning to meet Sol?
5. What is she going to buy for Max?

Hi Sol,

How are you? Did you hear the good news? Max passed his audition to the National Youth Theatre!

I'm planning a surprise for Max to celebrate his success and, of course, I'd like to invite you too! 😃 I'm going to invite Lily and Max's dad as well.

I reserved a table at Viva, the vegan café in the Arcade, for six o'clock on Friday. Let's meet under the bus station clock at quarter to six. I'm going to buy a card and ask everyone to sign it before we get to the restaurant. BTW, I'm not going to say anything to Max about this yet – it's a secret!

What do you think of my plan? Write back soon!

Love,
Eva

---

3 Study the Writing box. Find examples of the phrases in Eva's email.

Writing — An invitation email

Greetings/News
How are you?   I'm fine.   Did you hear the news?

Invitation
I'm celebrating (my birthday on) …
We're going to the cinema./I'm having a party./I'm planning a surprise.
… and I'd like to invite you./Can you come?/I hope you can come.

Meeting arrangements
The bus is leaving at …
My dad can give us a lift to …
Let's meet outside …

Other plans/More information
I'm going to bring/wear …
You don't have to bring/wear/buy …

4 Read the advert and complete the sentences. Write no more than three words in each gap.

ACE Go-karts for teenagers

We're the most popular go-karting track in town! We're open every weekend from 10 a.m. to 6.30 p.m. Please note all group members must be thirteen years old or more.

A session is two and a half hours long. Prices start at **£45**. We have a good choice of food and drinks in our café.

Click here to reserve a session.

1. On Saturdays Ace Go-karts opens at _____.
2. The minimum age is _____.
3. A session starting at twelve probably finishes at _____.
4. You don't have to bring _____.

Writing Time

5 You're celebrating your birthday this Saturday and you're inviting some friends to a go-karting session. Write an email inviting a friend to come. Use Eva's email, the Writing box and your answers in Exercise 4 to help you. In your email, you should:
- include greetings/news.
- invite your friend to the go-karting session and arrange how to meet.
- mention what he/she doesn't have to bring.

Unit 9

WORDLIST Transport | Travel | Holiday activities | The weather

bank /bæŋk/ n
bicycle/bike /ˈbaɪsɪkəl baɪk/ n
bike lane /baɪk leɪn/ n
bookshop /ˈbʊkʃɒp/ n
building /ˈbɪldɪŋ/ n
bus /bʌs/ n
bus stop /bʌs stɒp/ n
car /kɑː/ n
car park /kɑː pɑːk/ n
celebrate /ˈseləbreɪt, ˈselɪbreɪt/ v
(town) centre /(taʊn) ˈsentə/ n
cloudy /ˈklaʊdi/ adj
coach /kəʊtʃ/ n
cold /kəʊld/ adj
commuter /kəˈmjuːtə/ n
crazy about (sb) /ˈkreɪzi əˈbaʊt/ v
crossroads /ˈkrɒsrəʊdz/ n
cyclist /ˈsaɪkləst, ˈsaɪklɪst/ n
family holiday /ˈfæməli ˈhɒlədi/ n
far /fɑː/ adv
foggy /ˈfɒgi/ adj
get around /get əˈraʊnd/ v
hike/hiking /haɪk ˈhaɪkɪŋ/ v
hot /hɒt/ adj
invite /ɪnˈvaɪt/ v
metro /ˈmetrəʊ/ n
motorbike /ˈməʊtəbaɪk/ n
national park /ˈnæʃənəl pɑːk/ n
on the left/right /ɒn ðə left raɪt/ prep
opposite /ˈɒpəzət, ˈɒpəzɪt/ prep
pedestrian /pəˈdestriən, pɪˈdestriən/ n
plan /plæn/ n
promise /ˈprɒməs, ˈprɒmɪs/ v

public transport /ˌpʌblɪk ˈtrænspɔːt/ n
rainy /ˈreɪni/ adj
reserve (a table) /rɪˈzɜːv (ə ˈteɪbəl)/ v
sail/sailing /seɪl ˈseɪlɪŋ/ v
secret /ˈsiːkrət, ˈsiːkrɪt/ adj
shop/shopping /ʃɒp ˈʃɒpɪŋ/ v
sightseeing /ˈsaɪtˌsiːɪŋ/ v
sign (a card/letter) /saɪn ə kɑːd ˈletə/ v
ski/skiing /skiː ˈskiːɪŋ/ v
snowy /ˈsnəʊi/ adj
special /ˈspeʃəl/ adj
success /səkˈses/ n
sunbathe/sunbathing /ˈsʌnbeɪð ˈsʌnbeɪðɪŋ/ v
sunny /ˈsʌni/ adj
surf/surfing /sɜːf ˈsɜːfɪŋ/ v
swim/swimming /swɪm ˈswɪmɪŋ/ v
taxi /ˈtæksi/ n
traffic /ˈtræfɪk/ n
traffic lights /ˈtræfɪk laɪts/ n
train /treɪn/ n
tram /træm/ n
underground /ˈʌndəgraʊnd/ n
university /juːnəˈvɜːsəti, juːnɪˈvɜːsəti/ n
unusual /ʌnˈjuːʒuəl, -ʒəl/ adj
view /vjuː/ n
walk/walking /wɔːk ˈwɔːkɪŋ/ v
warm /wɔːm/ adj
weather /ˈweðə/ n
windy /ˈwɪndi/ adj

WORD FRIENDS

get a lift
get into a car/taxi
get married
get off a bus/train/bike
get on a bus/train/bike
get out of a car/taxi
give sb a lift
go by bus/car/bike
go on foot
go past (a place)
go straight on
go to the end of the road
in the mountains
late for (school)
learn to drive
live abroad
make a film
means of transport
move to (another country)
on the beach
park a car/motorbike
ride a bike/motorbike
start a business
study at university
take sb on holiday
take the (first) turning
take the bus/train (to)
turn left/right
visit a city
wait at the bus stop
wait for a bus
write a novel

VOCABULARY IN ACTION

1 Use the wordlist to find:
  1 eight holiday activities *sightseeing, …*
  2 eight means of transport *bike, …*
  3 three words to talk about temperature *cold, …*

2 Match the pictures 1–6 with words from the wordlist.

1 *windy* 2 _____ 3 _____
4 _____ 5 _____ 6 _____

3 Complete the words in the questions. In pairs, ask and answer the questions.
  1 What's the cheapest way to **get** around your town?
  2 Do you travel by public t_____?
  3 At what age do people usually l_____ to drive in your country?
  4 Would you like to live a_____?

4 🔊 3.40 **PRONUNCIATION** Listen to how we pronounce the /eɪ/ and /ɑː/ sounds. Look at the underlined letters and decide which sound you hear. Write the words in the correct column.

accommod**a**tion   bike l**a**ne   c**a**r
c**a**r p**a**rk   celebr**a**te   d**a**ngerous   m**a**ke
p**a**st   pl**a**ce   r**a**iny

/eɪ/	/ɑː/
accommodation	car

5 🔊 3.41 **PRONUNCIATION** In pairs, say the sentences. Listen, check and repeat.
  1 We st**a**rted walking to the c**a**r p**a**rk.
  2 Is this pl**a**ce d**a**ngerous?
  3 Is it f**a**r to the c**a**r?
  4 We're w**a**iting for a tr**a**in.
  5 What's the n**a**me of this pl**a**ce?
  6 Public transport can be f**a**ster than a c**a**r.

Revision

VOCABULARY

1 Complete the text with one word in each gap. In pairs, take it in turns to tell your partner how you get to school.

> Sometimes Mum gives me a ¹*lift* to school but I usually go ² _____ bus. I'm lucky – the bus ³ _____ is opposite my house. Sometimes the eight o'clock bus is really busy and I can't get ⁴ _____ it, so I have to wait ⁵ _____ the bus at ten past, but it's OK – I'm never late ⁶ _____ school. The bus takes about twenty minutes and I get ⁷ _____ in Duke Street, next to the school.

2 In pairs, explain the words below. Choose the two activities that you like best.

> hiking shopping sightseeing
> skiing   sunbathing

3 In pairs, complete gaps 1–3 with prepositions. Then complete gaps a–e with the activities in Exercise 2.

Place	Activity
¹*in* the town centre	ᵃ*shopping*, ᵇ _____
² ___ the mountains	ᶜ _____, ᵈ _____
³ ___ the beach	ᵉ _____

4 In pairs, take it in turns to tell your partner about your best holiday ever. Use these ideas.
- Where did you go?
- How did you travel there?
- What activities did you do?
- What was the weather like?

Last summer my family went to the mountains. We went by train to …

GRAMMAR

5 Iza and Tom are planning a day in London this Saturday. Look at the table and write about their arrangements. Use the Present Continuous.

7 a.m.	take a taxi to Newport bus station
7.30 a.m.	get the coach to London
5 p.m.	leave London
8 p.m.	arrive back in Newport

At 7 a.m. they're taking …

6 Look at the list of what Iza and Tom want to do in London. Write about their plans. Use *going to*.

> - visit the British Museum
> - meet Polly for lunch
> - go shopping in Oxford Street – don't spend too much money!
> - go sightseeing in Camden Town

They're going to visit …

7 Order the words to make questions. In pairs, take it in turns to choose five questions to ask your partner.
1. what / today / having for lunch / are / you / ?
   What are you having for lunch today?
2. getting / are / you / a lift home from school / this afternoon / ?
3. how / going to / are / celebrate your next birthday / you / ?
4. you / going to / are / this evening / do homework / ?
5. where / you / this year / going on holiday / are / ?
6. who in your family / celebrating a birthday / is / soon / ?
7. this weekend / what / your parents / doing / are / ?
8. in the future / you / going to / are / learn to drive / ?

SPEAKING

8 In pairs, take it in turns to ask for and give directions.

Student A
- Ask Student B for directions from the bus/train station in your town to your school.
- Give Student B directions from your school to the town centre.

Student B
- Give Student A directions from the bus/train station in your town to your school.
- Ask Student A for directions from your school to the town centre.

DICTATION

9 🔊 3.42 Listen. Then listen again and write down what you hear.

SELF-ASSESSMENT Think about this unit. What did you learn? What do you need help with?

Are there ghosts in the Underground?

BBC CULTURE

London Underground

People in towns and cities take public transport every day. In London four million people take the Underground! London Underground – Londoners call it 'the Tube' – is the oldest in the world. The first line opened in 1863. Now there are 11 lines, 270 stations and 400 kilometres of track.

The map

In 1931 Harry Beck designed the famous Tube map. Before that the map was complicated and difficult to understand. Beck put all the stations in straight lines with the same spaces between them. Undergrounds in other countries now use the same idea. It's easy to find your way.

The ghosts

People say there are lots of ghosts at stations on the Underground:

1 **Liverpool Street:** A man in white overalls sometimes waits for a train at night. A station worker first saw him in 2000 and the ghost was also on CCTV!

2 **Bethnal Green:** People often hear women and children screaming at this station. 126 people died there during the Second World War.

3 **King's Cross:** Here a well-dressed woman stands with her hands out and screams. Then she disappears!

4 **Covent Garden:** Workers often leave this station because they see the ghost. It's a tall man in a hat and coat with gloves. People say it's an actor. Someone killed him a long time ago.

5 **Aldgate:** 100 years ago an electrician nearly died. He fell onto the track. But he lived. His friends saw an old woman beside him. She touched his head. Then she disappeared!

GLOSSARY
ghost (n) the form of a dead person that some people think they can see
line (n) a track that trains travel on
overalls (n) a piece of clothing that covers your legs and body
scream (v) shout very loudly because you are angry, afraid or excited
track (n) metal lines that trains travel on

EXPLORE

1 In pairs, ask and answer the questions.
1. How many means of transport are there in your country?
2. How many did you use last week?
3. Do you like travelling on the underground? Why? / Why not?

2 Read the article. Match pictures A–E with ghosts 1–5 from the article.

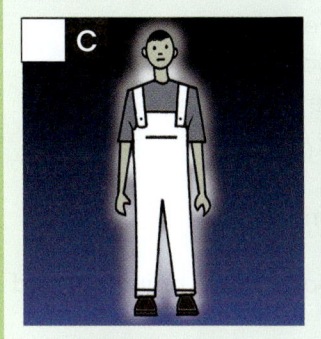

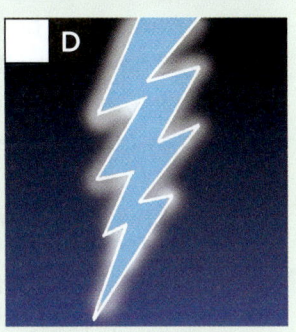

A
B
C
D
E

3 Read the text again. What do these numbers refer to?
1. 4,000,000 _____
2. 270 _____
3. 1863 _____
4. 400 _____
5. 2,000 _____
6. 126 _____
7. 100 _____

4 Do you believe there are ghosts on the London Underground?

EXPLORE MORE

5 You are going to watch part of a BBC programme about travelling on the Underground. Read an advert for the programme. What might the new technology be?

Tube Travel

New technology is helping blind people to travel on the Tube. Watch the programme on Tuesday!

6 ▶ 9.4 Watch or listen and tick the things Lauren does *not* do on her journey.
1. ☐ get on a train
2. ☐ get off a train
3. ☐ walk along a platform
4. ☐ go up an escalator
5. ☐ go down an escalator
6. ☐ go through a ticket barrier
7. ☐ buy a ticket
8. ☐ walk with a friend
9. ☐ go up some stairs

7 ▶ 9.4 Watch or listen again and answer the questions.
1. Why is a journey on the Underground usually scary for Lauren?
2. Who can the new technology also help?
3. Who helped design the new system?

8 Do you think this technology is a good idea for other means of transport? Discuss in pairs.

YOU EXPLORE

9 CULTURE PROJECT In groups, prepare a digital presentation about a means of transport in your country.
1. Use the internet to research a means of transport.
2. Find some pictures or videos.
3. Write a short script and record your presentation.
4. Share it with the class.

GRAMMAR TIME

1.2 can

+	I/You/He/She/It/We/They can speak English.
–	I/You/He/She/It/We/They can't (cannot) speak French.
?	Can I/you/he/she/it/we/they dance? Yes, I/you/he/she/it/we/they can. No, I/you/he/she/it/we/they can't.

1 Complete the sentences with *can* or *can't*.

1. Our dog Toby *can* swim – he's really good!
2. A: _____ your parents speak English?
   B: Yes, they _____ .
3. My sister can speak Italian but she _____ speak Spanish.
4. A: _____ you drive?
   B: No, we _____ .
5. My girlfriend _____ dance – she's fantastic – but I _____ .
6. A: _____ your brother use a computer?
   B: No, he _____ ! He's three!

2 Look at the table and make sentences about what the people can/can't do. In pairs, say which things *you* can/can't do.

	spell	read music	count to ten in a foreign language	use a computer
Billy	✗	✓	✓	✓
Aga and Suri	✓	✗	✓	✓

Billy can't spell. He can …

3 Complete the sentences with names of famous people in your country.

1. _____ can speak English very well.
2. _____ can't speak English.
3. _____ can play football very well.
4. _____ can dance but he/she can't sing.
5. _____ can play the guitar well.
6. _____ can swim really fast.

4 Look at Exercise 3. Make three similar sentences about your friends and family.

1. _____
2. _____
3. _____

1.4 have got

+	I/You/We/They've got (have got) blue eyes. He/She/It's got (has got) blue eyes.
–	I/You/We/They haven't got (have not got) blue eyes. He/She/It hasn't got (has not got) blue eyes.
?	Have I/you/we/they got blue eyes? Yes, I/you/we/they have. No, I/you/we/they haven't. Has he/she/it got blue eyes? Yes, he/she/it has. No, he/she/it hasn't.

1 Order the words to make sentences.

1. A: a pen / got / she / has / ?
   Has she got a pen?
   B: hasn't / no / she
   No, she hasn't.
2. got / any pets / haven't / they
3. have / new / got / books / we
4. a wallet / hasn't / he / got
5. A: they / got / have / a cat /?
   B: yes / have / they
6. got / have / lots of friends / I

2 Make questions with *have got*. In pairs, ask and answer the questions.

1. you / a laptop / ?
   Have you got a laptop?
2. your parents / brown eyes / ?
3. Beyoncé / blond hair / ?
4. you / a TV in your bedroom / ?
5. your friends / skateboards / ?
6. your mum / a mobile phone / ?
7. Homer Simpson / a small family / ?
8. you / a watch / ?

A: *Have you got a laptop?*
B: *No, I haven't. Have you got …?*

3 Write a short description of your best friend using *have got*.

Amy's tall. She's got long hair and green eyes.

GRAMMAR TIME

2.2 there is/there are

With *there is/there are*, before plural and uncountable nouns, we use:
- *some* in affirmative sentences.
- *any* in negative sentences and questions.

	Singular	Plural
+	There's (is) an apple. There's (is) a banana. There's (is) some water.	There are four carrots. There are some drinks.
–	There isn't (is not) a pizza. There isn't any pasta.	There aren't (are not) any noodles.
?	Is there a plate? Yes, there is./ No, there isn't.	Are there any forks? Yes, there are./ No, there aren't.

1 Look at the notes and make sentences about Layla's menu for her mum's birthday meal. Use *there is/there are*.

A special menu for mum's birthday

1. a cheese sandwich ✓
2. two muffins ✗
3. three boiled eggs ✓
4. a glass of cola ✓
5. a hot dog ✓
6. crisps ✓
7. a banana ✓
8. toast ✓
9. ice cream ✗
10. grapes ✓

1 There's a cheese sandwich on the menu.

2 Make questions with *there is/there are*. In pairs, ask and answer the questions.
1. a table / your kitchen / ?
   Is there a table in your kitchen?
2. fish fingers / your fridge / ?
3. a café / your school / ?
4. vegetarian meals / your school café / ?
5. a fridge / your bedroom / ?
6. a pizzeria / your street / ?
7. muffins / a pizza / ?
8. eggs / an omelette / ?

A: *Is there a table in your kitchen?*
B: *Yes, there is.*

2.4 Countable and uncountable nouns | Quantifiers

Some nouns are countable (e.g. *bananas*) but other nouns are uncountable (e.g. *bacon*).
Countable nouns can be singular (e.g. *a/one banana*) or plural (e.g. *bananas*). Uncountable nouns have no plural form.
I've got three bananas. NOT ~~I've got three bacons~~.

Singular	Plural	Uncountable nouns
a burger an egg	burgers eggs	bread, butter, cheese, cola, ketchup, soup

With uncountable nouns and plural countable nouns we use *some/any* instead of *a/an*.
I've got some bacon. NOT ~~I've got a bacon~~.

	Countable nouns	Uncountable nouns
+	There's a burger. There's an egg. There are some chips. There are a lot/lots of chips.	There's some cheese. There's a lot/lots of soup.
–	There aren't any cookies. There aren't many beans.	There isn't any bread. There isn't much butter.
?	Are there any forks? How many forks are there?	Is there any cola? How much cola is there?

1 Write the words below in the correct place in the table.

~~apple~~   brownie   crisps   glass   kebab   mayonnaise   noodles   salt   spaghetti   tomato   water

	Countable nouns	Uncountable nouns
Singular	apple	
Plural		

2 Write sentences with the words in Exercise 1. Use *there is/there are* and *a/an* or *some*.

There's an apple.

3 Choose eight words from Exercise 1 and make a shopping list. Write the quantities. In pairs, ask questions to find out what is on your partner's list.

A: *Are there any apples on your shopping list?*
B: *Yes, there are.*
A: *How many apples are there?*

119

GRAMMAR TIME

3.2 Present Simple (affirmative and negative)

We use the Present Simple to talk about routines and habits.

+	I/You/We/They get up late. He/She/It gets up late.
–	I/You/We/They don't (do not) eat breakfast. He/She/It doesn't (does not) eat breakfast.

Spelling rules: *he/she/it*
Most verbs add -s: eat – eats
Verbs ending in -ch, -o, -sh and -x add -es: wash – washes
Verbs ending in consonant + -y cut -y and add -ies:
study – studies

Time expressions
never, often, usually, sometimes, once a week, every three weeks

Adverbs of frequency (*never, often,* etc.) usually go before the main verb, but after the verb *to be*.
They sometimes complain.
They don't often go to the cinema.
She is often tired.

Longer phrases usually come at the end.
I go to the cinema once a week.

We don't use *not* with *never* because *never* already has a negative meaning.
She never eats meat. NOT ~~She doesn't never eat meat.~~

1 In pairs, say how often you do these things. Use a time expression from the box above.
- go to the cinema
- have breakfast
- help in the kitchen
- tidy your room
- browse the internet
- write long letters

I go to the cinema once a month. I usually …

2 Complete the text with the Present Simple form of the verbs in brackets.

Cody
Every morning my budgie Cody ¹*tells* (tell) us he's happy to see the sun and ² _____ (wake) us up! We ³ _____ (not have) a problem with this in winter. But in summer he ⁴ _____ (start) at 4 a.m. and he ⁵ _____ (not stop) – we ⁶ _____ (not like) it at all! When Dad ⁷ _____ (watch) football on TV, Cody sometimes gets very excited and Dad ⁸ _____ (shout) at him.
Cody ⁹ _____ (know) many words. He can say, 'Pretty boy!' and 'Lovely celery!' but his favourite words are 'Shut up, Cody!'

3 Think of a person you know very well. Write eight sentences about what he/she does/doesn't do on a typical day.

3.4 Present Simple (questions and short answers)

Yes/No questions and short answers

Do	I/you/ we/they	go to school?	Yes, I/you/we/they do. No, I/you/we/they don't.
Does	he/she/it	get up early?	Yes, he/she/it does. No, he/she/it doesn't.

Wh- questions
What time does he get up?
Where does she come from?
How often do you visit your grandparents?
Which languages do they speak?

1 Complete the questions with *do* or *does*. In pairs, ask and answer the questions.
1 *Does* your best friend live near you?
2 _____ your grandparents often visit you?
3 _____ your dad like sport?
4 _____ you like Mondays?
5 _____ your mum work in a bank?
6 _____ your parents speak a foreign language?

2 Complete the questions with the question words below. In pairs, ask and answer the questions.

~~how often~~   what   what time   where   which

1 *How often* do you text your friends?
2 _____ do your cousins live?
3 _____ do you usually do on Sunday's?
4 _____ do you go to bed on Friday's?
5 _____ countries do you want to visit in the future?

3 In pairs, write questions for these answers. Sometimes there is more than one possible answer.
1 I usually watch TV in the evening.
   When do you usually watch TV?
   What do you usually do in the evening?
2 My mum works in an office.
3 My brothers go to bed at ten.
4 I see my grandparents once a month.
5 No, we don't! We hate The Beatles!

4 Choose a favourite musician or sports star. Write six questions you would like to ask him/her about his/her life.

How often do you go to parties?

Grammar Time

GRAMMAR TIME

4.2 Present Continuous

We use the Present Continuous to talk about what is happening now.

+	−
I'm (am) working. You/We/They're (are) working. He/She/It's (is) working.	I'm not (am not) sleeping. You/We/They aren't (are not) sleeping. He/She/It isn't (is not) sleeping.
?	Short answers
Am I working? Are you/we/they working? Is he/she/it working?	Yes, I am./No, I'm not. Yes you/we/they are./ No, you/we/they aren't. Yes, he/she/it is./ No, he/she/it isn't.
What are you doing? Why are they smiling?	

Spelling rules: -ing
Most verbs add -ing: eat – eating
Verbs ending in -e cut the -e and add -ing: make– making
One-syllable verbs ending in vowel + consonant double the final consonant: sit – sitting

Time expressions
now, at the moment

1 Complete the sentences with the correct form of the Present Continuous.
1. Dana *isn't studying* (not study) – she _____ (browse) the internet.
2. Look! Two men _____ (run) out of that shop!
3. A: _____ (they/work?) hard?
   B: No, they _____ .
4. I can't speak to you now. I _____ (shop).
5. A: _____ (you/have?) a good time?
   B: Yes, we _____ . It's a great concert. All my friends _____ (dance)!

2 In pairs, take it in turns to mime one of the actions below for your partner to guess.

> check your email   drive a tractor   eat spaghetti
> feel bored   have a shower   make a pizza
> play a computer game   play with a cat
> walk in the rain

A: Are you making a pizza?
B: No, I'm not. I'm playing a computer game!

3 Think about a famous person in your country. What do you think they are doing at the moment? Write five sentences.

The President is having an English lesson.

4.4 Present Simple and Present Continuous

We use the Present Simple to talk about habits and routines.
I usually go to bed after midnight.
Jack never watches TV in the morning.

We use the Present Continuous to talk about something happening now/at the moment.
I'm playing a computer game at the moment.
Noah can't come to the phone right now – he's having a shower.

1 Read the information and make sentences about the people. Use the Present Simple and Present Continuous.

	Usually	At the moment
Jim	not eat meat	eat a hamburger
Gwen	feel happy	not feel well
Jack	not work hard at school	do homework
Luke and Seb	wear tracksuits	wear white shirts
Cara and I	not enjoy classes	have fun

Jim doesn't usually eat meat but he's eating a hamburger at the moment.

2 Make questions in the Present Continuous or Present Simple. In pairs, ask and answer the questions.
1. you / wear / trainers / at the moment / ?
   Are you wearing trainers at the moment?
2. your friends / usually / wear / trainers to parties / ?
3. when / you / usually / do / your homework / ?
4. your classmates / have / fun / now / ?
5. your parents / often / listen / to music / ?
6. how often / you / speak / English / after school / ?

A: Are you wearing trainers at the moment?
B: Yes, I am.

3 Choose three classmates you know well. Write sentences about what they often/ usually do in English classes. Use the Present Simple.

Igor usually sits next to the window.
Gabi always works hard.

4 Write sentences about what the people from Exercise 3 are doing now. Use the Present Continuous.

Igor is looking out the window.
Gabi is doing an exercise.

GRAMMAR TIME

5.2 Comparative adjectives

We use comparative adjectives to compare people, things or places. To form them, we use adjective + *-er* + *than* or *more* + adjective + *than*.
I'm *taller than* my mum.
English is *more interesting than* Maths.

Adjective	Comparative
Short adjectives: + *-er*	
strong	strong**er**
Short adjectives ending in *-e*: + *-r*	
cute	cute**r**
Short adjectives ending in vowel + consonant: double final consonant + *-er*	
big	big**ger**
Adjectives ending in *-y*: cut *-y* + *-ier*	
friendly	friend**lier**
Long adjectives: *more*	
intelligent	*more* intelligent
Irregular adjectives	
good	better
bad	worse

1 Write the comparative form of the adjectives.

bad – *worse*	happy –	sad –
brave –	lazy –	short –
cool –	nice –	successful –
fit –	old –	talented –
funny –	original –	thin –
good –	quiet –	young –

2 In pairs, compare these people, places and things. Use the adjectives in brackets.
 1 Canada / Ireland (small/big)
 Ireland is smaller than Canada. Canada is bigger than Ireland.
 2 Jennifer Lawrence / Brad Pitt (young/old)
 3 rap / reggae (good/bad)
 4 Beyoncé / Lily Allen (successful)
 5 Harry Potter / Homer Simpson (funny)
 6 Batman / Spider-Man (nice)

3 Write ten sentences about you and a friend. Use comparative adjectives.

I'm older than my friend Sarah. She's got longer hair than me.

5.4 Superlative adjectives

To form superlative adjectives, we use *the* + adjective + *-est* or *the most* + adjective.
I'm *the tallest* person in my family.
English is *the most interesting* subject at school.

Adjective	Superlative
Short adjectives: + *-est*	
strong	*the* strong**est**
Short adjectives ending in *-e*: + *-st*	
cute	*the* cute**st**
Short adjectives ending in vowel + consonant: double final consonant + *-est*	
big	*the* big**gest**
Adjectives ending in *-y*: cut *-y* + *-iest*	
friendly	*the* friend**liest**
Long adjectives: *most*	
intelligent	*the most* intelligent
Irregular adjectives	
good	the best
bad	the worst

1 Write the superlative form of the adjectives.

bad – *the worst*	happy –	sad –
brave –	lazy –	short –
cool –	nice –	successful –
fit –	old –	talented –
funny –	original –	thin –
good –	quiet –	young –

2 Make sentences with superlative adjectives. In pairs, compare your sentences.
 1 big / city / our country
 The biggest city in our country is …
 2 cool / person on TV
 3 interesting / film this year
 4 happy / person I know
 5 good / football team / world
 6 bad / pop group / world
 7 brave / person / history

3 Write ten sentences about your family. Use superlative adjectives.

The oldest person in my family is my great-grandfather – he's eighty-five.
The person with the biggest nose in my family is …

GRAMMAR TIME

6.2 was/were

The past form of the verb *to be* is *was* or *were*.

+	I/He/She/It	was in China.
	You/We/They	were at the match.
	There	was one team.
	There	were two teams.
−	I/He/She/It	wasn't (was not) in the team.
	You/We/They	weren't (were not) happy.
	There	wasn't (was not) a big crowd.
	There	weren't (were not) any goals.
?	Was he at the match? Yes, he was./No, he wasn't.	
	Were they good? Yes, they were./No, they weren't.	
	Was there a winner? Yes, there was./No, there wasn't.	
	Were there many goals? Yes, there were./No, there weren't.	

Time expressions
in 1991 (nineteen ninety-one), in 2016 (twenty sixteen)

1 Complete the dialogue with the correct form of *was* or *were*. In pairs, practise reading the dialogue.

A: Where [1]*were* the Olympic Games in 2012?
B: They [2]_____ in Rio, in Brazil, I think.
A: No, the 2012 Olympics [3]_____ in Rio. They [4]_____ in London.
B: So when [5]_____ the Games in Brazil? [6]_____ it in 2014?
A: No, it [7]_____ in 2014. It [8]_____ in 2016.
B: [9]_____ you there?
A: No, I [10]_____.

2 Complete the dialogue about the 2014 World Cup semi-final with the correct form of *there was* or *there were*. In pairs, practise reading the dialogue.

A: [1]*There were* five goals in the first half – all for Germany!
B: Wow! How many goals [2]_____ in the second half?
A: Three – the final score was Germany 7 Brazil 1.
B: [3]_____ a big crowd?
A: Yes, [4]_____. [5]_____ exactly 58,141 people in the stadium.
B: That's a lot! And [6]_____ any red cards?
A: No, [7]_____.

6.4 Past Simple (affirmative)

Regular verbs
To form the Past Simple of regular verbs, we usually add *-ed* to the verb.
I/You/He/She/It/We/They walked home.

Spelling rules
Most verbs add *-ed*: play – played
Verbs ending in *-e* add *-d*: move – moved
Verbs ending in vowel + consonant double the consonant and add *-ed*: stop – stopped
Verbs ending in consonant + *-y* cut *-y* and add *-ied*: carry – carried

Irregular verbs
Many common verbs are irregular in the Past Simple.
come – came   do – did   win – won (See page 127.)
I/You/He/She/It/We/They ran five miles yesterday.

Time expressions
this morning, yesterday, last night, last week, last month, last summer, last year

1 Write the Past Simple form of the verbs.

ask – *asked*	try –	dance –
do –	go –	win –
see –	jog –	come –
end –	put –	want –

2 Complete the text with the Past Simple form of the verbs in brackets.

Last Sunday I [1]*woke up* (wake up) at 6.30 a.m., [2]_____ (eat) an apple and [3]_____ (drink) some juice. Then I [4]_____ (take) a bag with some food and water and [5]_____ (run) to my friend Danny's house. His dad [6]_____ (drive) us to a mountain called Ben Nevis. We [7]_____ (arrive) there at 8 a.m. We [8]_____ (have) a snack and then we [9]_____ (start) walking. We [10]_____ (walk) for three hours and then we [11]_____ (stop) for lunch. We were tired when we [12]_____ (get) to the top but the view was fantastic!

3 In pairs, talk about what you did last Sunday. Use the text in Exercise 2 to help you.

4 Write two true Past Simple sentences for each of the time expressions below: one with a regular verb and one with an irregular verb.

last night   last week   last month
last year   this morning

My mum asked me a question this morning.
I had breakfast in a café this morning

GRAMMAR TIME

7.2 Past Simple (negative)

To form negative sentences in the Past Simple, we use *didn't* (*did not*) + infinitive.
I slept. – I didn't sleep.
She laughed. – She didn't laugh.

I/You/He/She/It/We/They didn't work.
I/You/He/She/It/We/They didn't go to school.

1 Complete the sentences with the Past Simple form of the verbs in brackets.
1. We *didn't go* (not go) to the park today.
2. Liz _____ (not like) her present.
3. You _____ (not finish) your breakfast.
4. I _____ (not get up) early yesterday.
5. The game _____ (not start) at six.
6. Tim _____ (not call) me last night.

2 Make the sentences negative.
1. We understood.
   We didn't understand.
2. She wrote to me.
3. They walked home.
4. We ate breakfast.
5. I bought a magazine.
6. He sold his laptop.

3 In pairs, correct the sentences.
1. William Shakespeare came from Canada.
   William Shakespeare didn't come from Canada. He came from England.
2. J.K. Rowling wrote *Game of Thrones*.
3. The British invented karate.
4. David Beckham played basketball.
5. Bill Gates started Apple.
6. Coca Cola came from Russia.
7. Leonardo Da Vinci lived in France.
8. Albert Einstein lived in the eighteenth century.

4 Write five sentences about the differences between your life and your parents' lives when they were your age. Use the Past Simple.

*My parents didn't go on holiday abroad.
They didn't learn English at school.*

7.4 Past Simple (questions and short answers)

To form questions in the Past Simple, we use *did* + subject + infinitive.
Did I/you/he/she/it/we/they go to school?
Yes, I/you/he/she/it/we/they did.
No, I/you/he/she/it/we/they didn't.
Where did you go yesterday?
When did you see her?
What time did you get up?

1 Complete the questions with the Past Simple form of the verbs in brackets. Then match questions 1–8 with answers a–h.
1. *Did you see* (you/see) Tom yesterday?
2. _____ (they/like) the party?
3. _____ (you/enjoy) the concert?
4. _____ (what/she/buy)?
5. _____ (they/go) to the shops?
6. _____ (what time/you/get up)?
7. _____ (you/wear) a dress?
8. _____ (where/he/stay)?

a. [1] No, I didn't, but I texted him.
b. [ ] I got up at six o'clock.
c. [ ] No, I didn't. I wore jeans.
d. [ ] Yes, they did – they really enjoyed it.
e. [ ] No, they didn't. They went to the cinema.
f. [ ] She bought a birthday present for her dad.
g. [ ] He stayed in a hotel.
h. [ ] No, I didn't. It was boring.

2 Complete the questions with the Past Simple form of the verbs below. In pairs, ask and answer the questions.

| buy   eat   get up   go   rain   wash   watch |

1. *Did you see* (you) any good films last week?
2. When _____ (you) to bed last night?
3. _____ (it) yesterday?
4. _____ (you) your hair this morning?
5. _____ (you) anything yesterday?
6. What time _____ (your parents) this morning?
7. What _____ (your family) for dinner last night?

3 In pairs, imagine that you work as reporters for a lifestyle magazine. Write an interview with your favourite music/sports star about his/her life. Write at least five questions.

Q: When did you start playing football?
A: I started playing football in …

Grammar Time

GRAMMAR TIME

8.2 Modal verbs: have to/don't have to, mustn't

Modal verbs come before other verbs.
When it is necessary to do something, we use *have to*.
When it is not necessary to do something, we use *don't have to*.
When it is important not to do something (e.g. it's a bad idea or it's against the law), we use *mustn't*.

I/You/We/They	have to	work harder.
He/She/It	has to	get up early.
I/You/We/They	don't have to	worry.
He/She/It	doesn't have to	come.
I/You/He/She/It We/They	mustn't	shout. be late.

1 Read the instructions for an exam and complete the sentences below with the correct modal verb.

> **Geography Exam: Room 4B, Tuesday 2 May, 9 a.m.**
> - Switch off your mobile phones.
> - There are four questions. Answer three of them.
> - Answer the questions with a pen, not a pencil.
> - The exam ends at 11 a.m. You can leave before the end if you like.

1 You *have to* switch off your mobile phones.
2 You _____ answer all the questions.
3 You _____ answer three questions.
4 You _____ use a pen.
5 You _____ use a pencil.
6 You _____ stay until the end of the exam.

2 In pairs, write sentences about your school. Use the ideas below and *have to*, *don't have to* or *mustn't*.

> ask the teacher questions   do a lot of homework
> eat during a class   run in the corridor   shout
> stand up when a teacher enters a room
> study two languages   wear a uniform

In our school you have to study two languages.

3 Complete the sentences so they are true for you.

1 Every morning before breakfast, I have to …
2 Every night before I go to bed, I have to …
3 At breakfast in my house, we don't have to …
4 When I'm on holiday, I don't have to …
5 At meals in our house, you mustn't …

Every morning before breakfast, I have to get dressed.

8.4 Articles: first and second mention

The first time we mention something, we use *a* or *an* for countable singular nouns, and *some* for plural and uncountable nouns.
The second time we mention something, we use *the*.
There's *a* lake near our town. There's *an* island on the lake. There are *some* trees on the island.
We go swimming in *the* lake. You can swim to *the* island. *The* trees are very old.

1 Complete the text with *a/an*, *some* or *the*.

> In my room there's ¹*a* cupboard. In ² _____ cupboard there's ³ _____ red suitcase. In ⁴ _____ suitcase there are ⁵ _____ books. In one of the books there is ⁶ _____ map. ⁷ _____ map shows ⁸ _____ island. ⁹ _____ island is in the Pacific Ocean. On ¹⁰ _____ map, in the centre of ¹¹ _____ island, there is ¹² _____ big red cross – like this: ✗. ¹³ _____ cross shows the location of ¹⁴ _____ box. In ¹⁵ _____ box there's a treasure!

2 In pairs, take it in turns to describe an object in your room. Use the text in Exercise 1 to help you.

3 In pairs, order the sentences to make a text about Edinburgh.

a ☐ The bridge is about 130 years old.
b ☐ On top of the hill there is a famous castle.
c ☐ There's a railway bridge over the river.
d ☐ The city has some ancient buildings.
e ☐ One of the buildings is a palace – Holyrood.
f ☐ **1** Scotland is a small country to the north of England.
g ☐ From the palace, a road – The Royal Mile – goes up a hill.
h ☐ **2** In the east of the country there is an amazing city – Edinburgh.
i ☐ From the castle there's a great view of a river – the Forth.

4 Write sentences about a place you know well. Use the sentences in Exercise 3 to help you.

Valencia is a city in the east of Spain. In the centre of the city there are some …

GRAMMAR TIME

9.2 Present Continuous for arrangements

We use the Present Continuous to talk about arrangements. We often mention a time and/or a place.
We're meeting at six o'clock.
Dad's taking me to London on the fifteenth.
They aren't coming with us – they're going on holiday.
Are you coming to my party on Sunday?
Yes, I am./No, I'm not.

Time expressions
this afternoon, tonight, tomorrow, next weekend

1 Complete the sentences with the Present Continuous form of the verbs in brackets.
1. Andy Murray *is playing* (play) Roger Federer on Saturday. Who _____ (Rafael Nadal/play)?
2. A: What _____ (you/do) on 30 October? We _____ (have) a Halloween Party!
   B: Oh that's a pity! We _____ (go) to a concert that evening.
3. A: _____ (you/come) with me and Jake to the cinema tomorrow evening?
   B: I can't. We _____ (take) our cat Rocky to the vet's.
4. A: What _____ (Jenny/do) for the Easter weekend?
   B: She _____ (spend) time with her dad.
5. Mike is very nervous – he _____ (see) the dentist this afternoon.

2 Complete your diary for the weekend with four arrangements. Use the ideas below or your own. In pairs, ask and answer questions about your weekend.

> go swimming   go to a birthday party   go to a disco
> go to the hairdresser's   have coffee with …
> meet a friend   watch a football match

FRIDAY	evening
SATURDAY	morning
	afternoon
	evening
SUNDAY	morning

A: What are you doing on Friday evening?
B: I'm going to a party! And what are you doing on…?

9.4 going to for plans

We use *going to* to talk about intentions and plans. (These plans can change in the future.)

+	I'm going to live abroad.
	You/We/They're going to live abroad.
	He/She/It's going to live abroad.
–	I'm not going to tell him.
	You/We/They aren't going to tell him.
	He/She/It isn't going to tell him.
?	Are you/we/they going to come?
	Yes, I am./Yes, you/we/they are.
	No, I'm not./No, you/we/they aren't.
	Is he/she/it going to come?
	Yes, he/she/it is./No, he/she/it isn't.
	Where are you going to stay?
	When are you going to visit us?

1 Complete the sentences with the correct form of *going to* and the verbs in brackets.
1. I*'m going to go* (go) skiing with my family next winter.
2. The youth hostel in Venice was terrible. Next time we _____ (not stay) at the youth hostel – we _____ (find) a cheap hotel.
3. I _____ (not play) football tomorrow. I _____ (revise) for my exams all weekend.
4. A: _____ (you/see) *Shrek 6* this weekend?
   B: No, we _____. We _____ (watch) the new Harry Potter film.
5. They _____ (go) to New York next summer.
6. A: _____ (Tom/go) to the new shopping centre?
   B: Yes, he _____. He _____ (buy) some new clothes.
7. We _____ (visit) my gran in hospital at the weekend.

2 In pairs, take it in turns to say what you are going to do in the next holidays. Use the ideas in below to help you.

> go to the seaside   learn a new language
> meet friends   read a lot of books
> sleep until noon   watch a lot of films

In the Christmas holidays I'm not going to read a lot of books but I'm going to watch a lot of films.

Grammar Time

IRREGULAR VERBS LIST

INFINITIVE	PAST SIMPLE
be [bɪ:]	was/were [wɒz/wɜ:]
become [bɪˈkʌm]	became [bɪˈkeɪm]
begin [bɪˈgɪn]	began [bɪˈgæn]
break [breɪk]	broke [brəʊk]
bring [brɪŋ]	brought [brɔ:t]
build [bɪld]	built [bɪlt]
burn [bɜ:n]	burned [bɜ:nd]/burnt [bɜ:nt]
buy [baɪ]	bought [bɔ:t]
can [kæn]	could [kʊd]
catch [kætʃ]	caught [kɔ:t]
choose [tʃu:z]	chose [tʃəʊz]
come [kʌm]	came [keɪm]
cost [kɒst]	cost [kɒst]
cut [kʌt]	cut [kʌt]
do [du:]	did [dɪd]
draw [drɔ:]	drew [dru:]
dream [drɪ:m]	dreamed [drɪ:md]/dreamt [dremt]
drink [drɪnk]	drank [drænk]
drive [draɪv]	drove [drəʊv]
eat [ɪ:t]	ate [et, eɪt]
fall [fɔ:l]	fell [fel]
feed [fɪ:d]	fed [fed]
feel [fɪ:l]	felt [felt]
fight [faɪt]	fought [fɔ:t]
find [faɪnd]	found [faʊnd]
fly [flaɪ]	flew [flu:]
forget [fəˈget]	forgot [fəˈgɒt]
forgive [fəˈgɪv]	forgave [fəˈgeɪv]
get [get]	got [gɒt]
give [gɪv]	gave [geɪv]
go [gəʊ]	went [went]
grow [grəʊ]	grew [gru:]
hang [hæŋ]	hung [hʌŋ]
have [hæv]	had [hæd]
hear [hɪə]	heard [hɜ:d]
hit [hɪt]	hit [hɪt]
hold [həʊld]	held [held]
hurt [hɜ:t]	hurt [hɜ:t]
keep [kɪ:p]	kept [kept]

INFINITIVE	PAST SIMPLE
know [nəʊ]	knew [nju:]
learn [lɜ:n]	learned [lɜ:nd]/learnt [lɜ:nt]
leave [lɪ:v]	left [left]
lend [lend]	lent [lent]
let [let]	let [let]
lie [laɪ]	lay [leɪ]
lose [lu:z]	lost [lɒst]
make [meɪk]	made [meɪd]
meet [mɪ:t]	met [met]
pay [peɪ]	paid [peɪd]
put [pʊt]	put [pʊt]
read [rɪ:d]	read [red]
ride [raɪd]	rode [rəʊd]
ring [rɪŋ]	rang [ræŋ]
run [rʌn]	ran [ræn]
say [seɪ]	said [sed]
see [sɪ:]	saw [sɔ:]
sell [sel]	sold [səʊld]
send [send]	sent [sent]
set [set]	set [set]
show [ʃəʊ]	showed [ʃəʊd]
sing [sɪŋ]	sang [sæŋ]
sit [sɪt]	sat [sæt]
sleep [slɪ:p]	slept [slept]
speak [spɪ:k]	spoke [spəʊk]
spend [spend]	spent [spent]
stand [stænd]	stood [stʊd]
steal [stɪ:l]	stole [stəʊl]
sweep [swɪ:p]	swept [swept]
swim [swɪm]	swam [swæm]
take [teɪk]	took [tʊk]
teach [tɪ:tʃ]	taught [tɔ:t]
tell [tel]	told [təʊld]
think [θɪnk]	thought [θɔ:t]
understand [ˌʌndəˈstænd]	understood [ˌʌndəˈstʊd]
wake [weɪk]	woke [wəʊk]
wear [weə]	wore [wɔ:]
win [wɪn]	won [wʌn]
write [raɪt]	wrote [rəʊt]

STUDENT ACTIVITIES

Unit 1 — Revision SPEAKING Exercise 9

Student B

Have a conversation with Student A, using these phrases in the correct order. Student A starts.
- Hi, … . I'm …/My name's …
- I'm fine, thanks.
- Hi, how's it going?
- See you!
- Hi, … . Pleased to meet you.

Unit 2 — Lesson 2.1, Exercise 10

Is your menu inside your calorie limit?

Calorie limits per day

Teenagers		
Age	Girls	Boys
13	2,223	2,414
14	2,342	2,629
15	2,390	2,820

Adults	
Women	Men
2,000	2,500

Unit 2 — Revision SPEAKING Exercise 9

Student B

You are a waiter in Student A's favourite restaurant.
- Say hello and ask him/her, 'What would you like?'
- Take his/her order.
- Ask him/her, 'Anything else?'
- Ask him/her if everything is OK.

Unit 3 — Lesson 3.1, Exercise 10

Quiz results

If your sentences are mainly from 1–4, you are definitely an early bird. If they're from 5–8, you are definitely a night owl. Many people are a mix of the two.

Unit 4 — Lesson 4.2, Exercise 2

I'm fine, you idiots! 😀 But I can't speak! Today is 5 March – the day of my sponsored silence for Sian's operation. Remember?! You're paying me 50p an hour to not speak! PS: Can I come with you to the snack bar too?

Unit 4 — Revision SPEAKING Exercise 8

Student B
- You're in a Maths lesson. Listen to Student A's problem. You have a pen and you're not using it at the moment.
- You don't have a dictionary. Ask Student A to lend you a dictionary. Thank Student A.

Unit 5 — Lesson 5.1, Exercise 6

Penny is thinking of Adele.

Unit 5 — Lesson 5.6, Exercise 7

Student B

1 Listen to Student A's situations. Make suggestions. Use the ideas below if you need to.
   - buy a ticket for a concert/get a CD/pay for a meal in a restaurant
   - make a sandwich/buy a packet of crisps/eat an apple

2 Read these situations to Student A. Respond to his/her suggestions.
   - It's a boring Sunday afternoon. I feel sad.
   - I've got an English exam tomorrow.

Unit 5 — Revision SPEAKING Exercise 6

Student B
- Listen to Student A's problem and make suggestions (e.g. give the ticket to a friend (me!), ask for your money back, sell the ticket online).
- Then ask Student A for suggestions for this problem: Your grandmother gives you a Miley Cyrus T-shirt for your birthday. You don't like Miley Cyrus. What do you do?
- Listen and respond to Student A's suggestions. (Don't accept the first one!)

Unit 6 — Lesson 6.4, Exercise 7

What	Where	When
eat some crisps	at home	this morning
go jogging	at school	last night
play football	in the town centre	yesterday
run 5 kilometres	in the park	last week
see a tennis match	on the bus	last month
win a medal	on TV	last year

STUDENT ACTIVITIES

Unit 6 — Lesson 6.6, Exercise 1

1. Max is in the skateboard park.
2. He's talking to a reporter from South Radio.

Unit 8 — Lesson 8.1, Exercise 6

Answers

1. Tokyo
2. Spain
3. Asia
4. Egypt
5. Italian
6. Amazon
7. dollar
8. mountain
9. four – French, German, Italian, Romansh
10. island

Unit 8 — Lesson 8.3, Exercise 1

Esperanto: fact file

- Esperanto is an invented language with simple grammar and vocabulary.
- Esperanto is easy. You can learn it quickly. You don't have to study irregular verbs!
- Esperanto isn't the language of any country.
- There are only a few thousand native speakers of Esperanto but there are probably about two million Esperanto speakers in the world.
- On Facebook there are over 300,000 people who have Esperanto as one of their languages and there's a Wikipedia site with about 230,000 articles.

Unit 8 — Lesson 8.6, Exercise 5

Student B

1. When Student A explains, say you understand or don't understand and ask for clarification if necessary. Use the Speaking box to help you.

   I'm not sure I understand. What do you mean?

2. Explain how to download a song from a music site. Use the Speaking box to help you.

   switch on your computer or tablet → connect to the internet → search for a music site that has the song you want → join the site → download the song

OK, to download a song from a music site, first you have to switch on your computer or tablet. Do you understand? Then you have to …

Unit 8 — Revision SPEAKING Exercise 7

Student B

- Student A tries to explain something to you. Use at least three of these phrases to say you understand/don't understand and ask for clarification.

   I'm sorry, I don't get it.
   I'm not sure I understand.
   What do you mean?
   Now I get it.   I see.   Oh right!

- Swap roles. Explain to Student A how to post a message on your favourite social networking site. Use these phrases to make sure Student A understands you.

   (Do you) know what I mean?
   Do you get it?   You see?

Unit 9 — Lesson 9.2, Exercise 5

Student B

- You are visiting a family member in hospital on Friday. Ask Student A if he/she is doing anything on Saturday.
- You don't have any plans for Sunday.
- You think Student A's suggestion is a good idea.

Student activities

EXAM TIME 1 — Listening and Speaking

1 🔊 **3.43** Listen to five short conversations. For each question, choose the correct answer, A, B or C.

Tip: Listen to the whole conversation. The right answer might be at the end.

Example: What does the boy want to do this evening?

A (circled) — B — C

1 What belongs to the girl?

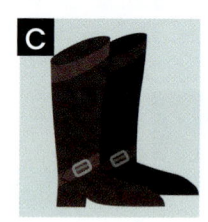

A — B — C

2 What's for dinner?

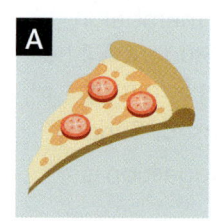

A — B — C

3 What does the woman give the boy?

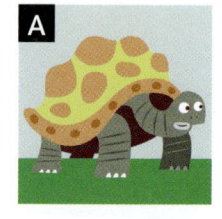

A — B — C

4 When does the boy's sister phone?

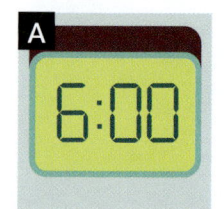

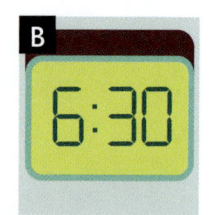

A 6:00 — B 6:30 — C 8:00

5 Where are the girl and boy?

A — B — C

2 🔊 **3.44** Listen to Katy talking to her friend Robby about the weekend. For each question, choose the correct answer, A, B or C.

Tip: All the words in options A–C are in the dialogue but only one is correct. Listen carefully.

Example:

Which day does Robby play football?
- A Friday
- B Saturday
- C Sunday (circled)

1 How much are the trainers?
- A £50
- B £30
- C £20

2 Where do they agree to eat?
- A the burger bar
- B the café
- C the new restaurant

3 What can they eat there?
- A chicken
- B burger
- C pizza

4 What time does Katy want to come home?
- A 12.30
- B 1.00
- C 5.00

5 Who goes to the same university as Katy's sister?
- A Dan
- B Helen
- C Sally

3 🔊 **3.45** Listen to a boy, Jed, talking to a friend about a meeting in town. Complete the gaps with the missing information.

Tip: Sometimes you need to write down a word that is spelled. Listen carefully and write it correctly.

New café	
When?	*Saturday*
Name of café:	1 _____
Where?	2 _____
Time:	3 _____
Meet where?	4 _____
Phone number:	5 _____

EXAM TIME 1 — Listening and Speaking

4 **Tip:** In Part 1 you have to answer personal questions about you. You know the answers, so don't worry!

Students A and B, answer the questions below.
1. What's your name? How do you spell that?
2. Where do you come from?
3. What are your favourite school subjects?
4. What other subjects do you study?

Student A, answer the questions below.
1. What do you do at the weekend?
2. Where do you go with your friends?
3. Do you go to music concerts?
4. Have you got a favourite T-shirt?

Student B, answer the questions below.
1. When do you do your homework?
2. What food do you like?
3. Tell me about your family.
4. Who is your favourite band or singer?

5a **Tip:** If you can't think what to say, pause and say, 'OK, just a moment,' and read your card again.

Student A, turn to page 133 for some information about a cookery course. Answer Student B's questions about it.

Student B, you don't know anything about the cookery course, so ask Student A some questions about it.

COOKERY COURSE
Who for? _____
Learn? _____
Where? _____
When? _____
Cost? _____

5b Student B, turn to page 133 for some information about a fashion show. Answer Student A's questions about it.

Student A, you don't know anything about the fashion show, so ask Student B some questions about it.

Fashion Show
Name/show? _____
Where? _____
When? _____
Phone? _____
Wear? _____

Exam Time 3, Listening and Speaking, Exercise 5a, Student A (page 135)

History of music
EAST GATE MUSEUM

Learn about songs, music and singers from the last 100 years.

Times: daily, 9.00–5.30

Prices: adults: £5; children: free

No cameras, please.

Exam Time 3, Listening and Speaking, Exercise 5b, Student B (page 135)

Adventure holiday

Do you want an exciting hiking holiday in the Black Mountains?

Choose July, August or September.

Each holiday is five days.

Price: £150

EXAM TIME 2 — Listening and Speaking

1 🔊 **3.46** Listen to five short conversations. For each question, choose the correct answer, A, B or C.

Tip: Read the questions and look at the pictures carefully before listening. Try to guess the words the speakers might use.

Example: What does the boy want to do this evening?

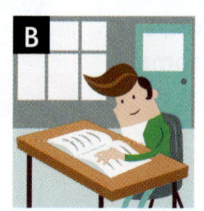

1 What subject was on the timetable today?

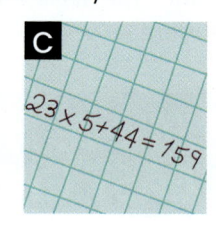

2 Which competition was the boy in last year?

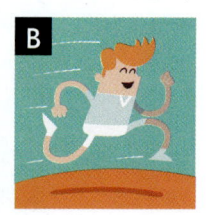

3 What time is it?

4 How many people are in the guitar club?

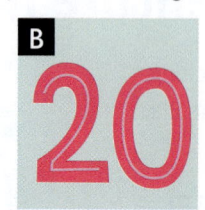

5 Where is Eva?

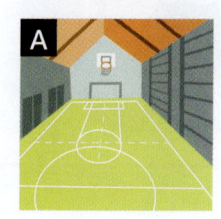

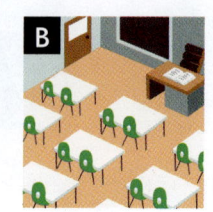

2 🔊 **3.47** Listen to Tommy talking to his friend Alison about his birthday. What did each person have? Match people 1–5 with dishes A–H.

Tip: The speakers talk about all the things in the list but only six things match the people.

PEOPLE

Example:

- G Tommy
- 1 ☐ sister
- 2 ☐ mum
- 3 ☐ dad
- 4 ☐ Mike
- 5 ☐ Timmy

DISHES

- A spaghetti
- B egg salad
- C fish and chips
- D carrot soup
- E hot dog and chips
- F fish fingers
- G kebabs
- H omelette

3 🔊 **3.48** Listen to a boy, Stuart, talking to a friend about a meeting for the school play. Complete the gaps with the missing information.

Tip: Think about what you need to write. For example, is it a name or a number?

Play meeting	
When?	*Friday*
Name of play:	1 _____
Where?	2 _____
Time:	3 _____
Teacher:	4 _____
Prepare what?	5 _____

EXAM TIME 2 — Listening and Speaking

4 **Tip:** Try to say more than one sentence. For example, if the question is, 'What's your favourite sport?', you can say, 'Football. I play football every weekend.'

Student A, answer the questions below.
1 What do you usually do after school?
2 What's your favourite sport?
3 Do you watch a lot of television?
4 What new film do you want to see?

Student B, answer the questions below.
1 What music do you like?
2 Do you like cooking?
3 Can you play a musical instrument?
4 What's your favourite day at school?

5a **Tip:** If you don't understand your partner, you can say, 'Can you repeat that, please?'

Student A, turn to page 135 for some information about a photo competition. Answer Student B's questions about it.

Student B, you don't know anything about the photo competition, so ask Student A some questions about it.

5b Student B, turn to page 135 for some information about a music school. Answer Student A's questions about it.

Student A, you don't know anything about the music school, so ask Student B some questions about it.

Music School

Name/school? _____
Which instruments? _____
When? _____
How much? _____
Email? _____

Exam Time 1, Listening and Speaking, Exercise 5a, Student A (page 131)

Cookery Course

Beginners' course

Learn some easy meals and surprise your friends!
Barton's Hotel, East Road
Mondays, 8.00–9.30
Cost: £20 for an eight-week course. You pay for the ingredients and eat the food!

Exam Time 1, Listening and Speaking, Exercise 5b, Student B (page 131)

Photo Competition

Who for? _____
What photos? _____
Website? _____
Date? _____
Win? _____

Fashion Show

Do you like clothes? Come to our fashion show, The Story of Fashion. Hilton School's fashion show is at the school, on Saturday 9 October.

You can see clothes from the last 200 years!
Phone 02456783912 for tickets.

Wear clothes from the past.
Ask your mum to help!
See you there!

EXAM TIME 3 — Listening and Speaking

1 🔊 **3.49** Listen to five short conversations. For each question, choose the correct answer, A, B or C.

Tip: You hear each conversation twice, so you can check your answers.

Example: What does the boy want to do this evening?

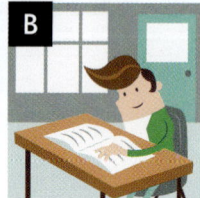

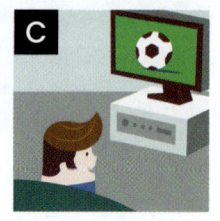

A ✓ / B / C

1 Where is the girl?

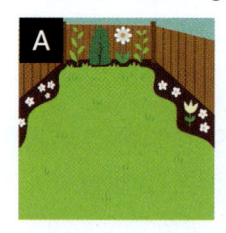

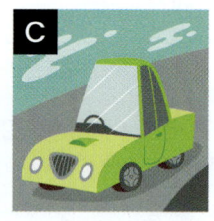

2 How did the girl travel home from Scotland?

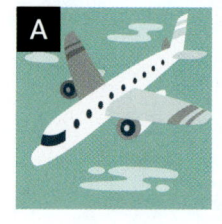

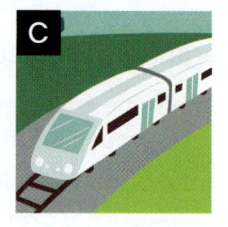

3 What present did the girl get today for her birthday?

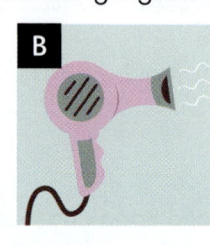

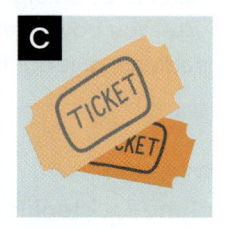

4 What's the weather like this afternoon?

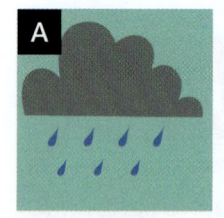

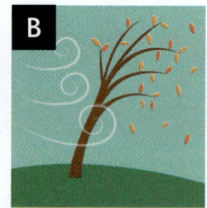

5 What's the password?

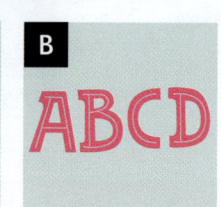

A 1981 B ABCD C 1234

2 🔊 **3.50** Listen to Karen talking to her dad about what happened at school this week. What did they do in each lesson? Match lessons 1–5 with activities A–H.

Tip: Read both lists carefully before you listen so you know what you are listening for.

LESSONS

Example:
- G English
1 ☐ Geography
2 ☐ History
3 ☐ Art
4 ☐ Maths
5 ☐ Biology

ACTIVITIES
A play a game
B write a story
C do homework
D do a test
E make a poster
F read a textbook
G watch a film
H revise for exam

3 🔊 **3.51** Listen to Danny having a video call with his friend Kathy. For each question, choose the correct answer, A, B or C.

Tip: The information in the recording comes in the same order as the questions.

Example:

Which city is Danny in at the moment?
- (A) Rome
- B Milan
- C Venice

1 Where is the house?
- A by the river
- B in the city centre
- C by the station

2 Who's in the photo in Danny's room?
- A Salvo
- B Salvo's mum
- C Salvo's dad

3 What is Danny eating tonight?
- A spaghetti
- B pizza
- C eggs and bacon

4 What's the time in Italy?
- A four o'clock
- B five o'clock
- C eight o'clock

5 What language do they all speak?
- A English
- B Italian
- C French

EXAM TIME 3 — Listening and Speaking

4 **Tip:** Try to use different tenses in your answers if possible.

Student A, answer the questions below.
1. What's your favourite website?
2. Do you prefer to travel by bus or by train?
3. Do you watch a lot of sport on television?
4. What are you going to do tomorrow?

Student B, answer the questions below.
1. What do you do in the school holidays?
2. Who's your best friend?
3. Do you play video games?
4. What's your favourite television programme?

5a **Tip:** If you give your partner a name, spell it for him/her.

Student A, turn to page 131 for some information about a museum exhibition. Answer Student B's questions about it.

Student B, you don't know anything about the museum exhibition, so ask Student A some questions about it.

MUSEUM EXHIBITION
- Name/museum?
- What/learn?
- When?
- Cost?
- Take photos?

5b Student B, turn to page 131 for some information about an adventure holiday. Answer Student A's questions about it.

Student A, you don't know anything about the adventure holiday, so ask Student B some questions about it.

Adventure holiday
- Type of holiday?
- Where?
- Which months?
- How long?
- How much?

Exam Time 2, Listening and Speaking, Exercise 5a, Student A (page 133)

PHOTO COMPETITION
For teenagers 12–16 years old

Our magazine wants your photos of animals! Send them to www.teen-mag.co.uk before 18 September. Win a new camera!

Exam Time 2, Listening and Speaking, Exercise 5b, Student B (page 133)

Top Class Music School
Want to learn piano, guitar or flute?

Classes every evening, 5.00–9.00

Prices: £10 a lesson

Contact mark@tcms.com.

ART — Still life

CLIL 1

Still life

Still life is a popular kind of painting for artists. Choose some objects – maybe some food or some flowers. Put them on a table and paint them! Easy? Oh no! Good still life painters are talented and hard-working.

Tjalf Sarnay is a famous still life painter today. He's fifty-four years old and he's Dutch, like a lot of famous still life painters from the past. But his paintings are different. In his pictures we can see ordinary objects like bread, burgers, cola cans, fried eggs, cheese and apples. His paintings are very clever. They are like photographs. Here are two pictures of a fried egg. Which is the photo and which is Tjalf's painting?

Tjalf has got four ideas:

1. Paint pictures like very good photographs.
2. Paint ordinary things.
3. Make those things beautiful.
4. Paint very big pictures.

Tjalf's paintings are called 'Megarealism'. They're very big and very real. One painting, of a burger with salt, pepper and ketchup is 823 x 550 cm! One look at Tjalf's paintings and you're very hungry!

---

1 Look at the still life paintings. Can you match the paintings with the dates?
1. ☐ eighteenth century
2. ☐ 2014
3. ☐ fifteenth century

A   B   C

2 Read the article above about an artist. One of the paintings in Exercise 1 is by Tjalf Sarnay. Which one?

3 Read the text again. Answer the questions.
1. What nationality is Tjalf Sarnay?
2. Name three things in his paintings.
3. Why are his paintings clever?
4. What is his style of painting called?
5. How big is one of his paintings?

4 Who is your favourite painter?

5 In pairs, follow the instructions below.
- Student A, choose one of these still life paintings and describe it to your partner. Can your partner guess the painting?
- Student B, cover the pictures on this page. How many items from the paintings can you remember in two minutes?

A   B

6 **PROJECT** Use the internet to research a famous still life artist from your country. Make notes about:
- what is in his/her paintings.
- what is special about them.
- any other interesting information.

7 **PROJECT** Write a paragraph about the artist and add some pictures. Show your project to the class.

LITERATURE   Poetry

The thin old man with snow white hair
Sits by the window frame
He sits there quite a lot, you know
Again and again and again

He looks across the hills and fields
The big wide-open plain
He sees it every day, you know
Again and again and again

He watches fat white cows go past
Their heads all wet with rain
They go by every day, you know
Again and again and again

In his head he walks the paths
And cycles down the lane
It's just a dream he has, you know
Again and again and again

1 Can you remember a poem from school?

2 Read the poem above and choose the best title.
   a Country life
   b My favourite day
   c The window

3 Read the poem again. Answer the questions.
   1 Where do you think the writer lives?
   2 How do you think the old man feels? Why?
   3 The word *frame* rhymes with *again*. Find two more words in the poem that rhyme (or nearly rhyme) with *again*.
   4 There are four lines in a verse. How many verses are there in the poem?
   5 Find two examples of repetition in the poem – where the writer repeats a word or phrase.
   6 Is the punctuation in the poem correct?

4 Do you like reading poetry? Why? / Why not?

5 In pairs, think of some words which rhyme (or nearly rhyme) with *again*. Then write another verse for the poem. Share it with the class.
   - *pain* , _____ , _____ , _____
   - *game* , _____ , _____ , _____

6 **PROJECT** Prepare a short presentation about a famous poem from your country.
   - Copy the poem onto a piece of paper.
   - Draw a picture to go with it.
   - Make notes about what it means.
   - Make notes about the rhymes, repetition and punctuation.

7 **PROJECT** Read your poem to the class. Use your notes to explain the poem to your classmates and say why you like it.

BIOLOGY — Exercise

Aerobic and anaerobic exercise

Everyone knows that exercise is good for us. But there are different kinds of exercise and they are good for different reasons.

Aerobic exercise
Aerobic exercise is when we use our arms and legs to do exercise. We move our whole body and use lots of different muscles. The word *aerobic* means 'with oxygen (O_2)'. We need lots of energy to do this kind of exercise. Oxygen burns fat and carbohydrates to give us energy. Aerobic exercise isn't always fast or difficult. Walking and jogging (even climbing stairs!) are examples of easy aerobic exercise. Then there is harder exercise, like dancing or swimming and the hardest aerobic exercise is when we do skilled sports like volleyball or tennis. This exercise is good for our hearts and can also help us get thinner.

Anaerobic exercise
When we do anaerobic exercise, we don't jump around a lot. We only use some muscles because we want them to get stronger. We don't use a lot of oxygen and we only burn carbohydrates. A lot of gym exercises and exercises we can do at home are anaerobic. Weightlifting, sit-ups and push-ups are examples of this. Anaerobic exercise is good for some muscles and also for our bones and joints.

1. **In pairs, ask and answer the questions.**
   1. What kind of exercise do you do?
   2. Do you know the difference between aerobic and anaerobic exercise?

2. **Read the article above and check your ideas from Exercise 1. Label the photos (A–E) A (aerobic) or AN (anaerobic).**

3. **Read the article again. Choose A (aerobic), AN (anaerobic) or B (both).**

   Which type of exercise:
   1. doesn't need a lot of oxygen?   A / AN / B
   2. is good for our heart?   A / AN / B
   3. is usually inside?   A / AN / B
   4. burns fat?   A / AN / B
   5. burns carbohydrates?   A / AN / B
   6. is good for our bones?   A / AN / B

4. **What kind of exercise do you like – aerobic or anaerobic? Why?**

5. **In pairs, read the text on the right about a test and order the pictures (1–5).**

How flexible are you?

Exercise is important for our flexibility and our balance. Here's a quick test. It shows how good your flexibility and balance are. Stand in the middle of the room. Cross your legs. Sit down but don't use your arms or knees. Then stand up. Again, don't use your hands, arms or knees. Can you do it? Don't try if you've got a bad leg or back!

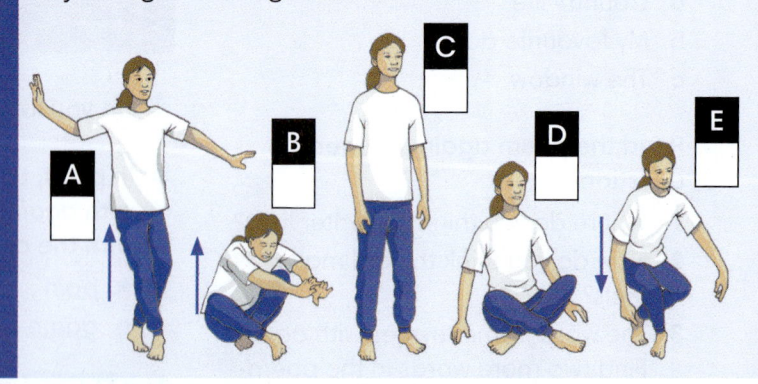

6. **PROJECT** Use the internet to research a useful exercise or fitness test. Make notes about:
   - what and how you do the test/exercise.
   - why it is good for you.
   - who can and can't do it.

7. **PROJECT** Write a paragraph about the exercise or test. Add some pictures. Show your project to the class.

HISTORY — Mummies

What is a mummy?

The Ancient Egyptians buried dead people in an interesting way. They prepared the body with special oils and put it in a stone or wooden box called a sarcophagus. These bodies lasted a long time and we can look at them in museums today. The bodies are called mummies. They also put food and valuable things with the bodies. Sometimes they put the dead person's pet cat there!

Why did they do this?

The Ancient Egyptians believed in an afterlife. They thought that the spirit of the dead person went to another world. They needed their body and lots of their things to use in this afterlife. They needed food and drink for the journey there.

Where did they put the sarcophagus?

They put poor people in the sand, but they buried rich people in tombs. They painted the walls with pictures from their lives. Between 2628 and 1638BC, the pharaohs (the kings) went into special tombs. They were great stone pyramids. This was to protect them. They painted the sarcophagus with a picture of the pharaoh, often with expensive gold paint. Very important pharaohs had gold masks on their faces.

A s_____
B t_____
C p_____
D s_____
E m_____

1 Do you know what an Egyptian mummy is?

2 Read the article above quickly and complete the labels for photos A–E.

3 Read the text again. Mark the sentences T (true) or F (false).
1. ☐ They buried animals with the people.
2. ☐ They thought that dead people had another life.
3. ☐ They buried all Egyptians in tombs.
4. ☐ They painted the bodies gold.

4 Read about the steps for 'mummification'. It took seventy days to prepare a body! In pairs, order the steps (1–6).
a ☐ They stuffed the body.
b ☐ They wrapped special cloth round the body.
c ☐ They put a special salt all over the body. This dried it.
d ☐ They put the body in the sarcophagus.
e ☐ After fifty days it was dry and they took out the old stuffing and put in new stuffing.
f ☐ 1 They washed the body and took out everything from inside.

5 PROJECT Use the internet to research a famous Egyptian mummy. Make notes about:
- who the person was.
- what things were with the mummy.
- where we can see it.
- any other interesting information.

6 PROJECT Write a paragraph about the mummy. Add some pictures. Show your project to the class.

SCIENCE — Hot-air balloons

CLIL 5

1 The hot-air balloon is not the fastest way to fly and it isn't the most direct. It depends on the wind. But the hot-air balloon was the first form of flying that carried people. It was a long time before aeroplanes. The first passengers were a sheep, a duck and a chicken! Then a few weeks later, on 21 November 1783 in France, a balloon carried two people.

2 The hot-air balloon uses science in a very easy but clever way. Hot air rises in colder air because it is lighter and less dense. Think about floating on water; our body floats because water is denser than we are.

3 The hot-air balloon has three main parts. There is a balloon envelope – this holds the air. The material is nylon and has sections called 'gores'. There is a valve at the top. Under the envelope there is a burner. This uses propane gas to heat the air in the balloon. There is a wicker basket to carry passengers. Wicker is strong and quite light.

4 When the pilot wants the balloon to go higher, he turns up the gas. This makes the air hotter and the balloon rises. To go down, he opens the valve at the top of the balloon. Some hot air leaves the balloon and it goes down. To go in the right direction, the pilot goes up or down to ride on the wind. Very clever!

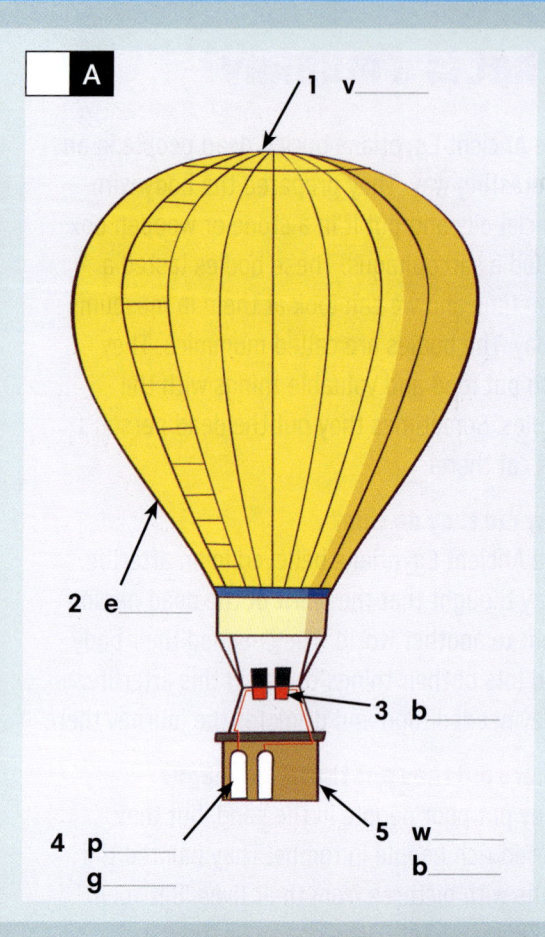

A
1 v_____
2 e_____
3 b_____
4 p_____ g_____
5 w_____ b_____

B NOT SO HOT AIR / HOT AIR

C First balloon flight

D

1 Read the article above. Match pictures A–D with paragraphs 1–4.

2 Complete the labels in picture A.

3 Read the article again. Answer the questions.
 1 Who were the first passengers in a hot-air balloon?
 2 When did the first hot-air balloon carry people?
 3 Why do hot-air balloons rise?
 4 Why do hot-air balloons have wicker baskets?
 5 How do hot-air balloons go down?

4 Would you like to travel in a hot-air balloon? Why? / Why not?

5 Work in pairs. Take turns to tell each other about the hot-air balloon. Talk about:
 - Student A: the first hot-air balloon.
 - Student B: the science behind the balloon.
 - Student A: the parts of the balloon.
 - Student B: how it goes up and down.

6 **PROJECT** Use the internet to research a famous airship (an aircraft that used hot gas). Make notes about:
 - its name and when it flew.
 - how it moved.
 - if it was safe.
 - any other interesting information.

7 **PROJECT** Write a paragraph about the airship. Add some pictures. Show your project to the class.

CULTURE 1 — Explore the English-speaking world

1 Read about the main English-speaking countries. Which country has the biggest population?

2 Read the text. Answer the questions.
   1 Which famous people came from Dublin?
   2 Which place in America sees the sun rise first?
   3 What is the capital of Australia?
   4 Which country has three capital cities?
   5 What was special about the 2010 World Cup?

3 In pairs, answer the questions.
   1 What is the capital of your country?
   2 What is the population and currency?
   3 What is interesting about your country?

4 Write a short fact file about your country. Use your answers to Exercise 3 and the examples in the text to help you.

The English speaking world

The UK
Capital of the UK and England: London (Edinburgh is the capital of Scotland. Belfast is the capital of Northern Ireland. Cardiff is the capital of Wales.)
Population of the UK: 63 million
Full name: United Kingdom of Great Britain and Northern Ireland
Currency: British pound
Extra interesting facts: The English like drinking tea. An English person drinks more tea than anyone else. They drink over twenty times more than Americans!

The Republic of Ireland
Capital of the Republic of Ireland: Dublin
Population of the Republic of Ireland: 4.8 million
Currency: euro
Extra interesting facts: In the Republic of Ireland people also speak Gaelic. English is the language of business. Ireland is famous for its writers. James Joyce and Oscar Wilde came from Dublin.

The USA
Capital of the USA: Washington DC
Population of the USA: 319 million
Full name: United States of America
Currency: US dollar
Extra interesting facts: The state of Maine sees the sun rise before the other states!

Canada
Capital of Canada: Ottawa
Population of Canada: 34 million
Currency: Canadian dollar
Extra interesting facts: They speak French and English in Canada.

Australia
Capital of Australia: Canberra
Population of Australia: 22.6 million
Currency: Australian dollar
Extra interesting facts: There are more sheep in Australia than people!

India
Capital of India: New Delhi
Population of India: 1.2 billion
Currency: Indian rupee
Extra interesting facts: India makes between 800 and 1,000 Bollywood films every year.

New Zealand
Capital of New Zealand: Wellington
Population of New Zealand: 4.5 million
Currency: New Zealand dollar
Extra interesting facts: It is the first country in the world to see the sun rise!

South Africa
Capital of South Africa: Pretoria, Cape Town and Bloemfontein
Population of South Africa: 53 million
Currency: South African rand
Extra interesting facts: The Football World Cup was in South Africa in 2010. This was the first Football World Cup in Africa.

CULTURE 2 — Explore the UK

1 Read the text and look at the map. Match the fact files (A–D) with the countries (1–4).

2 Read the text again. Answer the questions.
1. What languages do people speak in the UK?
2. Where are the following cities?
   a Aberdeen   c Leeds
   b Derry   d Cardiff

3 In pairs, answer the questions.
1. How many official languages are there in your country?
2. What are the main ethnic groups?
3. Write a fact file for your country. Include this information
   - location
   - population
   - main cities
   - languages

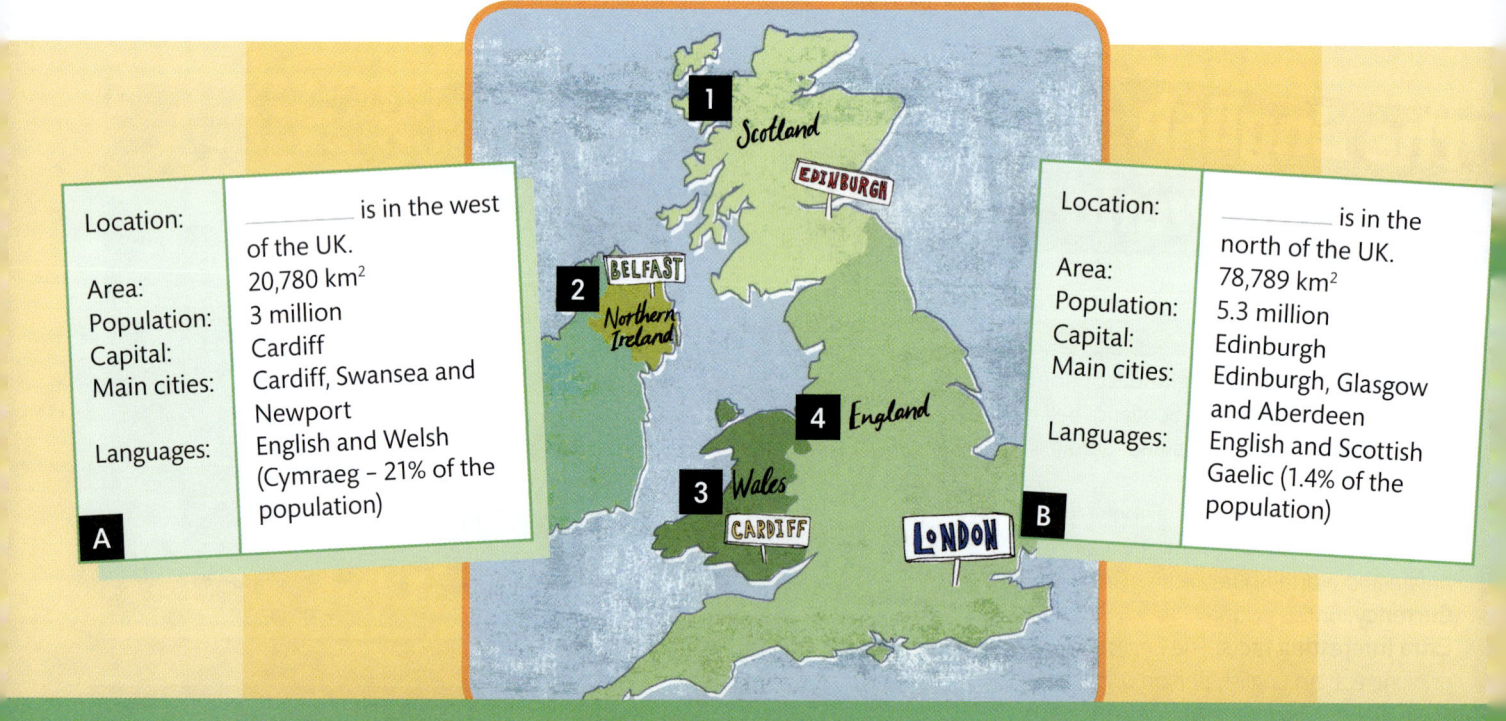

A
Location: _____ is in the west of the UK.
Area: 20,780 km²
Population: 3 million
Capital: Cardiff
Main cities: Cardiff, Swansea and Newport
Languages: English and Welsh (Cymraeg – 21% of the population)

B
Location: _____ is in the north of the UK.
Area: 78,789 km²
Population: 5.3 million
Capital: Edinburgh
Main cities: Edinburgh, Glasgow and Aberdeen
Languages: English and Scottish Gaelic (1.4% of the population)

C
Location: _____ is in the north-east of Ireland.
Area: 13,576 km²
Population: 1.8 million
Capital: Belfast
Main cities: Belfast, Derry and Lisburn
Languages: English and Irish Gaelic (7% of the population)

D
Location: _____ is in the south of the UK.
Area: 130,410 km²
Population: 53 million
Capital: London
Main cities: London, Birmingham and Leeds
Language: English

The United Kingdom: facts and figures

The United Kingdom is England, Wales, Scotland and Northern Ireland. The government of the UK is in London. The Prime Minister is the head of the government. Queen Elizabeth II is the Head of State. The United Kingdom is a multicultural society. There are many different ethnic groups. People from India, Bangladesh, the Caribbean, Africa and China live in the UK.